Assessment
for Education

Assessment
for Education
Standards, Judgement and Moderation

Valentina Klenowski and **Claire Wyatt-Smith**

Los Angeles | London | New Delhi
Singapore | Washington DC

Los Angeles | London | New Delhi
Singapore | Washington DC

SAGE Publications Ltd
1 Oliver's Yard
55 City Road
London EC1Y 1SP

SAGE Publications Inc.
2455 Teller Road
Thousand Oaks, California 91320

SAGE Publications India Pvt Ltd
B 1/I 1 Mohan Cooperative Industrial Area
Mathura Road
New Delhi 110 044

SAGE Publications Asia-Pacific Pte Ltd
3 Church Street
#10-04 Samsung Hub
Singapore 049483

Commissioning editor: Marianne Lagrange
Assistant editor: Kathryn Bromwich
Production editor: Thea Watson
Copyeditor: Christine Bitten
Proofreader: Jill Birch
Marketing manager: Catherine Slinn
Cover design: Wendy Scott
Typeset by: C&M Digitals (P) Ltd, Chennai, India
Printed in India by: Replika Press Pvt Ltd

© Valentina Klenowski and Claire Wyatt-Smith, 2014

First published 2014

Library of Congress Control Number: 2012930260

British Library Cataloguing in Publication data

A catalogue record for this book is available from the British Library

ISBN 978-1-4462-0840-3
ISBN 978-1-4462-0841-0 (pbk)

Contents

About the authors

Valentina Klenowski is Professor of Education at the Queensland University of Technology in Brisbane, Australia. She has research interests in curriculum and assessment reform and development, assessment and learning, evaluation and social justice. Recent research interests include fairness in classroom assessment, culture-responsive assessment and pedagogy, teacher judgement and social moderation in the context of standards-driven reform. Valentina has published in the fields of assessment and learning, curriculum and evaluation, and has held positions at the Institute of Education, University of London and the Hong Kong Institute of Education.

Claire Wyatt-Smith is Executive Dean and Professor of Educational Assessment and Literacy Education, Australian Catholic University, Faculty of Education. She first became interested in assessment and literacy as a high school teacher and Head of Department, English. Building on this foundation she developed her considerable expertise in researching professional judgement and teachers' assessment literacies, including the use of standards and social moderation. Claire's work in the field of professional judgement relates to teaching at all levels, including higher education and clinical practice. Current, large-scale funded projects include studies investigating digital assessment, gaming and the nature and effects of standardized testing upon learners and reluctant readers. Claire has an extensive history of working closely with the teaching profession and in advisory roles in curriculum and assessment policy, both within Australia and internationally.

Foreword

This is a remarkable book, not only because it presents a new and yet achievable vision for state assessment systems, but also because it presents, in its account of how this vision has been realized, the evidence of others who have found the system both practicable and rewarding. However, running through this account is a deeper lesson – that only teachers themselves can insightfully discern and so engage with the new problems and opportunities that society now presents to the work of teachers and schools.

In 1999, in an article entitled 'The knowledge creating school', David Hargreaves argued that schools now had to prepare students not just for increasingly higher levels of knowledge and skills, but also 'in the personal qualities that matter in the transformed work place – how to be autonomous, self-organising, networking, entrepreneurial, innovative'. To these he also added the capability to re-define the needs for skills and to find the resources to learn them. Whilst this is by now more widely recognized, Hargreaves took his argument further in the following way:

> It is plain that if teachers do not acquire and display this capacity to re-define their skills for the task of teaching, and if they do not model in their own conduct the very qualities – flexibility, networking, creativity – that are now key outcomes for students, then the challenge of schooling in the next millennium will not be met. (1999: 123)

One obstacle to the development of this process is that there are some who believe that they know and understand the new professional knowledge that is needed and, through their influence, seek to implement their recipes through state systems. The consequence is sadly familiar:

> An effect of recent educational reforms has been to discourage teachers from engaging in the process of professional knowledge creation by which, in rapidly changing social conditions in schools and society, the profession generates new knowledge to become more effective. (1999: 123)

Nowhere is this baleful influence more evident than in assessment. It is baleful because it discourages teachers from engaging in the generation of the new professional knowledge that is sorely needed in this key area.

Assessment is a key feature in this scenario because its role within a larger picture of pedagogy has always been distorted. In theoretical writing it has not been seen as central. In professional practice, it has come to be regarded as the negative dimension of learning, a view strongly enhanced by authorities who see in it no more than a tool to impose accountability and 'drive-up' standards. The toxic product of this process is the teacher who feels obliged to 'teach-to-the-test', where the test is often a collection of short written questions, structured so that they are easy to mark. Moreover, externally imposed accountability tests serve as a model for the year-on-year assessments which schools themselves compose and which are used to review the progress of their pupils. They thereby undermine the quality of that advice and of decisions which follow. This is a depressing picture, the more so because it is a fairly accurate account of the interaction between assessment and teaching in many state systems.

This book presents a very different picture. The authors bring together a strong positive vision of the central role of assessment in teaching and learning, and also an emphasis on the need to respect and support the professional autonomy and insights of teachers so that this vision can be realized.

What makes this book a uniquely valuable contribution to the field of assessment studies is that it combines a clearly articulated vision of how assessment could and should operate at the heart of pedagogy, with a wealth of practical experience of the operation, over many years, of a state system where this vision has been realized. The authors are fortunate in being able to work in the Australian state of Queensland, but have taken advantage of this opportunity to present concrete and detailed evidence, whilst drawing both on this experience and on the experience of initiatives in several other countries.

Several features of their account are crucial. One is that the summative assessments by teachers will only be trusted if they can be shown to be dependable on standards which are so shared between teachers that their interpretations are comparable across all of the teachers involved. This need can be met by moderation, the process in which teachers compare their grading of the same samples of students' work and, in the process of reaching agreement, develop a shared understanding of those standards. This may be seen as a burden of extra work, but the experience of teachers who have engaged in this process is that, as familiarity develops, it makes an increasingly positive contribution to many features of their work. It gives them confidence in their assessments, and it enables them, by drawing on their shared experiences and insights, to seek for validity in the assessment tools which they used.

This enhancement of validity is one of the main benefits that follows from giving teachers responsibility for summative assessments. The evidence that can be brought to moderation can reflect a variety of types of achievement: formal tests, projects requiring search for evidence and information (in libraries and on the internet), exploratory inquiries in science, creative writing in various genres, and so on. Each subject may define its own portfolio of tasks to reflect its particular learning aims. In producing such a portfolio, a student will be involved at several times and in several different contexts. All of these features strengthen the validity of the outcomes. At the same time, each student's portfolio becomes their personal product and the teacher can guide students to take personal responsibility for their portfolios by helping them to understand the aims and criteria of quality that are relevant to each component.

None of this is achieved easily or quickly. The successful examples all show that investment in supporting teachers to develop the skills, the practices and the confidence to make such an approach workable, has to be substantial and has to be sustained over several years. This book is a guide for those engaged in this process, for it contains a wealth of detail, grounded in experience, to help others foresee the needs and the pitfalls. But it is also rich in evidence of the rewards.

Many policy makers in education take the system, of high stakes account-ability through external testing, for granted: yet outside education there is no arena of human activity in which personal achievement is appraised by the capacity to produce in writing – on one's own, from memory and without access to resources – accounts of the products of several years of learning, within a situation made stressful because one's future opportunities depend on the outcome. One reason for this paradox is the failure to accept the alternative – which is to trust, and to invest in, the professional development of teachers. This is obviously a far better alternative, and this book helps to show both how such investment can be made to work and the fundamental rewards that it can secure.

Reference

Hargreaves, D. (1999) 'The knowledge-creating school', *British Journal of Educational Studies*, 47 (2): 122–44.

Paul Black
Emeritus Professor of Science Education,
Department of Education and Professional Studies, King's College London

Acknowledgements

Throughout the book we have referred to assessment as a social process involving judgement and participation in communities of practice. In the writing of this book we have been fortunate in our participation with a community of scholars, researchers, teachers and policy officers, all of whom have an interest in assessment for the improvement of student learning. Our understanding of assessment has benefited from conversations, challenges and feedback we have received from participating in this assessment community.

There are many colleagues, friends and family who have also supported and encouraged us throughout the writing process. It is not possible to name them all, but we do wish to acknowledge a few in particular. First, individually, we would like to thank our respective family members. Valentina's brother, George Klenowski, has offered kind support and read willingly draft chapters with careful attention to detail in his commentary. To David Smith, Matthew Smith and Rachelle Wyatt-Smith, Claire thanks them for their continuing support for her endeavours.

There are many colleagues we would like to acknowledge for their helpful contributions and support. Specifically, we wish to thank Professor Paul Black for agreeing to write the Foreword and for sharing his wisdom with us. Special thanks to Dr Kay Kimber for her work in pushing the boundaries of digital literacies and multi-modal assessment, with her research having direct application to classroom practice. As a longstanding, valued colleague at Brisbane Girls Grammar School and fellow researcher at Griffith University, the conversations we have enjoyed over many years have been foundational to the thinking in Chapter 8. Colleagues from the Department of Education and Training, the Catholic and Independent Education sectors, and the Queensland Studies Authority are also thanked sincerely for their educational ideals and professional values. Our thanks are also given to all of the teachers and students who allow us to study their assessment practices. The partnerships we enjoy with you and your professional values have made this book possible. We extend our thanks to Belinda Hampton for allowing us to reference her materials and those of her students in Chapter 7.

Special thanks to our long-term colleague, Dr Peta Colbert, who has assisted us with the book's creation and has facilitated our communications with our editorial consultant, Dr Renée Otmar. Renée's keen editorial eye has been invaluable and she has most assuredly enabled the smooth progression in preparing the manuscript for submission.

For permission to reproduce copyrighted materials, we wish to thank the following:

- Queensland Studies Authority – Figures 2.1 and 2.2
- Australian Curriculum Assessment and Reporting Authority – Figure 2.3
- Australasian Curriculum, Assessment and Certification Authorities – *Principles of Assessment F1–12* in Chapter 7
- Dr Kay Kimber – Table 8.1 on p. 148 and quotes on p. 139
- Department of Education, Training and Employment – materials included in Chapters 2 and 4
- Belinda Hampton – classroom materials in Chapter 7
- Figure 2.3 in this publication is subject to copyright under the Copyright Act 1968 (Commonwealth) and is owned by the Australian Curriculum, Assessment and Reporting Authority (ACARA). ACARA neither endorses nor verifies the accuracy of the information provided and accepts no responsibility for incomplete or inaccurate information. In particular, ACARA does not endorse or verify the work of the author. This material is reproduced with the permission of ACARA.

The transformation of assessment

Introduction

This book presents the case that intelligent accountability (O'Neill, 2002) involves high-quality assessment that can be inclusive of, but not restricted to, examinations. Our argument is two-pronged: first, high-quality assessment requires teachers to have well-developed assessment literacies and, second, teachers are central in creating much-needed assessment reform.

In taking up this case we aim to bring together the trilogy of standards, teacher judgement and moderation. Historically, these have been presented in the main as separate rather than intersecting fields. We bring them together in order to present new perspectives on quality assessment practice. In the chapters that follow, readers will encounter concepts traditionally associated with assessment, including validity and reliability, as well as new understandings about the global policy contexts of assessment and the associated demands on systems and classroom assessment practices in order to achieve equity. Also new is our introduction to ethical assessment, which attends to principles of social justice and equity. In the twenty-first century, concerns about validity and reliability, though essential, need to be complemented by a third and equally important feature of quality assessment: ethical practice.

Our focus is at the intersection of assessment standards–learning–teaching–judgement and moderation. We recognize this intersection as a new, interpretive space within which to see anew the dual purposes of assessment, namely for improvement and for determining or judging quality. Taking these purposes as complementary, we explore the space for its potential to achieve coherence between systems' and local site efforts to improve teaching and learning, and for accountability purposes.

Human judgement is central to assessment practice and, while the book is largely concerned with judgement and decision making in the field of education, we suggest that the messages are applicable to other professions and that the lessons, such as how to gain an understanding of the factors that influence professional judgement practice, extend to other fields.

The call for teachers to be assessment literate

For teachers to be 'assessment literate' they need to have a repertoire of skills and understandings to design quality assessments and to use achievement standards and evidence as a means by which to discern, monitor and improve learning as well as judge the qualities of student work. These capabilities and understandings are foundational to efforts to address issues of equity and social justice. They are also the means through which assessment can become a shared enterprise, with benefits accruing to all students, including those who are marginalized and disengaged and those who are identified as gifted and talented.

The book characterizes classroom assessment with the teacher at the centre. It presents ideas from a large body of assessment writing and empirically generated findings with direct application to the judgements and decision making that teachers are called on to do in their routine practice. Throughout the book we take the position that aligning assessment practice, curriculum and pedagogy is a main strategy for realizing learning improvement in accountability-driven systems, and beyond for enhancing learner engagement. Further, our aim is to connect the past and present – what we know about assessment and learning – to futures-oriented assessment possibilities and new contexts for learning, in order to meet the changing needs of the global society.

There is ample evidence that, in these times of economic uncertainty, many countries are increasingly concerned with the quality and effectiveness of their education systems. Through a range of strategies and investments governments across the world are seeking to develop an informed, skilled workforce that is productive and adaptable to changing global needs. Several developments have taken place in support of this priority, with three being directly relevant to this book. Major curriculum reform has been initiated in many parts of the world, with heavy investments in large-scale standardized testing for public reporting at local, regional, country and international levels. Also evident is the increasing role of new and emerging technologies, bringing with them capabilities to leverage changed assessment practices previously not imaginable.

The book is written against this background. It is also informed by the concerted move globally towards the development of inclusive educational policies, with reforms to maintain student participation in both senior secondary and higher education sectors. Globally, education policies have prioritized increased participation in all phases of formal education, extending from the early years through to higher education. This has attracted increased numbers and a greater diversity of students. In part, this has occurred through increased mobility and movement of peoples globally. The strong focus on inclusion and diversity also reflects diminishing employment opportunities in many countries as well as the demise of low-skill jobs in the wake of technological advances.

Given these changes, curriculum authorities and education departments throughout the world are seeking to take up futures-oriented perspectives to curriculum. Many have broadened the scope and demands of curriculum to include knowledges, skills and dispositions that enable participation in communities within and beyond the school. Further, there is growing recognition of the need to transform educational assessment and, in turn, instructional practice using new and emerging information and communications technologies (ICTs). Indeed, assessing and teaching twenty-first-century skills have been prioritized, nationally and internationally. Notable work includes the international project *Assessment and Teaching of 21st Century Skills* (Griffin et al., 2012) and the ETS research and development initiative *Cognitively Based Assessment of, for, and as Learning* (CBAL™). Projects such as these point to how ICTs offer opportunities to leverage change in assessment in ways previously not possible. They also show the strong and growing corporate business interest not only in educational assessment but also in investing in assessment innovation. This is hardly surprising. It has been clear for some time that education and assessment are big business. Such directions helpfully remind us that a quality education is about life futures: preparing a highly skilled, flexible workforce and an informed citizenry with capabilities that extend to innovation, creativity, collaboration and ability to use and create knowledge.

While assessment change is inevitable, the dominant view of assessment in many countries has tended to remain static and safe: examinations continue to be the traditionally safe choice for summative assessments bound up with reporting and certification. Indeed, many countries have seen a proliferation of examinations across the phases of education, with a concurrent press by the public for improved results. In many countries, despite the obvious societal changes over time, the changing needs of learners and the pressing global challenges of our time, examinations continue to offer the 'safe' and reliable assessment option, especially with regard to standards credentialing and the offering of university placements.

Taking account of the global development mentioned earlier, we seek to connect assessment past, present and futures. We build on ideas about the spaces and places 'beyond testing' and seek to reposition assessment in relation to new ideas about what we refer to as 'the masterful teacher'. Our interest is in quality assessment in which teachers, students and the wider community can have confidence. Quality assessment requires recursive decision making that takes into account expectations of assessment, including standards, learning opportunities, pedagogical approaches, curriculum and resourcing. Such approaches to decision making are critical to well-informed teaching that has rigour and quality, and is responsive to learners' diverse needs. We also seek to connect assessment to knowledges within and beyond the classroom, digital literacies and emerging technologies. In this way, we reframe assessment in relation to a much-needed move from knowledge acquisition, through participation, to knowledge creation. The position taken in this book recognizes how assessment has historically been grounded in theories of learning that understand knowledge to be acquired. Within this traditional framing of assessment, value has been ascribed to examinations and the measurement of learning. This has served the purposes of 'gate keeping' and selection for certification for the past two centuries. With developments in learning theory, sociocultural perspectives value student agency and participation in learning, which in turn call for different roles in assessment for teachers and students and different types of assessment. Within this alternative framing, value is placed on interactions between teacher and student, and student and peers, in assessment understood as a social act. It is through participation and dialogue that teachers and students can co-construct knowledge. Our interest is to transform the understanding of assessment to include knowledge creation, facilitated by new and emerging technologies. This represents a development of the field, recognizing the potential for technologies to leverage changed assessment practices and processes. It is indeed the affordances of technologies themselves that open up possibilities for assessment of student products, learning processes and the interactions, both individual and collective, which have occurred over time. It is now possible for us to 'see' achievement over time through a range of digital means, such as e-portfolios that include learning processes and completed works, and digital learning records.

Standards and judgement within this framing of assessment assume heightened importance. Our interest is in bringing about change in teaching through deliberately aligning or connecting assessment and curriculum in teaching and, further, by 'front-ending assessment' (Wyatt-Smith and Bridges, 2007) with related foci on quality task design and the pedagogical utility of summative standards. These elements contribute to sustainable assessment cultures, with coherence between system and site assessment practices. Underpinning this call for change is a sociocultural orientation to learning, moderation practices and the use of standards. Such changes are facilitated by new and emerging technologies. However, in and of themselves, the technologies are mere tools. The masterful teacher will be able to design interdisciplinary learning opportunities that enable students to both use existing knowledge and create new knowledge. This calls for teachers who are able to develop quality learning through well-developed disciplinary knowledge and an appreciation of how such knowledge intersects with community knowledge, digital literacies, criterial knowledge and understandings about quality.

Consistent with this approach, we explore opportunities to assess vital attributes and capabilities for an informed twenty-first-century citizenry. New understandings are presented about how achievement standards can engage with creativity, innovation and design capability, and critical thinking. The book charts new territory, exploring how assessment can incorporate ways in which students work individually and in teams, using both traditional and new technologies. The discussion therefore includes consideration of new and emerging technologies, their convergence and their effect both on teaching and learning, and what counts as quality assessment.

The book also takes into account the global context of testing and classroom assessment. We consider large-scale international testing, including Programme for International Student Assessment (PISA), Trends in International Mathematics and Science Study (TIMSS) and Progress International Reading Literacy Study

(PIRLS), as well as national testing initiatives employed in several countries. In the discussion we open up the utility of standards-referenced data for informing and changing governmental policy and assessment practice in the classroom. We consider how, in these ways, standards contribute towards systems-level expectations and improvement initiatives at the local, site level.

The alignment of assessment, curriculum and pedagogy is also important and acts as a powerful driver for change in all phases of education. In fact, alignment – or, more aptly, the extent to which it is achieved – is a marker of good education. It lies at the heart of the teaching–learning dynamic. Within this dynamic the relationship between the learner, learning and assessment is integral to teacher judgement at the local, professional level. In moves towards standards-referenced assessment systems, teacher judgement is critical for both curriculum and assessment design. Teacher judgement in this context refers to decision making regarding how assessment, curriculum and pedagogy align in practice. This is because standards can be used to indicate the desired qualities and levels of achievement within a learning area of the curriculum. They can also be used in relation to interdisciplinary studies in all phases of education. Essentially, standards work to indicate student learning and achievement in relation to the constructs being assessed. In turn, student achievement, as reflected through assessment requirements and tasks, is referenced to the standards.

The opportunities for assessment to broaden what it values as evidence of learning and achievement have been a catalyst for this book. Also to the fore have been attempts in several countries to focus on, value and strengthen teacher judgement, standards and moderation in order to develop more intelligent accountability systems. A main characteristic of education systems in which such developments have occurred is the recognition of the need to support the professional judgement of teachers, particularly with the introduction of standards-related accountability. This requires appropriate support of quality assurance measures, which, in turn, will help build dependable teacher judgements in which the public can have confidence. The relationship between the teacher and the student matters, as does the teacher's discipline or subject content and pedagogical content knowledge. Standards-driven reform and increased emphases on teacher judgement and moderation practice bring with them new demands of teachers, students, parents, carers and the public. Assessment literacies and skills in the use of standards are some of the emergent needs in this changing climate of curriculum and assessment reform that have prompted the writing of this book. Accordingly, we aim to address the conditions under which assessment and judgement practice can be valid and dependable for both local and systems reporting. Insights derived from research of social moderation practices and developed from analysis of moderation in different contexts, including educational authorities, regional organizations and schools, are offered to promote further understanding.

In discussions of educational opportunity, many writers have recognized the need to emphasize quality. Similarly, there is a clear impetus internationally to deliver both high-quality and high-equity outcomes. In this context, the book explores how quality assessment can extend well beyond basic literacy and numeracy to include complex reasoning and critical thinking skills, and a broadened notion of education that quite properly factors in student attributes of resourcefulness and resilience.

The book addresses approaches to assuring quality and standards, and presents the role of review through moderation practices. The main interest is in how educational professionals engage with standards in their own practice, and not simply as a regulatory mechanism mandated by policy. That is, our interest is in the self-regulatory use of standards to build a networked community of judgement practice.

In exploring moderation as involving networked professional discipline communities, we invite readers to consider the interpretation required in the use of standards, and how standards themselves acquire meaning through use. The argument developed in this book is threefold: teacher judgement, informed by standards, lies at the heart of quality learning opportunities; moderation provides the means for teachers to review their interpretation and application of the stated standards; and moderation supports system efforts to promote consistent use of standards, both over time and across sites. This is not to suggest that the function of teacher judgement and moderation is narrowly understood as serving accountability alone. Nor is it to argue a case against external examinations and large-scale tests. Both can play a part in quality assessment, including monitoring trends for reporting at particular phases. Our argument is that teacher use of standards in moderation practices can have a direct flow on to systems-wide efforts to improve curriculum design and development in the classroom. Specifically, it is in the context of standards-based moderation talk that teachers can explore the meaning and use of standards as this relates to construct validity. Standards and moderation work together to enable teachers to achieve clarity of expectation for themselves and their students, especially in relation to task design. Further, moderation can function as a main means through which teachers reach agreement regarding the qualities of the learning being assessed. Moderation practice therefore involves practitioners in explicating the basis for their judgements, including how they have drawn on the standards to arrive at a judgement of quality. This position holds at all levels of education, from early years of schooling through to postgraduate programmes at regional, state, national and international levels.

The chapters in outline

In conclusion, we introduce readers to the suite of chapters. They do not need to be read in a specific order, and we encourage readers to 'dip into' the ideas of the book in ways that are responsive to their contexts and practices. For the purpose of this introduction, however, we outline each chapter in turn as a guide to the focus and ideas explored in the respective chapters.

Chapter 2 considers why teachers need to understand standards. Certain twenty-first-century trends in education, such as the increased use of standards for improved learning, and for system and individual accountability and evaluative purposes, have required teachers to develop new skills and understandings in their practice. These include what counts as quality in assessment and how assessment and curriculum align. In this chapter we discuss the nature and functions of standards and how teachers can use them as part of their repertoire for analysing and interpreting achievement data. Specific quality assessment issues are discussed, with some examples provided to support this approach.

Chapter 3 presents a sociocultural perspective of teachers' judgement practice. We take a sociocultural perspective of learning and assessment and provide examples of teacher assessment that involve both the judgement and the decision levels of the purposes of assessment. Judgement procedures are articulated using the sociocultural theoretical perspective that identifies the importance of the interaction of teachers' tacit knowledge and explicit knowledge of curriculum, achievement standards and pedagogy. How judgements are defended and deprivatized is made explicit, with reference to research findings and examples of practice. The important question of fairness in assessment that includes key ideas relating to cultural difference and equity are also presented. Assessment issues of validity, access and literacy demands are defined and discussed in relation to studies of culture-responsive assessment.

Chapter 4 is concerned with the integration of assessment and instruction, and presents two related concepts for the maintenance of dependable and sustainable assessment cultures: the alignment of assessment curriculum and pedagogy and the front-ending of assessment, mentioned earlier. Designing effective, suitably demanding assessment tasks becomes a major skill within curriculum planning and teaching. Quality assessment task design requires teachers to consider the evidence to be collected and the methods by which the information is to be collected to assess student learning. This chapter presents design decisions that teachers could consider as part of their repertoire of practice.

Chapter 5 extends to the purposes of moderation. We address questions of how moderation practice attends to accountability and improvement priorities. The discussion includes how moderation is one means to achieve reliable and valid judgements with high levels of inter-rater reliability. Moderation is defined and the processes and the role of standards described. Use of evidence and exemplars are extrapolated with issues of consistency, comparability and agreement addressed. The chapter introduces various models of moderation and describes specific moderation systems.

Chapter 6 considers the pedagogical utility of summative achievement standards in improving learning and teaching. The discussion addresses what is involved in a dialogic inquiry approach to classroom assessment that has at its heart intentional and artful connections across curriculum, instruction and assessment. Teacher judgement and standards are presented as central to a long-overdue focus on quality in the classroom, with direct benefit to teacher and student efforts to improve student learning. At issue is how teachers and students can work purposefully with standards to develop student knowledge about the expectations or characteristics of quality, their capabilities in recognizing quality, and their 'know-how' in applying standards to improve performance.

In Chapter 7 we offer insights into the building of sustainable assessment cultures, and consider coherence between system and site. With the emergence of the need for more intelligent accountability systems and a greater recognition of the professionalism of teachers we explain how teachers can use standards and achievement data to make more discerning decisions for a variety of assessment and learning purposes. A case study of exemplary classroom assessment practice is used to illustrate the concept of front-ending assessment as used at the local professional level to achieve coherence with system-level accountability demands. We explain how teachers can develop their judgement practice so that it is explicit and defensible, using achievement standards with students in classroom assessment practice. We introduce different approaches and models of judgement that relate to decision making for both summative and formative learning purposes. The use of exemplars with students is also discussed. Strategies are presented for ensuring that the judgement practice is rigorous and addresses equity issues.

In Chapter 8 readers are offered new ways to think about assessment in the digital, screen-based age. Rapid changes in ICTs have challenged educators in many ways. There are the obvious infrastructure issues, including the initial investments required in hardware and software, and the related costs of maintenance and replacement. These budgetary issues are significant. There are also equally significant challenges of integrating the technologies into what and how students learn and are assessed. In this chapter we recognize that new practices that students and teachers use when working online call for fundamentally different notions of assessment. New ways to think and talk about features of quality are also needed from those that have been used in assessing traditional demonstrations of knowledge and skills. With this in mind, we move into a new assessment space to explore multi-modal ways of working online.

In concluding the book, Chapter 9 revisits the notions of assessment literacies and intelligent accountability to explore characteristics of a futures-oriented approach to assessment in classroom practice.

References

Griffin, P., McGaw, B. and Care, E. (eds) (2012) *Assessment and Teaching of 21st Century Skills*. Dordrecht: Springer.

O'Neill, O. (2002) *A Question of Trust: The BBC Reith Lectures*. Cambridge: Cambridge University Press.

Wyatt-Smith, C.M. and Bridges, S. (2007) 'Evaluation study report', in *Meeting in the Middle – Assessment, Pedagogy, Learning and Educational Disadvantage. Literacy and Numeracy in the Middle Years of Schooling Initiative – Strand A*. Australian Government, Department of Education, Employment and Workplace Relations and Queensland Government. Available at: http://education.qld.gov.au/literacy/docs/deewr-myp-final-report.pdf.

Web extra

Daly, A.J. and Finnigan, K.S. (2011) 'The ebb and flow of social network ties between district leaders under high-stakes accountability', *American Educational Research Journal*, 48 (1): 39–79.

2

Why teachers need to understand standards

Overview

In this chapter we set out the rationale for standards-based assessment and the need for teachers to understand the roles and functions of standards. We discuss ideas central to an understanding of standards and their relationship to curriculum, accountability, improvement and equity, and provide examples of how standards are represented and promulgated and how teachers use standards in making judgements about students' work.

Introduction

Trends in education, such as the increased use worldwide of standards for improved learning, and for systems and individual accountability and evaluative purposes, have required teachers to develop a repertoire of new skills and understandings in their teaching and assessment practices. These include knowledge and understandings about what counts as *quality* in assessment, and capabilities in aligning or connecting assessment and curriculum in a standards-based system. Such connections are essential in efforts both to diagnose students' learning needs and to use assessment to improve learner outcomes and achievement. This chapter outlines how teachers can build on their existing assessment repertoire to include the use of standards for analyses and interpretation of achievement. Specific quality and equity assessment issues in different European countries, Australia and New Zealand are included to illustrate developments in standards-based curriculum and assessment.

Aims of the chapter

This book aims to raise awareness about the unintended consequences of previous curriculum and assessment reforms, and suggests ways to avoid such outcomes.

When educational change takes place, such as the introduction of a system of standards-referenced assessment, it is imperative that teachers and policy makers understand the rationale for such an approach and are knowledgeable about the implications for practice. Also necessary is clarity about the role and purposes of standards in educational reform. The point is therefore self-evident: the publication of standards in and of itself is only part of the story. Their intended uses, and especially how teachers are expected to use standards to inform judgement, is another part. These parts can be overlooked in periods of heightened educational accountability, where the focus may be on measuring the rise and fall of standards as indicative of the health of education systems. The position that we take in this book is that standards are at the very heart of systems and local action for improvement for all students and in meeting accountability parameters.

In this chapter we present ideas central to the concept of standards, their relationships to curriculum, accountability, improvement and equity. This is followed by an explanation of the conditions required in order for standards to be used in measuring improvement and in informing student learning and teaching for improvement purposes in contexts of curriculum and assessment reform. Research evidence is included to support our argument that teachers' use of standards for systems reporting is part of a desired evidence-based judgement and, in turn, valid and reliable assessment practice.

The chapter addresses the following issues:

- the development of standards, by whom, and how they will be used in practice
- the assessment evidence used to inform the development and use of standards
- the communication of measures of quality, represented as standards
- the 'fit' between how standards are formulated and how they are used in practice, by whom and for what purposes.

We begin with an explanation of why there has been a global movement towards standards-based curriculum and assessment.

Rationale for the emergence of standards

Increasingly, governments worldwide are meeting public accountability demands by introducing standards to demonstrate transparency in relation to educational policies, and to maintain public confidence in the standards of schooling. The issue for educators is whether such efforts to meet accountability demands are achieved without negatively affecting the quality and equity of teaching and learning. Much has been written about the unintended consequences of high-stakes accountability policies and how they can undermine quality teaching and learning, and equity related efforts (Nichols and Berliner, 2005; Stobart, 2008). It is important to understand the directions countries are taking in terms of high-stakes assessment programmes, which involve standards-referenced assessment, in order to protect schools and teachers from negative or inadvertent effects.

In recent times, public education policy has been characterized by standards-referenced accountability testing and assessment. For example, in Germany, national educational standards for seven subjects were introduced in 2003 and 2004 (Henning, 2004; Köller, 2009). In Norway, the development of a national curriculum and achievement standards is currently taking place. In New Zealand, national standards in literacy and numeracy are being implemented and, in Australia, the country's first national curriculum and achievement standards are being implemented.

What has prompted such changes to assessment and curriculum provision? The answer can be found in analysing the shifts in education policy processes. In the twenty-first century, a global education policy community has emerged (Rizvi and Lingard, 2010), so that today there exists a community in education policy creation that includes policy agents and agencies, beyond the individual nation. The context of policy production now includes a rescaling across local, regional, national and global spheres bringing with it concepts of global competitiveness and global imperatives.

The most evident examples of global competitiveness are programmes for international measures of educational attainment, such as the Programme for International Student Assessment (PISA) developed by the Organization for Economic Cooperation and Development (OECD) and the Trends in International Mathematics and Science Study (TIMSS) of the International Association for the Evaluation of Educational Achievement (IEA). These international programmes have had a major impact on curriculum and assessment reform and policy development worldwide. For example, in Germany, the OECD annual report in 2000, entitled *Education at a Glance: OECD Indicators*, reported that 'Germany's education system is outmoded, overburdened and desperately in need of an overhaul' (Deutsche Welle, 2003a). The identification of this implication for reform by the OECD led the Standing Conference of Ministers of Education and Cultural Affairs to approve major reforms to the German education system with the introduction of 'nationwide curriculum that sets the standards for the knowledge and capabilities students are expected to possess at the end of each level of education' (Deutsche Welle, 2003b). The president of the Standing Conference in Germany stated:

> ... it's gotten to the point where academic levels in the different states can vary as much as two years. Now we want curriculum standards, in other words, we want to specify competencies that should be achieved by the end of the certain phases of schooling. But they also give schools considerable leeway in how to achieve them. (Deutsche Welle, 2003b)

The OECD reported in 2000 that:

> In searching for effective education policies that enhance individuals' social and economic prospects, provide incentives for greater efficiency in schooling and help to mobilise resources in order to meet rising demands for education,

governments are paying increasing attention to international comparative policy analysis. This attention has resulted in a major effort by the OECD to strengthen the collection and reporting of comparative statistics and indicators in the field of education. (OECD, 2000: 5)

With the emergence of a global community in education policy, economic values appear to dominate the foundations of policy, such that 'market efficiency concerns seem to override equity ones' (Rizvi and Lingard, 2010: 16). In this evolving global context we should note Reid's (2011: 3) warning that 'unless and until there is a serious attempt to theorise equity as a concept and a practice, the policy rhetoric about equity is unlikely ever to be realised'.

Global considerations, then, have underpinned the values of current policies, and the reframing of education in economic terms has led to an emphasis on policies of education as production of human capital in order to ensure the competitiveness of the national economy in the global context. It is in this global education policy community that policy agents and agencies such as the OECD can have an influence on education policy development and implementation at a national level.

Our argument is that defined standards can inform professional judgement of systems-level expectations. This has implications not only for efforts to realize curriculum intent and the design of quality assessment tasks, but also for understandings of the relationship between curriculum and assessment in a standards-referenced system. Students, too, need to take part in the use of standards for self-assessment and peer assessment, and to learn about the standards through their application in assessing their own and their peers' work. Involving students in the processes of standards-referenced curriculum and assessment reform helps to address equity concerns by emphasizing that achievement should be a priority for all students, and that teachers should raise their expectations for all students to improve.

What are standards?

The meaning of the term 'standards' varies according to the context in which it is used and also the purpose (goal) and function (role) it fulfils. The word 'standard' is universally used yet has different meanings, dependent on historical and social contextual derivation. Different countries, and even different states or districts within countries, can have varying views about what constitutes a 'standard' (Goldstein and Heath, 2000). The concept of standards is thus elusive, and confusion can occur when the term is used in official documents or when making comparative judgements, for it is not always clear which meaning is intended.

In this book we are concerned with explicit or stated standards for quality judgements. In the field of education, standards are understood to be 'fixed points of reference for assessing individual students' (Sadler, 1987: 191) and cohorts. We understand standards to be vital in systems-wide efforts to serve consistent judgements. Judgement is inherently a private practice: the actual influences on and bases for judgement typically remain private. It is only when standards are defined and applied in standards-referenced judgement practice that standards can become published indexes or features of quality against which judgement can be made available for scrutiny and, thereby, made defensible. It is in this broadened sense that standards can serve to support the development of productive assessment cultures in schools. It is also through such a focus on standards in classroom assessment that they can serve the best interests of learners and the broader community. 'Assessment' here is used broadly to refer to any decision or judgement of student work or student performance made by a teacher for formative or summative purposes. 'Standards-referenced assessment' focuses attention on desired features or characteristics of quality. It directly connects a student's actual achievement with a set of specified indicators, grades or levels. It requires teachers to draw on their professional knowledge and expertise to arrive at judgements of quality, or grading decisions. The decision can be recorded in a range of ways, including numerical scoring, alpha rating, grades or percentages. In a standards-referenced system it is essential to understand the difference between a 'criterion' and a 'standard':

- *criterion* A distinguishing property or characteristic of anything, by which its quality can be judged or estimated, or by which a decision or classification may be made. (From the Greek *kriterion*, 'a means for judging'.)
- *standard* A definitive level of excellence or attainment, or a definite degree of any quality viewed as a prescribed object of endeavour or as the recognised measure of what is adequate for some purpose, so established by authority, custom or consensus. (From the Roman *estendre*, 'to extend'.) (Sadler, 1987: 194)

Standards can differ in the following dimensions:

- the *type* of standard
- the *focus*; that is, the thing or event to which the standard is applied
- the underlying characteristic or *construct*
- the *purpose* or use to which the standards will be put. (Maxwell, 2009: 264)

The various types of standards can include:

- standards as moral or ethical imperatives (what someone *should* do)
- standards as legal or regulatory requirements (what someone *must* do)
- standards as target benchmarks (expected practice or performance)
- standards as arbiters of quality (relative success or merit)
- standards as milestones (progressive or developmental targets). (Maxwell, 2001)

The last two types are of central interest as these standards represent 'different levels of learning, performance or achievement' (Maxwell, 2009: 265). 'Quality' and 'progress' represent different constructs used by teachers in assessing the educational outcomes of students. Maxwell (2009) indicates that the important difference in these standards is the time frame for referencing them. That is, for *merit standards* that indicate the levels of quality or success achieved, these are referenced at the completion of a task, course or programme. *Developmental standards,* or sequential stages of improvement, however, are referenced over time to assess development or improvement.

Content standards and *achievement* standards differ in focus. Content standards apply to schools and systems, and attend to the knowledge and/or processes that are taught. Maxwell (2009) emphasizes that these standards help schools to develop their curriculum in relation to their local contexts. Achievement or performance standards refer to student work and the defined qualities and features of the work. Achievement standards establish the knowledge, understandings and skills that students are expected to develop, and the quality of achievement that is evident in the work. Achievement standards as indicators of quality are referenced when teachers are judging students' work. Optimally, the standards come into play when teachers are planning their curriculum and, in particular, the assessment tasks they expect students to complete. By considering the use of standards in this way and at the outset, teachers plan for assessment as part of their learning and teaching, and directly connect assessment tasks with the full requirements of the standards. The extent to which the tasks connect with (or align with) the requirements of the standards requires the teacher to understand the relationship between the demands of the tasks and the evidence base required by those standards. That is, the evidence required to classify the work against the standards. Such evidence can be formulated to be task-specific, or provide for a portfolio of evidence compiled over time. The portfolio is used to judge the standard of student work at a terminal or end point. For these summative purposes, only representative student work samples should be included in the portfolio for the purpose of awarding a final grade. Standards can also be used formatively, to inform students of their strengths and areas needing further development; however, they tend to be used primarily for summative assessment and to report on the quality of the achievement or performance of the student.

In a standards-driven accountability system, everyone needs to understand that different representations may have unintended consequences, particularly for individual students. If this is the case it may be that systems and teachers need to consider alternative approaches to their assessment, reporting, policies and practices. For example, several countries, including Germany, have introduced standards to help achieve greater consistency and comparability in levels of achievement. The approach taken to assessing student outcomes differs according to whether the focus is on the individual student or on the system as a whole. Rather than adopting a *full-census* approach or a *whole-of-cohort* approach (year or grade level) to assessing and monitoring an education system, a *sampling* of students can be used, as is the case in New Zealand.

The sample approach, as exemplified in New Zealand, is implemented through the National Educational Monitoring Project (see National Education Monitoring Project, http://nemp.otago.ac.nz/). The project has allowed for a wide range of assessment types, such as one-to-one, group, pencil-and-paper and stations with four students working independently on a series of authentic and rich, hands-on activities. Principles of equity in assessment can be addressed through the diversity of assessment types.

How are standards represented?

Defined standards are textual artefacts that seek to convey expectations of quality and value in assessment of achievement. Standards are socially constructed and historic in nature. As such, they achieve acceptance at a point in time, and can also change over time. The ways in which standards are formulated influence not only their representation but also suggest a particular approach to judgement. The ways in which standards are represented convey expectations of quality and levels of performance.

Standards come to be accepted and salient through judgement practice. In effect, they become legitimated in communities of judgement over time. The extent to which expected features or qualities can be wholly anticipated and pre-specified remains a contentious issue in policy and in judgement practice. From one vantage point, stated standards should be adhered to strictly, and only those features or characteristics that are stated can be properly considered in arriving at a decision about the grade to be awarded to a piece of work. In this technicist view, judgement is prescribed practice – able to be regulated – and some would argue that such regulating is central to quality assurance measures and public confidence in reported standards. From a different vantage point, it is potentially self-limiting to adhere in a narrow or prescriptive way to stated features of quality. From this perspective, the brain is understood to be the primary instrument of decision making (not the statement of standards *per se*) and it is entirely proper for assessors to remain 'open to the surprise' or unanticipated features that may emerge in some students' approaches to set tasks.

Also at issue is the way in which standards are derived; that is, the evidence base used to inform their development. For example, are standards empirically developed and validated through use over time, or are they constructed from expert or connoisseur knowledge about expectations at certain year levels?

As emphasized by Sadler (1987), the main function of a set of achievement standards is to enable a statement to be made about the quality of performance, or degree of achievement, without reference to other students' achievements. That is to say, in a standards-referenced system the point of reference is each standard by itself. Student work is compared directly with the qualities or features of the standards. As such, standards-referenced judgement is not determined by comparing a student's work with that of other students. This is not to suggest that such comparison has no place in quality judgement practice. Rather, defined standards in standards-referenced practice constitute the prime reference point. This approach allows for a distribution of grades that is reflective of the qualities or specifications of the standards themselves and how students' work satisfies these requirements. Standards-referenced approaches to judgement are distinctive from a norm-referenced approach, whereby grading decisions tend to be regulated by scales and numerical cuts-offs. However, predictably, standards-referenced assessment tends to lead to the classification and categorisation of students, even though this is not the main aim.

Standards are derived from what is known to be feasible and desirable. Ideally, they are 'grounded in field experience rather than in theory and theorising' (Sadler, 1987: 196); that is, they are generated empirically, with direct connections to actual learners' work. When this occurs, it is more likely that what is represented in the standards corresponds to what is achievable in the field. As a set, standards provide the necessary framework according to which teachers might ascribe student work to a category or classification such as a grade or level of achievement. The idea of standards as stable or fixed reference points at any given point in time characterizes a standards-referenced assessment system. Over time, it is possible to evaluate changes in a phenomenon from the use of fixed standards.

With standards-referenced curriculum reform, the representation of standards has significant implications for teachers' assessment practice. No matter the context or the purpose of standards, professional judgements involve teachers in interpreting the standards' descriptors. In a standards-referenced system, teachers' qualitative judgements can be made dependable if certain conditions exist. First, standards need to be developed and promulgated in appropriate forms. This relates to the way that they are represented. Second, teachers need the support of conceptual tools and practical training (Sadler, 1987). These conditions raise the relevance of the distinction between standards as cultural artefacts and their use in applied judgement practice. The remainder of this chapter addresses the first condition of the development and promulgation of standards in appropriate forms.

Annotated samples or exemplars can also represent standards. Carefully chosen, annotated work samples can provide useful and concrete examples to show the desired features or characteristics of the standards. While the combination of standards and examples is useful, an overall commentary can be added to this approach to standards, with the commentary detailing how the standards have been interpreted and applied to arrive at an overall judgement. More critically, such explanations make available insights into the compensatory factors or trade-offs that have influenced the decision regarding the grade or level and, more specifically, how these have been combined in practice. This explication is a form of *cognitive commentary* that illustrates how trade-offs have been enacted in the application of the standards during acts of judgement. These cognitive commentaries provide a lens by which to view the complexities of judgement practice in standards-referenced assessment. The provision of exemplars and associated commentaries help to improve and support teachers' judgement practice.

The way the features of the standard are distinguished and communicated can affect teaching and student learning. Standards in this context can have a regulatory function. For example, if teachers provide students with feedback according to the specified features, then this is standards-referenced. Additionally, if teachers engage students in self-assessment or peer assessment that is standards-referenced, then students can gain an awareness of their performance in relation to that which is expected, or to which they aspire. In this way the standards help to focus their efforts towards production or performance (Sadler, 1987). For teachers, the implication is that standards-referenced assessment has an impact on pedagogy such that teachers present opportunities for students to develop understandings of quality to inform and monitor their learning. In effect, there is a partnership between students and teachers in learning and, in particular, a joint understanding about how to apply the standards and in so doing build their evaluative experience and capability.

Promulgation of standards

It is worth emphasizing that standards are understood differently, depending on the context, purpose and intention for use in practice. The different representations and models of standards therefore need to be defined and understood in relation to the context and the purpose for which they are used. The methods of promulgation include: numerical cut-offs, tacit knowledge, exemplars and verbal descriptors (Sadler, 1987).

In order to achieve high reliability while preserving validity, teacher assessors need to develop common understandings of mandated standards and reach 'similar recognition of performances that demonstrate those standards' (Maxwell, 2001: 6). However, clear communication about the nature of standards and the levels and related qualities they seek to specify is not necessarily achieved through the provision of stated standards alone. Sadler (1987) argued, for example, that exemplars or samples of student work provide concrete referents for illustrating standards that otherwise remain tacit knowledge. He made the point that the stated standards and exemplars work together to show different ways of satisfying the requirements of say, an A or C standard. Standards written as verbal descriptors call for qualitative judgements. Exemplars help to explicate judgement practice and form one part of a comprehensive approach to moderation. As such, the standards necessarily remain open to interpretation, and common understandings of the terms used to capture notions of quality in the standards need to be developed over time.

What are the purposes of standards?

There are many purposes for standards, and some of these range from: making explicit the expected quality of learning in terms of knowledge, understanding and skills to be achieved; providing the language teachers need to discuss with students, and their parents, the student's current achievement level or progress to date, and what should come next; and to identify students whose rate of progress puts them at risk of being unable to reach satisfactory achievement levels in later years. These purposes for standards can be categorized with others to:

- set targets for student learning
- demonstrate progress
- promote consistency and comparability in judgement of achievement and/or progress

- set requirements for certification
- interpret and reference performance on examinations or tests
- set benchmarks for monitoring the system
- provide for accountability by schools and systems. (Maxwell, 2009: 269)

This range of purposes reflects how standards can be used to support learning by making explicit what is to be taught (*content standards*), by identifying the levels or progression points in assessing progress (*development standards*) and by identifying the typical or targeted level for each year (*expected standards*) (Maxwell, 2009: 280).

Across this range of purposes, standards are intended to be used as the basis for judgements of student achievement. The results from assessment tasks are meant both to inform the teaching and learning process and to monitor and report student progress. The role and reliability of teacher judgement therefore is fundamental. Issues relating to validity and reliability as well as dependability of judgement are considered in further detail in Chapter 5.

Standards for learning improvement

Standards provide descriptors of student achievement. They are useful in informing teachers' classroom practice and thereby contribute to quality teaching and learning experiences (Sadler, 2005; Klenowski, 2006, 2007). They function by indicating the level accomplished and by providing information about the quality of student work. Standards are also used to assess the quality of learning, and support teachers in identifying areas for improvement in teaching, curriculum design or development. In a related function, standards indicate what teachers are expected to teach and the level of performance expected for a particular age group. In this way they help to meet the demand for public accountability at the local professional level of the teacher (Wilson, 2004; Harlen, 2005).

Standards support learning improvement. Particular constructs, or underlying dimensions of students' learning such as concepts and skills, are represented in the standards by multiple criteria and non-numerical forms. Teachers' professional judgement is required to evaluate the student's learning or performance. In Queensland, Australia, senior secondary teachers have been working with standards in an externally moderated, school-based system for 40 years. The levels of achievement reported on the Queensland Certificate of Education at the end of Year 12 are referenced in teachers' professional judgements of student achievement and the quality of that achievement. The standards framework is referenced by teachers in describing how well students have achieved the objectives in the syllabus; however, it does not indicate how teachers are to interpret the standards. Teachers' interpretations of the standards are negotiated and made public in the external moderation processes.

The Queensland Studies Authority states that the predefined standards ensure that:

- students and teachers know what is expected for each level of achievement and can work together to achieve the best result for the student
- comparability from school to school can be achieved
- teachers can discuss standards with parents/carers when reporting a student's achievements. (www.qsa.qld.edu.au)

Each syllabus has general objectives that state what must be taught and assessed. These general objectives are categorized into dimensions or the most important aspects of the subject. A standard is given for each dimension, expressed as an A–E grade. Teachers use the standards at the level of the individual assessment instrument and for decisions about overall achievement across a range of assessment instruments towards the end of the course of study. An overall judgement about how the qualities of the student's work match the standards descriptors in each dimension is made. On completion of a senior secondary course of study, teachers award one of five levels of achievement:

Very High Achievement (VHA)

High Achievement (HA)

Sound Achievement (SA)

Limited Achievement (LA)

Very Limited Achievement (VLA)

Each level indicates what constitutes achievement and provides the benchmark against which student achievement is referenced. In this assessment system, teachers are required to provide students with standards specifications for each significant assessment task that contributes towards interim and terminal reporting prior to students commencing work on the task. These specifications include statements of criteria and related standards.

Another example of the use of standards for learning improvement purposes is assessment of the Queensland Comparable Assessment Tasks (QCATs). These tasks are defined as assessment instruments:

which are authentic and performance-based, designed to provide students in Years 4, 6 and 9 with the opportunity to demonstrate what they know, understand and can do in a selection of Essential Learnings in English, Mathematics and Science. (www.qsa.qld.edu.au)

The standards as used in the context of QCATs have been defined as achievement standards linked to the *Essential Learnings*. Using a five-point scale, the *Standards* describe how well a student has demonstrated their learning based on a collection of evidence. The standards can also be used to report student progress and achievement (see www.qsa.qld.edu.au).

The Queensland standards are intended to promote teachers' professional learning, focused on learning supportive assessment practices and judgement of the quality of student achievement against systems-level benchmarks or referents. In addition, it is expected that teachers using the standards will present meaningful reports and engage with assessment as a learning process.

To illustrate how these standards are represented, two examples (see Figures 2.1 and 2.2; QSA, 2007 and 2009, respectively) are provided, both relating to Year 6 English. Both examples have a clear aim of informing, even regulating, judgement. The examples illustrate two organizational structures for representing standards and the descriptors or terms used to capture the standards. In example one, the overall rating scale is A–E; there are also five assessable elements or criteria, and each of these is unpacked on this scale and referred to task-specific descriptors. Also evident is the explicit connection of particular criteria to questions of the task. For example, the criterion 'expression of personal opinion about the appeal of a favourite fictional character' is related to questions 1 and 2 (Q1, Q2). Implicit in this representation is that the approach to judgement is to identify performance on each assessable element using an A–E scale. The implied use of this structure or representation is that the teacher will mark the cells within the grid in making the judgement on each assessable element. As a result, a pattern of achievement across the elements emerges as a tangible record of judgement. Missing, however, is explicit guidance about how teachers combine decisions on

Guide to making judgments — Year 6 English

Student _____

Overall grade   A   B   C   D   E   N

ASSESSABLE ELEMENTS	TASK-SPECIFIC DESCRIPTORS				
	A	B	C	D	E
Expression of personal opinion about the appeal of a favourite fictional character. *Q1, Q2*	Explains fictional character's appeal in insightful, relevant, succinct and direct terms.	Explains fictional character's appeal in relevant and comprehensive terms.	Identification and/or basic description of character's appeal.	Basic statement made about character or appeal.	Inconsistent reference to character or character's appeal.
Justification of favourite fictional character's unappealing action/s. *Q3*	Logical, well-substantiated and relevant justification to describe, in detail, the valuable unappealing actions of character.	Justification is relevant, organized and describes most of the important unappealing actions of character.	Statement/s describe/s some basic or obvious unappealing actions of character.	Simplistic ideas to describe character.	Inconsistent ideas to describe character.
Description of a character for chosen medium and audience. *Q4*	Description is highly appropriate for chosen audience and medium. Uses a variety of vivid, effective and original descriptive words, noun and verb groups.	Description is appropriate for audience and medium. Descriptive words, noun and verb groups used to describe character are mostly correct.	Description is generally appropriate for audience and medium. Descriptive words, noun and verb groups are sometimes correct.	Description relies on verbs to explain actions of the character.	Describes by stating character's basic features.
Control of structure and textual resources to create a description. *Q4, Q5*	Applies consistent and effective punctuation and derivational spelling strategies. Uses paragraphs, description structure and varies sentence length to great effect.	Applies effective punctuation and spelling strategies in multisyllable words. Uses paragraphs successfully. Adheres to description structure. Some variety in length and structure of sentences to achieve some effect.	Applies some punctuation and spelling strategies in multisyllable words. Uses simplistic sentences and occasional lapses in paragraphing and structure.	Applies only basic punctuation and sound/ letter pattern strategies which detract from meaning. Description does not use paragraphs correctly. Sentences are short, simplistic and repetitive in structure.	Limited understanding of punctuation and spelling which impedes meaning. Disjointed sentences and lack of structure and paragraphs impede meaning.
Critically reflects on the appeal of new character. *Q5*	Insightful identification of character's appeal/actions: relevant evidence to support.	Useful identification of character's appeal/actions and evidence to support.	Basic identification of character's appeal/actions and brief or simplistic statement to support.	Identification of character's appeal/ actions: merely an obvious statement to support.	Inconsistent identification of character's appeal/ actions.

(Left vertical axis label: DIMENSIONS – KNOWING AND UNDERSTANDING; WAYS OF WORKING)

Figure 2.1   Year 6 English – Grid example one

Source: Queensland Studies Authority 2007

separate assessable elements (criteria), trading off strengths and limitations in performance to arrive at an overall judgement of quality (standard). The representation promotes the view that the whole is (or should be) the sum of the parts. This tends to preference an analytical approach to judgement.

In the second example (Figure 2.2), the overall rating scale remains as A–E, and three explicit assessable elements (criteria) are identified. For example, the criterion of *Knowledge and Understanding* is elaborated as 'selects language and textual features (vocabulary, grammar, punctuation, spelling, sentence and paragraph structure) to create a description of the student's favourite place'. In turn, the features are presented on a continuum, connected (shaded arrow) to an A–E scale. The continuum aims to represent increasing cognitive demand. The implied use of this structure is for the teacher to record student achievement on each of the three criteria. The expected use is that the teacher will indicate a position on each continuum and arrive at an overall judgement by looking across the continua. As was the case in the first example (Figure 2.1), there is no explicit instruction about how to combine aspects of performance. However, the representation itself suggests a more open, interpretative approach and appears to invite an holistic approach to judgement. In this approach, the whole is not necessarily treated as the sum of the parts, and the judgement process allows for emergent criteria or features that arise from the quality of the student work itself. That is, they represent previously unspecified criteria.

The examples provided in Figures 2.1 and 2.2 are taken from the Queensland Essential Learnings, which have been replaced by the Australian Curriculum:

Guide to making judgments — Year 6 English   Student ....

Purpose: To demonstrate how well you can construct texts for different purposes and that match your audience.

Knowledge and understanding	Constructing texts	Constructing texts	
Selects language and textual features (vocabulary, grammar, punctuation, spelling, sentence and paragraph structure) to create a description of the student's favourite place. *Q1*	Uses details and descriptive language in a text to attract visitor to come to the student's favourite place. *Q1*	Selects and sequences details in an itinerary, and gives logical justification of the most interesting place. *Q2, 3*	
◄Cohesive and evocative description written with well-controlled, varied and effective sentence structure.	◄Detailed, evocative and descriptive language used to perceptively explore how the place is special for the student.	◄Selection and sequencing of itinerary details is thoughtful and logical. Selection and justification of an interesting local place to visit is considered and appropriate for the visitor.	A
◄Imagery created using a variety of adjectives, verbs and emotive language. Control of grammar, punctuation and spelling is effective.	◄Convincing and interesting descriptions.	◄Detailed itinerary. Justification of a local place is appropriate.	B
◄Appropriate language elements selected to create a picture of a favourite place. Sentence structure is mostly controlled.	◄Credible descriptions that consider how the place makes the student feel.	◄Credible structure with appropriate activities and places chosen. Selects an interesting place with a reason given.	C
◄Simple vocabulary chosen. Choices in grammar, punctuation and spelling may sometimes hinder meaning.	◄Superficial or repetitive selection of ideas. Length may be inappropriate. Mainly recounts events.	◄Limited details of places and activities with little scope for justification.	D
◄Language choices hinder meaning.	◄Superficial description that names location and lists some features.	◄Activities and places chosen are repetitive, narrow or unsuitable.	E

Feedback...

....

Figure 2.2   Year 6 English – Continuum example two

Source: Queensland Studies Authority 2009

English. The Queensland Studies Authority has developed similar resources to support the Australian Curriculum achievement standard. These are called Standards Elaborations, which use task-specific standards rather than guides to making judgements, and work in the same way as the examples given but use the Australian Curriculum achievement standards as the reference point. The Standards Elaborations are available on the Queensland Studies Authority website (www.qsa.qld.edu.au).

Standards for accountability

Systems, schools and teachers use standards to demonstrate accountability internationally, publicly and to parents. Governments are increasingly anxious about education standards as reflected in national or international comparisons of student achievement because of the expected critical contribution to economic growth and competitiveness. There are also individual anxieties (particularly parental), given the growing importance of formal qualifications in determining success in life. In this intense education policy environment, key issues are the nature and extent of the evidence base used to inform the development of standards and related trialling and validation processes. Related to this is the evidence used to report student achievement using the standards. It can be the case that standards assume high public confidence and policy importance that is detached from the evidence base from which they derive meaning.

Testing for accountability has assumed prominence in public Australian education policy, with the implementation of the National Assessment Program – Literacy and Numeracy (NAPLAN) and the publication of results in literacy and numeracy on the MySchool website in 2010 (see www.myschool.edu.au). Since 2008, NAPLAN tests have been administered to students in Years 3, 5, 7 and 9 nationwide, every year, in the second full week in May. These tests assess the domains of reading, writing, language conventions (spelling, grammar and punctuation) and numeracy (www.nap.edu.au).

The NAPLAN results are reported on scales that demonstrate how students have performed when compared to established standards. The assessment scales are used to map the achievement of students as they progress through schooling. There are five scales: one for reading, writing and numeracy and two for language conventions (one for spelling and one for grammar and punctuation). Each assessment scale spans the full year from Year 3 to Year 9 along a 10-band scale (Australian Curriculum Assessment and Reporting Authority, 2009). These scales have been developed such that any given score, such as 700 in reading, will represent the same level of achievement over time so that the score will have the same meaning in 2012 as it did in 2010. Monitoring of literacy and numeracy achievements over time occurs with the use of this common scale that spans Years 3, 5, 7 and 9 as both the status of, and gain in, individual student achievement is monitored and reported throughout each student's years of schooling. The achievement of all students can also be monitored, and it is possible to gauge the achievement of the most able group of students and, at the same time, to pay attention to the group of students who have yet to reach the agreed national minimum standard.

For each domain, the scale is divided into 10 bands to cover the full range of student achievement in the tests. The bands map the increasing complexity of the skills assessed by NAPLAN. Six of the bands are used for reporting student performance at each year level. The Year 3 report shows Bands 1 to 6, the Year 5 report shows Bands 3 to 8, the Year 7 report shows Bands 4 to 9 and the Year 9 report shows Bands 5 to 10. For each year level, a national minimum standard is located on the scale. For Year 3, Band 2 is the national minimum standard; for Year 5, Band 4 is the national minimum standard; for Year 7, Band 5 is the national minimum standard; and for Year 9, Band 6 is the national minimum standard (see www.nap.edu.au).

The NAPLAN standards fulfil an accountability function and are used as benchmarks for systems-wide monitoring. These standards represent increasingly challenging skills and require increasingly higher scores on the NAPLAN scale (see www.nap.edu.au/results-and-reports/how-to-interpret/how-to-interpret.html). The minimum standards and common scales for NAPLAN results across all year levels are illustrated in Figure 2.3.

NAPLAN test results are reported for individual student performance and are provided to all students and parents/carers by the states and territories. The results are also reported nationally through a summary report each September and later in the year, a full national report. The publication of results has given rise to a number of unintended consequences. It was intended that information would be

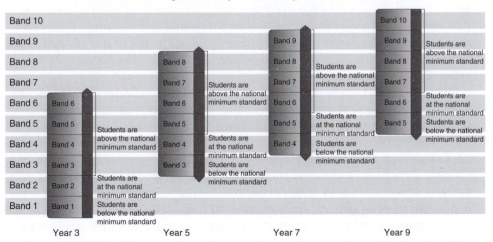

Figure 2.3   NAPLAN national assessment scale

Source: http://www.nap.edu.au/results-and-reports/how-to-interpret/how-to-interpret.html; © Australian Curriculum, Assessment and Reporting Authority 2011

provided on how students are performing in the areas of literacy and numeracy, to support improvements in teaching and learning and so that schools and systems could measure their students' achievements against national minimum standards and student performance in other states and territories (see www.nap. edu.au/results-and-reports/how-to-interpret/how-to-interpret.html).

In 2010, the high-stakes nature of NAPLAN testing was confirmed with the publication of results on the MySchool website (www.myschool.edu.au). The Australian Government has consistently reported high levels of parental support for the MySchool website, indicating that it serves the best interests of transparency and accountability by enabling parents to have access to evidence of schools' performance in the national literacy and numeracy testing. The publication of these results was a claim to support parental access to information about the quality of schooling; however, the results themselves have become codes or indexes for the quality status of individual schools and education systems more generally.

It is this use of standards for accountability that has proven to be most controversial because of the unintended consequences arising from high-stakes pressures. These can be acute when performance-based remuneration is associated with required improvement as measured by the standards. Often, the targets set are unachievable and the consequences of such policies have not been thoughtfully considered at the outset of implementation.

Unintended consequences of standards for high-stakes accountability

Several researchers have identified unintended consequences as they have occurred in other countries, including the United States (Darling-Hammond, 2010), England (Stobart, 2008) and Singapore (Kramer-Dahl, 2008). In these contexts of high stakes and high accountability, the nature of testing has led to a narrow set of outcomes that tend to distort learning and teaching. It should be noted that not all education systems have made public the results of high-stakes testing in league tables: New Zealand, Scotland, Wales and the Republic of Ireland being notable examples.

In England and the United States, simple and narrow indicators used to identify targets have resulted in numerical indicators of test results that are considered to be external measures of school performance. Such measures distort the image of improvement because the stakes attached to the targets, or the improved results, are so high that they become the focus in themselves. This is to the detriment of learning as they lead to perverse effects, such as cheating or manipulation of course entry, or choosing courses to maximize results. Grade inflation occurs and is evident when there is dramatic improvement on high-stakes tests, yet there is a lack of corresponding improvement on the low-stakes assessments. This would suggest that the improvements are more attributable to the students becoming increasingly proficient in test-taking than the subject itself (Stobart, 2005: 176).

In the United States, the No Child Left Behind Act (NCLB), which became law in 2002, requires public schools to demonstrate regular progress for all children towards achieving high standards. The target was that by 2014 all children would attain proficiency. All school districts and states were required to show Adequate Yearly Progress (AYP) towards this 2014 target for each subgroup (ethnicity; gender; English as a Second Language (ESL); special needs; status as economically disadvantaged) (Stobart, 2005: 119–20). Such pressure for achievement had many unintended consequences. For example, Amrein-Beardsley and colleagues (2010) researched how pressures on teachers to ensure improved tests results led to cheating. These researchers studied the types and degrees to which a sample of teachers was aware of – or had participated in – these practices in the context of the NCLB high-stakes testing policies. A taxonomy of cheating based on definitions of first-, second- and third-degree offences in the field of law was identified. Amrein-Beardsley and colleagues (2010: 27) concluded that:

> Policies that clearly undermine the moral and professional behavior of America's teachers need to be debated more thoroughly, and such policies must be challenged if their negative effects outweigh their positive effects on the educational system of our nation. It serves no one's interest to have policies that inherently promote cheating, and even justifications for cheating by educators, because the policy environment in which they work has become so onerous. There are better ways to design accountability systems.

The NCLB exemplifies how the push to raise standards has led to enormous pressure on teachers and distortions in the teaching of an holistic curriculum and the reduction in authentic and challenging learning experiences for students (Marsh, 2009). In fear of job losses and school closures, teachers have resorted to test irregularities such as providing answers to exam questions and reducing teaching responsive to Indigenous language and culture (McCarty, 2009).

The negative impact of high-stakes assessment on the quality of teaching and learning becomes evident with the shift to a focus only on the results in the evaluation of school performance and when sanctions are imposed. The unintended consequences that have been identified by the Australian Primary Principals Association (APPA, 2010) include:

- the narrowing of the curriculum as teachers teach only that which is to be tested
- the neglect of curriculum areas that are not tested
- the neglect of higher-order thinking skills that are difficult to assess in paper-and-pencil formats
- time spent on coaching and practice tests
- participation by schools in perverse practices designed to improve achievement data
- negative impacts on teachers, including public perception of the standing and quality of the profession
- the growth of a testing industry driven by commercial interests.

Other negative outcomes that have emerged in Australia include pressures on leaders to lift performance, threats to their jobs if results do not improve, more attention given to those students who are more likely to achieve better grades, neglect of those students who have the greatest need for support, the emergence of commercial tests that have not been quality assured, increased absenteeism by low-performing students on the day of the test and increased instances of cheating.

A set of guiding principles governing the reporting and use of NAPLAN has been developed by APPA (2010: 2) in an attempt to protect primary schools from these unintended consequences and to ensure that the national transparency agenda has a positive impact on the primary curriculum. These principles include: 'making informed and balanced judgements' that involve evaluations of schools' and systems' performance based on multiple sources of reliable evidence that relate to not just the academic goals but include the key socio-emotional goals of schooling. This is recommended to be a responsibility of the school and to take place through the development of appropriate appraisal systems, rather than having the Australian government develop more quantitative indicators.

Conclusion

In this chapter we discussed the reasons teachers need to understand standards and their relationship to curriculum, accountability, improvement and equity. We have outlined international trends in the use of standards and explained why standards have emerged as an important consideration for policy and teachers' assessment practice.

We have defined standards, discussed the different types of standards and the importance of understanding how they are represented and promulgated. We have indicated our concern with explicit or stated standards for quality judgements and have introduced the various ways in which standards are used for the improvement of learning and accountability. We concluded by illustrating how education systems, in pursuing efforts to raise standards in education, can have a negative effect and unintended consequences upon curriculum, teaching and learning.

Review questions

What has prompted some education systems to introduce standards-referenced assessment in the form of achievement or performance standards?

Why have standards become an important consideration in teachers' assessment practice?

Why do teachers need to understand standards and how they are represented?

How do teachers use defined standards in judgement practice?

What are some of the unintended changes that can be brought about when systems link standards to high-stakes accountability?

References 📖

Amrein-Beardsley, A., Berliner, D. and Rideau, S. (2010) 'Breaking professional law: Degrees of cheating on high stakes tests', *Education Policy Analysis Archives*, 18 (14): 2–33.

Australian Curriculum Assessment and Reporting Authority (2009) *NAPLAN National Assessment Scale*. Available at: www.nap.edu.au/results-and-reports/how-to-interpret/how-to-interpret.html.

Australian Primary Principals Association (APPA) (2010) *The Reporting and Use of NAPLAN*. APPA: Kathleen, Australian Capital Territory (see www.appa.asn.au).

Darling-Hammond, L. (2010) *The Flat World and Education: How America's Commitment to Equity will Determine Our Future*. New York: Teachers' College.

Deutsche Welle (2003a) *Report lambastes German school*. Available at: www.dw.de/dw/article/0,,993336,00.html.

Deutsche Welle (2003b) *Germany to introduce federal school standards*. Available at: www.dw.de/dw/article/0,,1050915,00.html.

Goldstein, H. and Heath, A. (eds) (2000) 'Educational standards', *Proceedings of the British Academy 102*. Oxford: Oxford University Press.

Harlen, W. (2005) 'Trusting teachers' judgement: Research evidence of the reliability and validity of teachers' assessment used for summative purposes', *Research Papers in Education*, 20 (3): 245–70.

Henning, D. (2004) *Germany: New education standards – perfecting the system of social selection*. Available at: www.wsws.org/articles/2004/jan2004/germ-j30.shtml.

Klenowski, V. (2006) *Evaluation report of the pilot of the 2005 Queensland Assessment Task (QAT)*. Brisbane: Queensland Studies Authority. Available at: www.qsa.qld.edu.au/3514.html.

Klenowski, V. (2007) *Evaluation of the effectiveness of the consensus-based standards validation process*. Available at: http://education.qld.gov.au/corporate/newbasics/html/lce_eval.html.

Köller, O. (2009) 'Using computer-based assessment to test listening and visual comprehension in large-scale assessments of foreign languages'. Keynote presentation at the 10th annual Association for Educational Assessment – Europe conference, Malta.

Kramer-Dahl, A. (2008) 'Still an examination culture – for most: Singapore literacy education in transition. Point and counterpoint', *Curriculum Perspective*, 28 (3): 82–8.

McCarty, T. (2009) 'The impact of high-stakes accountability policies on Native American learners: Evidence from research', *Teaching Education*, 20 (1): 7–29.

Marsh, C. (2009) *Key Concepts for Understanding Curriculum*. London: Routledge.

Maxwell, G.S. (2001) *Are Core Learning Outcomes Standards?* Brisbane: Queensland Studies Authority. Available at: www.qsa.qld.edu.au/downloads/publications/research_qscc_assess_report_1.pdf.

Maxwell, G.S. (2009) 'Defining standards for the 21st century', in C.M. Wyatt-Smith and J.J. Cumming (eds), *Educational Assessment in the 21st Century*. Dordrecht: Springer International. pp. 263–86.

Nichols, S.L. and Berliner, D.C. (2005) *The Inevitable Corruption of Indicators and Educators Through High-Stakes Testing*. Michigan: Great Lakes Center for Education Research and Practice.

OECD, Organization for Economic Cooperation and Development (2000) *Education at a Glance: OECD Indicators, Education and Skills*. Available at: www.oecd.org.

QSA, Queensland Studies Authority (2007) *Guide to Making Judgements*. Brisbane: QSA.

QSA, Queensland Studies Authority (2009) *Guide to Making Judgements*. Brisbane: QSA.

Reid, A. (2011) 'What sort of equity?', *Professional Educator*, 10 (4): 3–4.

Rizvi, F. and Lingard, B. (2010) *Globalizing Education Policy*. London: Routledge.

Sadler, D.R. (1987) 'Specifying and promulgating achievement standards', *Oxford Review of Education*, 13 (2): 191–209.

Sadler, D.R. (2005) 'Interpretations of criteria-based assessment and grading in higher education', *Assessment and Evaluation in Higher Education*, 30 (2), 175–94.

Stobart, G. (2005) 'Fairness in multicultural assessment systems', *Assessment in Education: Principles, Policy and Practice,* 12 (3): 275–87.

Stobart, G. (2008) *Testing Times: The Uses and Abuses of Assessment*. London: Routledge.

Wilson, M. (ed.) (2004) *Towards Coherence Between Classroom Assessment and Accountability*. Chicago: University of Chicago Press.

Web extras

Delandshire, G. and Arens, S.A. (2003) 'Examining the quality of the evidence in pre-service teacher portfolios', *Journal of Teacher Education,* 54 (1): 57–73.

Linn, R.L. (1993) 'Educational assessment: Expanded expectations and challenges', *Educational Evaluation and Policy Analysis,* 15 (1): 1–16.

3

A sociocultural perspective on teachers' judgement practice and learning

Overview

In this chapter we describe teachers' judgement in assessment practice as understood from a sociocultural perspective. We present assessment as a situated practice, providing examples that involve the judgement and decision purposes of assessment (Newton, 2007, 2010). The explanatory power of sociocultural theories of learning and knowing (Murphy and Hall, 2008) illuminates assessment as a situated practice. We analyse the notion of teachers' judgement by focusing on the interactions between teachers' tacit and explicit knowledge of curriculum, achievement standards and pedagogy in assessment communities. With reference to evidence from research, we consider how such communities of practice develop within and between schools and work to support teachers' judgements in assessment. We also discuss the importance of an understanding of culture, situated views of learning, assessment and related equity issues.

Introduction

In this chapter we introduce some key terms and related issues that connect with a sociocultural perspective of learning and assessment. These are defined at the outset, and are followed with illustrative examples of how teachers' professional judgement – as enacted in the assessment process – can be understood and explained from this theoretical perspective.

In contexts of high-stakes testing and accountability, reliance on assessment data and evidence of student learning have highlighted a significant priority for many countries in identifying the low level of equity achieved through current systems of assessment. Within such contexts, countries including Australia, New Zealand and

Canada have introduced national curricula and performance or achievement standards. In order to identify the disparities that continue to exist between the highest and lowest achievers, we analyse equity concerns regarding fairness, validity, cultural difference and access. Taking a sociocultural theoretical approach, we also explore why it is not possible to produce culturally neutral or fair assessment (Klenowski, 2009).

Key terms

It is useful to define some key terms from the underpinning sociocultural theory of learning and knowing adopted in this book.

Assessment

Assessment has been defined as taking place whenever:

> ... one person, in some kind of interaction, direct or indirect, with another, is conscious of obtaining and interpreting information about the knowledge and understanding, or the abilities and attitudes of that other person. (Rowntree, 1987: 4)

Teachers in schools are aware that assessment involves the collection of information and evidence of students' achievements in a purposeful and often systematic manner. Teachers are familiar, also, with how the judgement-level of assessment purpose (Newton, 2010) provides evidence of an individual student's achievement that is reported, for example, as an A–E grade. This is summative assessment.

In classroom practice, teachers are familiar with the use of evidence or assessment data to monitor students' achievements throughout the course or year. Teachers often draw upon their observations of students completing assessment and learning tasks, and other assessment information collected during classroom teaching, learning and assessment activities, to decide whether a student is experiencing difficulty in learning a particular concept or idea. At this decision-level of assessment purpose (Newton, 2010), the teacher provides appropriate feedback to the student about how to take the next steps in her learning, or the teacher may decide to intervene to scaffold the student's learning. The teacher may also take this as an opportunity to engage the student in discussion about her demonstrated knowledge, understanding and capabilities, as reflected in her work. Such engagement with the student by the teacher aligns with the sociocultural view of learning that values the collaboration of expert and novice for joint problem solving, in creating and sharing meaning. This decision-level of purpose is formative and is similar to student monitoring, diagnosis and continuous assessment. From a sociocultural perspective, such assessment is defined as a social practice that is interactive and contextual (Stobart, 2008; Mahuika et al., 2011).

Too often, constructivist discourse is evident in the specified curriculum but absent from the assessment of the curriculum (Murphy, 1996). Broadly speaking, assessment systems reflect a psychometric tradition '… that saw ability as an innate trait that could be measured' (McCormick and Murphy, 2008: 10). This measurement approach differentiated students on the basis of their ability, located on a 'normal' distribution curve that supposedly was representative of the population. Students were 'streamed' into classes in which a particular curriculum was taught, or they were separated into employment or academic pathways considered appropriate to their abilities. These psychometric views have been challenged (Gipps, 1994), and sociocultural theorizations of assessment have emerged (Murphy and Hall, 2008; Pryor and Crossouard, 2008). From these perspectives, learning and assessment are situated and the agency of both teacher and student are recognized. That is, learning is seen as a 'process of participation in cultural activity' (McCormick and Murphy, 2008: 5). Participation in the interaction becomes fundamental. The classroom learning activities and associated assessment provide opportunities for participation or learning, and 'what is experienced is determined by the participants and the nature of the participation in the arenas in which curricula are enacted' (McCormick and Murphy, 2008: 3).

Achievement

Achievement has been defined as 'the extent to which a student has demonstrated knowledge, skills, values and attitudes as the result of the teaching/learning process' (Queensland Studies Authority, 2012: 13). An important understanding identified in recent research is that there exists a strong association between a student's background and identity, and achievement, regardless of the level of schooling (McCormick and Murphy, 2008; Murphy and Hall, 2008; Pryor and Crossouard, 2008; McNaughton, 2011). Assessment information can therefore only provide an indicator or understanding of achievement: it is 'not actual achievement' (McCormick and Murphy, 2008: 12). A number of explanations for this proposition relate to a sociocultural view of learning.

Sociocultural views of learning and assessment

To understand learning through the lens of assessment, we need to focus on the interactions between '… the learner, the teacher and the assessment task in the social, historical and cultural context in which it is carried out' (Elwood, 2006: 231). These interactions are important considerations in a social theory of learning (Wenger, 1998) and a sociocultural perspective of assessment (Murphy and Hall, 2008). Learning viewed as an active construction of knowledge in social and cultural environments is integral to understanding how assessment and learning connect (Elwood, 2006; Klenowski et al., 2006). Sociocultural and situated or non-local views of mind (Murphy and Hall, 2008), and learning in the context of assessment frameworks, are significant in this active view of knowledge construction. These theoretical perspectives help to enhance our understanding of teachers' assessment practices, their use of achievement or performance standards to improve learning, and the manifestation of these standards in the judgement practice and moderation processes. Additionally, how this stance relates to assessment issues of fairness, validity and equity is exemplified using recent research findings that demonstrate how teachers engage in culturally responsive pedagogy and assessment cultures to improve their judgement practice and learning experiences for all their students.

From a sociocultural position, learning is understood as 'becoming' a full participant (Murphy and Hall, 2008) in the community of learners of the school or the classroom. This can refer to a teacher who is 'becoming' more competent in teaching and assessing through the use of achievement standards or more culturally relevant pedagogy to build her assessment identity and assessment repertoire. Or it can refer, for instance, to an Indigenous or Māori student whose identity as a learner strengthens and whose sense of 'belonging' develops through greater participation and engagement involving interaction and negotiation with other learners during classroom teaching, learning and associated assessment activities.

A sociocultural perspective, then, defines learning in terms of this sense of 'becoming' and 'belonging' (Murphy and Hall, 2008) through participation and changing of identity (or identities) with acceptance into the community of learners through developing relationships, effortful teaching and assessment. Assessment, as theorized from a sociocultural view of learning, views the individual's historical, social and cultural contexts to be influential in the development of their values, beliefs, understanding and sense-making of the world, and their identity and position within it (Rogoff, 2003; Murphy and Hall, 2008; Mahuika et al., 2011).

A sense of community that is inherent in the learning process is valued from sociocultural conceptions of learning and assessment practice. Lave and Wenger (1991) proposed that learners gain experience through a 'community of practice' that involves a form of apprenticeship through a process of 'legitimate peripheral participation'. Teachers are also learners, as they participate in a new form of assessment and judgement formation. Although there are experienced teachers and those who are new to the profession, if the majority is using a new mode of assessment, such as achievement or performance standards to assess learning, then many will have limited experience with the practice of using, for example, folios of work, authentic performance tasks or social moderation in assessment. In this respect teachers themselves are apprentices.

A sociocultural positioning of judgement practice

According to Wenger's social theory of learning (Wenger, 1998: 5), four components are integral to learning and knowing processes: community (learning as belonging); identity (learning as becoming); meaning (learning as experience); and practice (learning as doing). To illustrate these components, two examples of communities are given.

First is an assessment 'community' of teachers who interact with one another in the social practice of moderation to 'deprivatize' their judgement practices.

This involves explicating their interpretations of the standards by identifying the qualities of the student work in defence of their judgement, which is reflected in their award of a particular grade. The teachers negotiate their understanding of the meaning of the standards in this 'assessment community' through practice and, in so doing, develop their identities as assessors.

Second, community can be used to refer to students in the 'learning community' of the classroom, where teachers engage students in assessment activities to increase their participation and sense of belonging. Students, too, develop their identities based on their participation and the extent to which they feel as though they belong. In both examples of community, an 'assessment identity' in context of the particular community evolves. This can occur through a range of interactions including moderation 'practice', whereby a level of competence that is recognizable is established through participation, or through practice or doing on the part of the student to gain experience and develop an identity as learner.

In these communities, the historical, social and cultural influences on judgement and assessment practices become apparent and are often dependent on the levels of assessment purpose. For example, at the summative, judgement-level, reporting of student achievement for accountability occurs. At the formative, decision-level, the improvement or development of learning is the teacher's focus. A teacher may, for example, adapt the learning activity and associated assessment for students with learning difficulties, in order to provide more opportunities for these students to participate in the achievement of learning goals that are realistically attainable for them, though different to those of other students. Such adaptations permit learning and assessment to be tailored to the interests and needs of individual students, and serve the purpose of promoting and monitoring participation in learning for these individuals who, over time, may well achieve the learning goals and standards expected at a given year level.

Moderation as a community of practice

The concept of 'bridging epistemologies' (Cook and Brown, 1999) provides an explanatory framework by which to understand the sociocultural processes and interactions of teachers in moderation meetings. From this concept the interplay of knowledge and knowing is seen as 'a potentially generative phenomenon' (Cook and Brown, 1999: 54). As teachers meet in their moderation groups to develop and articulate their understanding of the standards, their purpose, function, nature and meaning, the interplay of individuals' explicit and tacit knowledge of the standards with the group's explicit knowledge and tacit knowledge of understanding is revealed. For while teachers use the standards and related textual resources such as annotated student responses and the guides to making judgements, they also actively refer to other tacit knowledges. These tacit understandings are either individual tacit knowledge such as a teacher's personal knowledge of particular students, or individual tacit knowledge of standards not specified elsewhere. The group's tacit understandings include knowledge of curriculum and teaching contexts where teachers have delivered the curriculum and their prior evaluative experiences of judgement practice. The individual tacit and group tacit understandings are often used in combination, and sometimes in opposition to the explicit achievement standards. Teachers identify how, at times, the tacit understandings are used to discount or even subvert the achievement standards (Wyatt-Smith et al., 2010). This is why it is crucial that guidelines and professional development opportunities are provided for teachers, so that they can experience and practise their judgement skills and utilize the various resources available to draw upon.

For those participating in moderation, new knowledge about standards and knowing how to use standards in the approach to making judgements is an outcome from 'the use of knowledge as a tool of knowing within situated interaction with the social and physical world' (Cook and Brown, 1999: 54). In other words, moderation as social practice or a community of learners provides an opportunity for teachers as assessors to develop and articulate their understanding of the standards as used in the assessment of student work. The moderation meeting itself also provides an opportunity for the generation of new knowledge and new ways of knowing as teachers draw on their individual tacit and explicit knowledge and the group's tacit and explicit knowledge, and use this knowledge as a tool of knowing within situated interaction in the social and physical world. This is what Cook and Brown (1999) called 'knowing in action', and leads to the production of new knowledge and knowing about standards, in relation to their judgements, in the practice of moderation.

Teachers' engagement in moderation practice and the new knowledge and ways of knowing that are generated include the following.

- Teachers are able to check that similar skills are taught and the levels of skills achieved are comparable.

- Teachers can also check that similar learning outcomes are assessed as equitable and of a comparable quality.

- Fairness for all students is extended beyond the classroom or school to between schools, as teachers focus on quality and how judgements of quality are reached.

- Teachers, parents, students and other staff members can develop increased confidence in that common standards are expected and being achieved by a particular year group of students.

- Teaching and assessment practices are made visible in that teachers' work is made public and open to scrutiny and critique, which helps to address accountability and quality assurance demands.

- Gaps or omissions in the teaching programme can be identified, particularly if the director of curriculum or head of department participates in the moderation meetings.

- A sense of community develops as teachers negotiate their understanding and seek clarification and advice when they are unsure of the standard itself or the standard of work. There is a shift from individual practice to shared practice, and the improvement of that practice.

- Teachers' attention can be focused on assessment and its place within the teaching and learning programme.

- Teachers are motivated to teach a topic when they realize the results achieved by other teachers using different approaches.

- Teachers learn new ways of teaching, and diversify to improve their practice in order to meet the needs of individual students. (Klenowski and Adie, 2009)

Culture and situated learning

Culture influences students' learning and their assessments. Bruner (1986: 65) described culture as 'the implicit semi-connected knowledge of the world, from which through negotiation people arrive at satisfactory ways of acting in given contexts' (cited in McCormick and Murphy, 2008: 5). A sociocultural perspective has a view of 'learning as a process of participation in cultural activity' (McCormick and Murphy, 2008: 5). From this vantage point, meaning comes through interaction and participation in social activity. Knowledge is therefore not transferred from expert to novice; rather, it is in the interaction or, as expressed by McCormick and Murphy (2008: 5) 'engagement in the culturally authentic activity'. Such activity is seen as part of a community of practice.

Students who wish to understand and learn mathematics, for instance, become members of a community of learners of mathematics and, as suggested by Lave and Wenger (1991), a novice starts at the 'periphery' of the community and as participation and understanding develop moves to 'central participation' of the community. McCormick and Murphy (2008: 5) explained that 'mutual understanding, or "intersubjectivity" comes through participation' and 'with it a transformation of identity'. If learning is viewed as a transformation of identity and enculturation into communities of practice, then knowledge is viewed as situated in learning. That is to say, the learning or associated assessment activity in which students engage to develop knowledge is integral to that learning and cognition (Brown et al., 1989 cited by McCormick and Murphy, 2008: 6).

This situated view of learning has implications for how teachers organize their classroom teaching, learning and assessment practices. From this view, peers and others are involved in joint problem solving, with collaboration and the development of intersubjectivity as the intended goals. When students participate in group or peer work by attending to a common focus with shared understandings about the learning activity or task such that they focus and communicate with one another to develop a solution, then intersubjectivity is realized. This view of learning is important when considering the equity issues associated with cultural difference and efforts to achieve fairer assessment practices.

Cultural difference and equity

Many teachers are unaware that there is no cultural neutrality in assessment or in the selection of what is assessed. In this light, Cumming (2000) asks 'When setting standards and test content, are we really sure that this is the knowledge we need?' or 'Are we really privileging certain knowledges to maintain a dominant culture, and, in so doing, ensuring perpetuation of ourselves, as people who have succeeded in the formal educational culture to date?' (Cumming, 2000: 4). These questions, while they relate to considerations of fair and valid assessment, high-light the importance of cultural difference and equity concerns. Equity does not mean treating students all the same or seeking equality of outcomes. Rather, the concept relates to cultural difference, access and justice.

Students from a non-dominant culture may 'experience testing as a form of cultural intimidation ... students from particular ethnic and racial groups may actually develop attitudes and practices of resistance to the surveillance, judge-ment and categorisation practices that are affiliated with large-scale testing' (Berlack, 2001, as cited in Luke et al., 2002: 11). Fair assessment does not favour culturally different groups above others. On the contrary, it recognizes cultural differences and investigates the possible effect on student performance in the context of assessment and standardized tests. Culture-specific variables said to influence test performance include those related to: content knowledge, the framing of the task, the design of the task including the terms used to commu-nicate task requirements, the normative models of development reflected in the domain or constructs of the test, and linguistic codes and conventions of the test (ACACA, 1995; Luke et al., 2002).

In the contexts of assessment and curriculum reform, policy and research to sup-port and manage issues of equity are helpful in up-skilling teachers in inclusive and ethical assessment practices. Positive support of cultural and social diversity in policy, practice and principles is required. A fair educational and assessment envi-ronment supports teachers to develop a sense of social, legal and ethical respon-sibility to promote equity. In a changing educational context, equity as a concept and a practice must be theorized in order to influence policy (Reid, 2011).

However, many teachers are unaware of how to deal with the cultural diversity of their students in the way they teach and assess. Due to this lack of understand-ing teachers often fail to respond to the specific cultural needs of their students (Mahuika and Bishop, n.d.: 6). A sociocultural view of learning and knowing recognizes the cultural variations inherent in learning as well as what constitutes valued knowledge (Murphy and Hall, 2008). This position also values the cultural legacies an individual learner may draw upon and the connections made by prior generations, which are often mediated by the cultural tools inherited (Rogoff, 2003, cited by Murphy and Hall, 2008).

Equity and assessment

Fair and valid assessment

Teachers assess students' learning to identify what they have learned, what they have not learned and where they are experiencing difficulty. Assessment, because of its concern with what students have learned, is also based on a conception of the nature of learning and learners. When considering the fairness of the assessment, there is a need, then, to be clear about the concepts underlying the specific assessments (Gipps and Murphy, 1994). In addition to these conceptions of the nature of learning and learners, it is important, in terms of equity, to consider the choice of knowledge and skills selected for the assessments. To achieve equity, the curriculum needs to include valued knowledge and skills consisting of different kinds of cultural knowledge and experience, reflective of the diversity of groups, and not privilege one group over others.

Research to date has identified fair assessment as a qualitative concern related to equity and justice, and considers how this influences access to learning and the curriculum (Gipps and Murphy, 1994; Stobart, 2005). As expressed by Gipps and Murphy (1994: 273) there is '[n]o such thing as a fair test and nor could there be as the situation is too complex and the notion too simplistic'. However, as Stobart (2008: 113) suggested '[w]e will never achieve fair assessment but we can make it fairer'.

Assessments have to be as fair as we can make them, and issues of student access to curriculum and the design of assessment tasks require teacher understanding of the relationships between teaching, curriculum and assessment, particularly in high-stakes accountability contexts. The fairness of any test or assessment depends on whether the students are able to make sense of what is required. It is important for those students from culturally and linguistically diverse groups and those from backgrounds of poverty and social disadvantage to be provided with opportunities to offer evidence of their expertise. In order to achieve assessment that is as fair as possible, teachers need to use a range of modes and task styles. The use of rich tasks and authentic assessments is an attempt to achieve forms of assessment with high site validity (as distinct from system validity); that is, assessment that is contextually relevant and relates directly to students' own community contexts.

In 1989 it was Michael Apple who expressed how important it was for curricular questions to address equity issues related to gender and race:

- Whose knowledge is taught?
- Why is it taught in a particular way to this particular group?
- How do we enable the histories and cultures of people of colour, and of women, to be taught in responsible and responsive ways?

Caroline Gipps and Patricia Murphy (1994) later built on these questions and suggested several significant questions related to assessment that are equally relevant to teachers' practice today:

- What knowledge is assessed and equated with achievement?
- Are the form, content and mode of assessment appropriate for different groups and individuals?
- Is this range of cultural knowledge reflected in definitions of achievement?
- How does cultural knowledge mediate individuals' responses to assessment in ways that alter the construct being assessed?

Gordon Stobart (2005) raised the following questions regarding access, which also need to be understood by teachers as they underpin the curriculum, assessment practice and related literacy demands:

- What is incorporated from the cultures of those attending?
- Who gets taught and by whom?
- Are there differences in the resources available for different groups?

Together, these questions highlight how all students need opportunities to demonstrate their learning through valid tasks and assessments designed and developed at local and regional levels. For, as expressed by Gipps (1999: 385) '[o]penness about design, constructs and scoring, will bring out into the open the values and biases of the test design process, offer an opportunity for debate about cultural and social influences, and open up the relationship between the assessor and the learner'.

The focus on these curricular and assessment questions has increased awareness of the need for strategies to develop assessment practices that address equity issues more effectively. For example, in Australia the Australian Curriculum, Assessment and Certification Authorities (ACACA) guidelines recommend that assessment agencies:

> evaluate the occurrence in assessment instruments of reproductions of gender, socioeconomic, ethnic or other cultural stereotypes; conduct equity scanning of assessment instruments before use; promote research into the validity and fairness of assessment items for which the agency is responsible and employ specialist editors to examine the language of assessment instruments in terms of possible barriers to equal opportunity for all students. (ACACA, 1995: 1)

Teachers need to be aware of group and cultural differences, and to understand the interaction of the mode of assessment with the construct assessed and student experience, to ensure that there is access for all, in terms of what is being asked in the assessment task or test. They should also be aware of their society's views and expectations of the abilities of different student groups, and how this influences expectation, teaching and the curriculum offered (Gipps and Murphy, 1994: 277).

Access issues and literacy demands

All assessment makes demands on students' literacy. Literate practices are often invisible as they are context-specific and constructed through social interactions. Assessment tasks are saturated with literacy demands; teachers often are not aware of them or assume that these skills have been developed at another time and in another context (Wyatt-Smith and Cumming, 2003). Literacy demands vary from student to student, and it is difficult to say what these demands are until teachers have what Reid (2001) called, insights into students' extra-textual knowledge.

Failure to teach explicitly the literacy demands of assessment may seriously inhibit students' reported learning because of their inability to access what is being asked of them in the assessment item or task. Students may 'fail', or in the case of school-based assessment may not submit, because they are uncertain or do not understand the assessment question or requirements of the assessment task. In other words, some students cannot access the literacy demands, which Hipwell and Klenowski (2011) called the *'silent assessors'*. Literacy and illiteracy are manifest when situations allow or disallow literate practices to be used. If students are placed in situations in which their literacy skills do not match the demands of that situation, then they can be positioned as failures (McDermott, 1999; Stobart, 2008).

The prominence of large-scale testing for accountability purposes has heightened the need for teachers in their classroom assessment practices to be aware and skilled to understand and teach the literacy demands for both tests and assessment tasks. Ensuring that all students are able to understand and access the test question or assessment task is fundamental in addressing equity concerns (Hipwell and Klenowski, 2011). Findings from recent research conducted in Queensland, Australia emphasized the significance of this problem, as it links to culture and assessment.

Australian research

Patterns of under-achievement by Australian Indigenous students are reflected in national benchmark databases such as NAPLAN and international testing programmes like TIMSS and PISA. A trend of under-performance in terms of equity has continued over the past six years, as is evident from the comparative analyses of PISA results, first administered in 2000, then again in 2003, 2006 and 2009. However, too often, little attention is given to better performances by Australian Indigenous students and to the similarity of spread across percentiles for both Indigenous and non-Indigenous students. On this, De Bortoli and Thomson stated:

> Although many Indigenous students performed at very low levels (in PISA), there were also some Indigenous students who performed very well … there was a spread of 304 score points between the 5th and 95th percentile for Indigenous students. The spread of scores for non-Indigenous students between the 5th and 95th percentile was similar, at 310 score points … On the mathematical literacy proficiency scale in PISA 2003, only a small proportion of Indigenous students achieved Level 5 or 6, while around one in five non-Indigenous students were performing at these levels. At the lower end of the mathematical literacy scale, 43 per cent of Indigenous students did not achieve a proficiency of Level 2 compared to 14 per cent of non-Indigenous students. (2009: 26)

There is no denying that Australian Indigenous children score significantly lower than non-Indigenous children in tests and that the performance of Indigenous students declines in numeracy and literacy relative to that of the rest of the school population as the period of time spent at school increases. Classroom teaching and assessment, and the conditions and organization of schools in which the performances of Indigenous and non-Indigenous students vary and fluctuate, have been the subject of recent research (Klenowski et al., 2010). How and why fluctuations occur need to be contrasted against factors such as the students' first language and their sociocultural and socioeconomic circumstances.

Language study

McTaggart and Curro (2009), in a north Queensland participatory action research study conducted by teachers, suggested that differences between home and school are a fundamental factor.

> [T]here are many complex and interacting causes of the underachievement of Indigenous students ... a vast number of Indigenous Australian students are speaking at least one Indigenous language and no English when they are not in classrooms ... The languages used, orally only, by students in schoolyards, at home and in recreation may range from traditional languages, through clearly identifiable creoles, to several dialects, sometimes termed 'Aboriginal Englishes' which are similar to each other but locally specific. Students may use any or all of these, together, or separately, or intermittently with subconscious code-switching. Standard Australian English is almost never used. So, in schools, students are usually learning English as a second or third language. (McTaggart and Curro, 2009: 6)

This study which was sponsored by the Queensland College of Teachers (see www. qct.edu.au) aimed to determine how to prepare teachers with the skills required to teach students whose first language is not English, particularly in relation to pre-service teacher education and professional development. The Cairns-based, Far North Queensland Indigenous Schooling Support Unit (ISSU) (see www.issu. com.au) provided rich case material and helped in the selection of the teachers, principals and other participants for this study. Teacher participants were selected from a broad range of schools on the basis of at least five years of teaching experience and their work on English as Second Language (ESL) with ISSU staff, with evident changes in practice and learning as a result of that experience. These criteria for selection were important as the researchers wanted to obtain 'before and after' thinking of the participants. The researchers focused on staff development designed to assist educators to improve their language awareness and to adopt the principles and strategies of Teaching English as Second Language (TESL) in the teaching and learning for Australian Indigenous students.

A review of the literature raised the researchers' awareness of how the relevance of ESL for Indigenous learners was lost in the multiple discourses of 'cultural differences, behaviour management, morale, literacy, attendance, hearing, disability, traditional language maintenance, socio-economic status and NAPLAN scores' (McTaggart and Curro, 2009: 4). The action-research perspective adopted was used to interpret the information collected from the participants, and the review of the research literature, to outline an approach to monitor and consolidate changes in educational practice. These researchers concluded that while there is an abundance of ideas about Indigenous education there are 'few resources to support the use of ESL ... strategies readily available' (ibid.). They found that many participants had commenced their teaching careers knowing very little about the needs of Indigenous students. While some had significant understanding about Indigenous culture, languages, the low achievement of Indigenous students and the many causes, fundamentally these teachers had not been given any useful strategies. McTaggart and Curro (2009) emphasized how many Indigenous students were failing to achieve sufficient English proficiency to gain access to the curriculum. It follows from this that many Indigenous students fail to access the literacy demands of the assessment tasks, such as those items that make up PISA, TIMSS and NAPLAN tests. 'Teachers are poorly prepared to solve the problem which is caused by unjustified assumptions made by system curriculum makers, not by the children themselves, or their families (McTaggart and Curro, 2009: 6).

Language of mathematics study

Facility with Standard Australian English (SAE) appears to be assumed in the ACARA curriculum, NAPLAN and state-based curricula. Students whose first language is not SAE require sensitive teaching and learning strategies to gain an understanding of how to communicate (mathematically and linguistically) in classrooms (Jorgensen, 2011). *The Language of Maths* study (DEST, 2009), which was included in the Department of Education, Science and Training's Literacy and Numeracy in the Middle Years Cluster Project, was also conducted in northern Queensland. This project involved 14 teachers and 260 Indigenous students from Year 1 through to Year 9, two rural/remote schools with 100 per cent Indigenous students and three urban schools with a diverse student population. Four of the schools were state schools and one was a Catholic primary school.

The study adopted an action-research approach, which was informed by a review of recent relevant research and data collected by the project teachers about the students they teach. Teachers completed contextual analyses of their respective schools by answering questions related to their teaching and their professional learning aims. The data from the teachers was augmented by a comparative analysis of Indigenous student assessment data with state data of the standardized numeracy tests. Language difference was highlighted as a significant issue in assessing learner performance and achievement, having a negative effect on Indigenous students' test performance. The test items that required articulation of 'thinking, processing, and reasoning by students were the items that the students experienced most difficulty with and "failed", along with not understanding the test questions due to the complexity of language used' (DEST, 2009, Appendix 5: 7).

Developing the students' use of the language of mathematics while recognizing and valuing the Indigenous language spoken at home by using the home language as a bridge to the language of school and wider society was identified as a priority for development. The action-research programme incorporated discovery tasks for students and teacher reflection, followed with the need to focus on language. Teachers found that the '... students demonstrated that they may have the requisite knowledge and skills, but language can be a barrier to communicating knowledge' (DEST, 2009, Appendix 5: 8).

The teachers worked in collaboration with colleagues, a linguist, and mathematics mentor to develop a scaffolded support document to help them appreciate linguistic differences and how these differences can affect the teaching and learning of mathematics. The approach adopted used these differences as productive resources to plan for and scaffold students' understandings and knowledge of the English language of mathematics and to develop effective ways to assess and report student achievements. Importantly, it was recognized and emphasized that Indigenous students are not an homogeneous group at either the system or the school level. It was understood that 'language, knowledge and experience varies from community to community, student to student and categorizing students and applying a generic approach is counterproductive' (DEST, 2009, Appendix 5: 10).

The project's mathematics mentor helped the teachers to identify and explicitly teach language in relation to:

- mathematical content language (for example, 'average', 'multiply', 'compare', 'more', 'less')
- topic language ('round trip', 'leg of a journey')
- grammar in which this language is connected and embedded (If … then … because)
- task language (design a 'table', present your 'data' in 'columns')
- procedural language (present, explain, describe, calculate). (DEST, 2009, Appendix 5: 15)

In summary, the major findings of this project concluded that:

- It is important to incorporate and value the entering behaviours of students so that teachers do not make assumptions about content knowledge, learning and associated understandings; the use of discovery tasks as formative assessment to help inform planning, teaching, assessment and reporting is also important.
- Quality assessment tasks need to be authentic and meaningful, and to be engaging for students.
- Assessment needs to provide opportunity for all students to demonstrate success, which includes:
  - explicit teaching of language and bridging from the shared language
  - identified in discovery tasks to abstract the symbolic language of mathematics
  - open-ended tasks that encourage engagement and risk taking
  - clear expectations of criteria and standards for students and teachers
  - contexts that promote engagement and risk taking

    ○ opportunities for oral language use and development so that students can demonstrate understandings (valuing home language and school language)

    ○ ensuring validity of assessment.

Teachers are expected to meet curriculum outcomes and national testing expectations with the diverse range of students who make up their classes. However, as evident from studies such as these conducted for the Queensland College of Teachers in 2009 and for DEST in 2005, teachers are often unaware or not knowledgeable about how to address language and literacy related issues.

Culture-responsive assessment

Teaching and assessment practices that are responsive to sociocultural contexts, and cultural and social difference, help to address questions of equity. Learning for *all* students occurs with greater responsiveness to cultural and social difference in classroom teaching and assessment. Care in how the achievement results are interpreted and presented is essential in order to see beyond the raw scores and to understand the related equity issues, without over-interpretation of students' results in terms of innate ability and limitations (Murphy, 2009). Assessment is integral to the teacher's repertoire of practice and provides an important means by which to understand the learning needs of the students and to modify teaching accordingly.

    The concepts of 'cultural capital' and 'social capital' (Bourdieu and Passeron, 1977; Bourdieu, 1986) help illustrate how one group (socioeconomic, cultural or gender) can be situated such that greater resilience, perseverance or competence than another is required to succeed. 'Cultural capital' can take the form of knowledge, skills, education or values, which can give an individual an advantage or a disadvantage, or a higher or lower status in society. For example, if students have not developed certain skills, or have not had access to certain knowledge because of their cultural background or gender, then they are at a disadvantage when those skills, or that knowledge, are valued and assessed in high-stakes tests. Such examinations for selection purposes can favour those who have access to the 'cultural capital' that is considered of value. It is in this way that the dominant group is privileged. Bourdieu's work illustrates how internal processes of schooling, including assessment for selection purposes and the attainment of formal qualifications, provide for the reproduction of the elite rather than being genuinely meritocratic. His work showed how such processes favoured bourgeois 'cultural capital' and experience, such that working-class students had to have greater persistence and ability than those from favoured backgrounds in order to reach the same level in the education system (Broadfoot, 1996). These insights have implications for our assessment systems and signal a need for culturally responsive assessment.

    Mahuika and colleagues (2011), who have reviewed culture and assessment in New Zealand, referred to the disparity that exists in their country between their highest and lowest achievers, which they suggested exists within rather than between schools. These researchers support teacher use of culturally responsive pedagogies and assessment to meet the specific needs of their Māori students. According to Mahuika and colleagues (2011: 185), these students are 'to be targeted by teachers through the implementation of culturally responsive pedagogies that include assessment practices'. They did not, however, suggest that Māori or Indigenous students 'are so different that they need some different, and as yet undiscovered, "recipe" for addressing these differences' (ibid.). Rather, from a sociocultural view it becomes apparent that some teachers are unaware of how the education system supports the dominant group's cultural values and beliefs. However, although teachers want the best for all of their students they continue to use teaching and assessment strategies that do not recognize the cultural variations of their Indigenous students and how these differences mediate the Indigenous students' learning and assessment outcomes.

Internationally, an important understanding of cultural difference has occurred in that there has been a shift from a deficit view of the learner to a more considered view of how the school or the system can take responsibility for the development of culturally responsive models and quality teaching programmes that incorporate formative assessment (Comber and Kamler, 2004; Ainscow, 2010; Bishop et al., 2010; Mahuika et al., 2011). Too often, teachers or principals will indicate that very little can be done to improve the achievement of Indigenous students with explanations for low achievement directed at the student, the student's home circumstances or outside-of-school experiences. As expressed by Mahuika and colleagues (2011: 189) in relation to the teachers of their review '... teachers pathologized Māori students' lived experiences by explaining their lack of educational achievement in deficit terms as something within the child or the child's home', with the consequence of '... the creation of negative and problematic relationships between teachers and Māori students; lowered teacher expectations of Māori students' abilities; and a loss of an appreciation of how powerful agentic teachers can be in bringing about change in learning outcomes for students previously denied access to the benefits that education has to offer.' These authors emphasized how teachers who adopt this view tend to blame someone or something beyond their influence and in so doing suggest that they are unable to take responsibility for the outcomes of these influences.

Schools and teachers need to develop their capacity to identify *deficit views of difference* (Ainscow, 2010), which position students as *lacking in something*. These assumptions are challenged from a sociocultural perspective of learning and assessment that gives greater respect to the valuing of difference. A diagnostic and holistic view of the student's background, culture, language and demeanour is seen as more beneficial for the teacher, to gain a better understanding from their use of formative assessment to identify the student's learning needs. Assessment and pedagogy that is responsive to cultural variations and that helps to build supportive relationships between teachers and their students acknowledges that culture is central to learning. Indigenous students who are supported to draw on their 'funds of knowledge' (Moll, 1992) or what they know, or their ways of sense making from their culture, gain in terms of classroom learning. Effortful teaching and assessment that is culturally responsive and allows for different ways of knowing facilitates increased agency for Indigenous students. Culturally inclusive assessment does not attempt to favour different cultural groups; rather, it is recognized that cultural differences can affect performance, such as on standardized tests.

Implications for practice

Culturally responsive assessment implies that teachers are assessment literate with respect to their understanding of cultural and linguistic differences. These teachers provide pedagogic support for students to access the literacy demands of assessment tasks or items. They have expertise in task design, and attend to the validity and fairness of assessment practices. Culturally responsive assessment practice requires teachers to be fully aware of the needs of their students whose first language is not English, and to use appropriate strategies. For example, each set of assessment and teaching tasks or instruments that is designed to assess a student's achievement in a subject should use:

- a range and balance of background contexts in which assessment items or tasks are presented;
- a range and balance of types of assessment tasks or instruments and modes of response, including a balance and range of visual and linguistic material; and
- involve a range and balance of conditions. (ACACA, 1995: 1)

It is important to understand the student's understandings, dispositions and self-beliefs, and acknowledge her personal view of the value of learning. The teacher's use of assessment formatively helps him to interact with the student in ways that facilitate the student to re-imagine an identity as a successful learner through appropriate feedback and goal setting. Such formative assessment practice also helps to develop a relationship that is not dominating, and that encourages student agency.

To become members of the learning community, students need to decode the cultural relay of the language of the classroom and align their behaviour with the accepted norms of that classroom. This is not always possible for Indigenous students who have different cultural and language experiences to others in the classroom. Achieving a sense of cultural awareness together with classroom teachers and Indigenous education aides (in Australia, Aboriginal Education Workers) is a fundamental goal for pedagogical and assessment decisions, and for gaining greater awareness of what individual students might be capable of and how they might best learn. A culturally responsive approach to assessment acknowledges the importance of identity and background, the central constituents of teacher assessment literacies. As much as literacy is an issue for the students in terms of the demands of assessment and the curriculum, it is an issue for teachers in their efforts to align their teaching practices with the current curriculum and standards reform.

Conclusion

Teachers need to be aware of the accountability contexts within which they work. Their assessment and pedagogic practices are mediated by structures beyond their control, such as national policy about what they should assess, and how that is to be recorded and reported. However, teachers also need to be aware of the diverse nature of the learners in their classrooms and how culture and language mediate their students' learning and assessment. It is important that teachers do not see Indigenous students as an homogeneous group, for much diversity exists in terms of Indigenous students' backgrounds and cultural influences.

The students' sociocultural circumstances need to be understood, considered and valued by teachers and school leaders, as students' attitudes to learning are directly affected by the value they place on the learning and the success that they believe they might have in reaching a satisfactory goal. From research, it appears that a majority of teachers have had limited professional development in relation to cultural awareness, culturally inclusive strategies, language issues and literacy demands of assessment tasks or tests. Effortful teaching and practices that encompass the complex nature of the classroom environment by engaging in culturally responsive approaches to assessing students through rich and challenging tasks and open-ended questions are part of the teacher's responsibility in developing his professionalism.

Review questions

From a sociocultural view of learning, how can assessment be described as a social practice?

Why are communities of practice important for an understanding of assessment from a sociocultural perspective?

How does moderation practice constitute a community of learners?

What are the important implications for classroom teaching, learning and associated assessment activities from a situated view of learning?

How can assessment practice be made fairer for those students who come from different racial, ethnic, cultural or social backgrounds?

Why have the literacy demands of assessment tasks and tests been named 'the silent assessors'?

References

Ainscow, M. (2010) 'Achieving excellence and equity: Reflections on the development of practices in one local district over 10 years', *School Effectiveness and School Improvement,* 21 (1): 75–91.

Apple, M.W. (1989) 'How equality has been redefined in the conservative restoration', in W.G. Secada (ed.), *Equity in Education.* London: Falmer Press. pp. 7–35.

ACACA, Australian Curriculum, Assessment and Certification Authorities (1995) *Guidelines for Assessment Quality and Equity.* Available at: http://acaca.bos.nsw.edu.au/go/acaca-documents/.

Berlack, H. (2001) 'Race and the achievement gap', *Rethinking Schools Online*, 15 (4). Available at: http://www.rethinkingschools.org/archive/_04/Race154.shtml.

Bishop, R., O'Sullivan, D. and Berryman, M. (2010) *Scaling Up Education Reform: Addressing the Politics of Disparity*. Wellington: NZCER Press.

Bourdieu, P. (1986) 'The forms of capital', in J.G. Richardson (ed.), *Handbook of Theory and Research for the Sociology of Education*. New York: Greenwood Press. pp. 241–58.

Bourdieu, P. and Passeron, J.C. (1977) *Reproduction in Education, Society and Culture*. London: Sage.

Broadfoot, P. (1996) *Education, Assessment and Society*. Buckingham: Open University Press.

Brown, J.S., Collins, A. and Duguid, P. (1989) 'Situated cognition and the culture of learning', *Educational Researcher*, 18 (1): 32–41.

Bruner, J. (1986) *Actual Minds, Possible Worlds*. Cambridge, MA: Harvard University Press.

Comber, B. and Kamler, B. (2004) 'Getting out of deficit: Pedagogies of reconnection', *Teaching Education*, 15 (3): 293–310.

Cook, S.D.N. and Brown, J.S. (1999) 'Bridging epistemologies: The generative dance between organizational knowledge and organizational knowing', *Organization Science*, 10 (4): 381–400.

Cumming, J. (2000) 'After DIF, what culture remains?' 26th International Association for Educational Assessment Conference, Educational Assessment in a Multicultural Society: Integrating Unique Perspectives and Shared Values, Jerusalem.

De Bortoli, L. and Thomson, S. (2009) *The Achievement of Australia's Indigenous Students in PISA 2000–2006*. Melbourne: ACER Press.

DEST, Department of Education, Science and Training (2009) *The Language of Maths*, A DEST Literacy and Numeracy in the Middle Years Cluster Project: Appendix 5. Available at: http://education.qld.gov.au/literacy/docs/deewr-myp-final-report.pdf.

Elwood, J. (2006) 'Formative assessment: Possibilities, boundaries and limitations', *Assessment in Education: Principles, Policy and Practice*, 2: 215–32.

Gipps, C. (1994) *Beyond Testing: Towards a Theory of Educational Assessment*. London: Falmer Press.

Gipps, C. (1999) 'Chapter 10: Socio-cultural aspects of assessment', *Review of Research in Education*, 24 (1): 355–92.

Gipps, C. and Murphy, P. (1994) *A Fair Test? Assessment, Achievement and Equity*. Buckingham: Open University Press.

Hipwell, P. and Klenowski, V. (2011) 'A case for addressing the literacy demands of student assessment', *Australian Journal of Language and Literacy*, 34 (2): 127–46.

Jorgensen, R. (2011) 'Language, culture and learning mathematics: A Bourdieuian analysis of Indigenous learning', in C. Wyatt-Smith, J. Elkins and S. Gunn (eds), *Multiple Perspectives on Difficulties in Learning Literacy and Numeracy*. Dordrecht: Springer. pp. 315–29.

Klenowski, V. (2009) 'Australian Indigenous students: Addressing equity issues in assessment', *Teaching Education*, 20 (1): 77–93.

Klenowski, V. and Adie, L. (2009) 'Moderation as judgement practice: Reconciling system level accountability and local level practice', *Curriculum Perspectives*, 29 (1): 10–28.

Klenowski, V., Askew, S. and Carnell, E. (2006) 'Portfolios for learning, assessment and professional development in higher education', *Assessment and Evaluation in Higher Education*, 31 (3): 267–86.

Klenowski, V., Tobias, S., Funnell, B., Vance, F. and Kaesehagen, C. (2010) 'Culture – fair assessment: Challenging Indigenous students through effortful mathematics teaching', in *AARE International Education Research Conference*, Melbourne.

Lave, J. and Wenger, E. (1991) *Situated Learning. Legitimate Peripheral Participation*. Cambridge: Cambridge University Press.

Luke, A., Woods, A., Land, R., Bahr, M. and McFarland, M. (2002) *Accountability: Inclusive assessment, monitoring and reporting*. Research report prepared for the Queensland Indigenous Education Consultative Body. Queensland, Australia.

Mahuika, R. and Bishop, R. (n.d.) *Review Paper 6: Issues of Culture and Assessment in New Zealand Education pertaining to Māori Students*. Available at: www.assessment.tki.org.nz.

Mahuika, R., Berryman, M. and Bishop, R. (2011) 'Issues of culture and assessment in New Zealand education pertaining to Māori students', *Assessment Matters*, 3: 183–98.

McCormick, R. and Murphy, P. (2008) 'Curriculum: The case for a focus on learning', in P. Murphy and K. Hall (eds), *Learning and Practice Agency and Identities*. London: Sage. pp. 3–18.

McDermott, R.P. (1999) 'On becoming labelled – The story of Adam', in P. Murphy (ed.), *Learners, Learning and Assessment*. London: Paul Chapman. pp. 1–21.

McNaughton, S. (2011) *Designing Better Schools for Culturally and Linguistically Diverse Children: A Science of Performance Model for Research*. New York and London: Routledge.

McTaggart, R. and Curro, G. (2009) *Book Language as a Foreign Language: ESL Strategies for Indigenous Learners*. Toowong: QCOT.

Moll, L.C. (1992) 'Bilingual classroom studies and community analysis', *Educational Researcher*, 21 (2): 20–4.

Murphy, P. (1996) 'Integrating learning and assessment – the role of learning theories', in P. Woods (ed.), *Contemporary Issues in Teaching and Learning*. London: Routledge. pp. 173–93.

Murphy, P. (2009) 'Applying a sociocultural approach to assessment theory and practice: Issues for summative and formative assessment', The Open University, presentation at Queensland University of Technology, Brisbane.

Murphy, P. and Hall, K. (eds) (2008) *Learning and Practice: Agency and Identities*. London: Sage.

Newton, P.E. (2007) 'Clarifying the purposes of educational assessment', *Assessment in Education: Principle, Policy and Practice*, 14 (2): 149–70.

Newton, P. (2010) 'The multiple purposes of assessment', *International Encyclopedia of Education*, 3: 392–6.

Pryor, J. and Crossouard, B. (2008) 'A socio-cultural theorisation of formative assessment', *Oxford Review of Education*, 34 (1): 1–20.

Queensland Studies Authority (2012) 'Reporting student achievement and progress P–10 Advice and Guidelines' (Draft): 13. Available at: www.qsa.qld.edu.au.

Reid, I. (2001) 'Framing literacy demands', in J.J. Cumming and C. Wyatt-Smith (eds), *Literacy and the Curriculum: Success in the Senior Secondary Schooling*. Melbourne: ACER Press.

Reid, A. (2011) 'What sort of equity?', *Professional Educator*, 10 (4): 3–4.

Rogoff, B. (2003) *The Cultural Nature of Human Development*. Oxford: Oxford University Press.

Rowntree, D. (1987) *Assessing Students: How Shall We Know Them?* London: Kogan Page.

Stobart, G. (2005) 'Fairness in multicultural assessment systems', *Assessment in Education: Principles, Policy and Practice,* 12 (3): 275–87.

Stobart, G. (2008) *Testing Times: The Uses and Abuses of Assessment.* London: Routledge.

Wenger, E. (1998) *Communities of Practice: Learning, Meaning and Identity.* Cambridge: Cambridge University Press.

Wyatt-Smith, C.M. and Cumming, J.J. (2003) 'Curriculum literacies: Expanding domains of assessment', *Assessment in Education: Principles, Policy and Practice,* 10 (1): 47–59.

Wyatt-Smith, C.M., Klenowski, V. and Gunn, S.J. (2010) 'The centrality of teachers' judgement practice in assessment: A study of standards in moderation', *Assessment in Education: Principles, Policy and Practice,* 17 (1): 59–75.

Web extra

Wilson, M. (1992) 'Educational leverage from a political necessity: Implications of new perspectives on student assessment for Chapter 1 evaluation', *Educational Evaluation and Policy Analysis,* 14 (2): 123–44.

4

Alignment and front-ending assessment

Overview

This chapter has a focus on how assessment and instruction can be integrated in classroom practice to improve learning and student engagement. We present two main concepts for building and sustaining high-quality assessment cultures: the alignment of assessment, curriculum and pedagogy, and the 'front-ending' of assessment with a sharp focus on task-design processes as the anchors for curriculum planning and teaching.

Introduction

The ideas discussed in this chapter draw from a range of assessment studies and engage in particular with the insights of a large-scale, one-year study funded by the Australian government. The aims of the Department of Education, Employment and Workplace Relations (DEEWR) and the Queensland Department of Education, Training and the Arts (DETA)[1] in this initiative were 'to increase teachers' knowledge, understanding and professional skill development about best practices in literacy and numeracy assessment, curriculum and teaching instruction for their particular middle years of schooling contexts' (DEEWR and DETA, 2007: III). We have drawn on this study as it represents empirically based findings about applications for classroom practice as found in the evaluation report undertaken by Wyatt-Smith and Bridges (2007) as a part of this larger government initiative and related report.

'Front-ending' assessment is a deliberate action to connect curriculum planning, assessment, task design and evidence collection in the classroom (Wyatt-Smith and Bridges, 2007). Main reference points for the teacher, then, are what students will be expected to learn and how the teacher will know whether and how well students

---

[1]Now the Department of Education, Training and Employment

have learned what was intended, as well as other incidental or unplanned learning that may occur. Put simply, the change in classroom practice explored in the chapter is threefold: first, before teaching begins, quality teaching is understood to extend to the teacher's work in directly aligning or connecting assessment and the intended curriculum. So, assessment is not an endpoint or terminal activity, something tacked onto the end of the unit, or done after teaching and learning have taken place. Instead, assessment comes to the fore when planning. The quality of assessment tasks that students are to complete becomes a feature of quality teaching, vital in establishing *what evidence* the teacher wants to collect, when and why this particular evidence. Also at the planning stage is teacher consideration of how the quality of the information gathered will be interpreted to indicate not only how far learning has progressed (distance) but also how well (quality). Fundamental and productive changes in teaching practice and learning can result from critical reflection on the assessment evidence to be collected *before* teaching begins.

Second, for teachers, designing suitably demanding assessment tasks becomes a major skill. Strategies are presented in the chapter to support teacher decision making in assessment design, the aim being to ensure such tasks are rigorous, carry forward the intent of the curriculum with related issues of community and student relevance, and that equity issues are addressed.

Third, the related idea explored is that, optimally, the teacher also develops task-specific features of quality for significant pieces that students are asked to complete: the standards and criteria that can accompany classroom tasks. This is not to take a prescriptive or limiting view of how students might approach project work or classroom assessments. Instead, it is to foster opportunities for teachers to bring into their planning how they might engage students in consideration of quality performance as part of classroom teaching. The intention is that standards are taken up by teachers and students to foster conversations about quality. As discussed elsewhere in this book, standards are also best understood as part of a suite of resources to support such conversations, other resources including authentic exemplars of student work used as concrete referents for the standards. Alignment of curriculum, pedagogy and assessment through a focus on how teachers design assessment tasks with accompanying statements of standards is enabling. It is through this work that teachers address as part of their practice the knowledges and capabilities that students will need in order to be successful. The notion of alignment and the idea that students will be offered and will engage with information about expected features of quality before they commence work on summative assessment activities are consistent with the view of assessment as situated practice whereby classroom assessment can work to inform teaching practice and also to engage students in their own learning in new ways.

The teacher-as-researcher movement came to the fore in the 1970s (Stenhouse, 1975), and attracted considerable attention in the 1980s (Schön, 1983; Cole, 1988). Schön claimed that the reflective practitioner uses dialogue with colleagues and students as part of the continuous assessment of both student achievement and teaching performance. Further, the work of Glaser (1963, 1976, 1986) and others (Glaser and Nitko, 1971) established a strong research interest in the integration of assessment and instruction.

Discussions of how to integrate assessment and instruction led to considerations of assessment purposes and the concepts of *reliability and validity*. It has been argued that 'the quality of any particular assessment is typically addressed in terms of measures of reliability and validity', which often follow from the uses of assessment practices (Broadfoot and Black, 2004: 14). Broadly speaking, whereas classroom assessment is said to support higher validity, for large-scale testing, issues of reliability are central. Sadler (1989: 122) explained that:

> Reliability is usually (and correctly) said to be a necessary but not sufficient condition for validity, because measurements or judgments may be reliable in the sense of being consistent over time or over judges and still be off-target (or invalid). Reliability is therefore presented as a precondition for a determination of validity. In discussing formative assessment, however, the relation between reliability and validity is more appropriately stated as follows: validity is a sufficient but not necessary condition for reliability. Attention to the validity of judgments about individual pieces of work should take precedence over attention to reliability of grading in any context where the emphasis is on diagnosis and improvement. Reliability will follow as a corollary.

Hence, for formative and instructional purposes, the main focus is properly on validity, while in high-stakes testing high reliability is of key importance. Others (Linn, 1989; Messick, 1989; Torrance, 1997; Wilson, 2004; Newton, 2012) have written in detail about theories of validity and reliability, explored in terms of two-value systems or paradigmatic views: standardization and traditional psychometric test theory, and contextualized judgements and hermeneutic theory. Broadly speaking, the case is well supported in the literature that both 'value systems' have a role in maintaining validity and reliability but assert that validity should play a greater role than in the past (Matters et al., 1998). While a full overview of these arguments cannot be presented here, essentially the argument is that by applying the 'Cronbach-Moss framework' tighter notions of validity and broader notions of reliability are possible. Pitman and colleagues stated that:

> at the centre of our construction of validity is the assertion that the worth of assessment lies fundamentally in its contribution to learning ... [and] the *consequences* of assessment both for individuals and for institutions ... In the Cronbach-Moss framework, questions about appropriateness as well as adequacy are raised ... reliability is generally seen as a necessary but insufficient condition for validity [but] an important guarantor of fairness. (1999: 2)

So, while emphasizing the importance of reliability, without validity, reliability is viewed as trivial.

More recently, Matters (2006) argued that factors such as rigour, accountability, credibility and authenticity (another way to view reliability and validity) are more useful constructs. She suggested that system and teacher energy should primarily go into effective assessment, with teachers designing and critiquing, at both design and item levels. This work would extend to instruments developed and administered by others, and would be a more productive focus than arguing about the relative merits (and limitations) of different purposes of assessment. Related to this, of course, is the key capability for teachers to collect and interpret data on student achievement, including data generated at both system and local levels. Essentially, the focus needs to shift to the nature of the evidence generated in the various assessment programmes, from standardized testing to classroom-based programmes. We need to know how they interface, 'and what they tell us, separately and together, so that we know the whole assessment story' (Wyatt-Smith, 2000: 125). Several authors (Moss, 1994; Matters, 2006) have recognized the importance of validity. While there is a range of arguments put forward in support of validity, broadly speaking there is agreement with Cronbach and Meehls' (1955) teaching that the validity of the interpretations of measurements and how they are used are priority concerns.

While not focusing on validity in particular, Black and Wiliam (1998a) took up the metaphor of the 'black box' to focus attention on the essential connection between assessment and learning. Through examination of the impact of specific actions of educators, from policy makers to teachers, they and other writers have given impetus to the discourse on assessment for learning. Close scrutiny of the classroom assessment 'black box' was required in order to identify how learning was occurring and the role of assessment in informing and supporting learning. This brings to attention what is actioned or deposited into the classroom (for example, policy decisions, anxieties, standards, high-stakes tests), the social interactions in the course of learning, and what was generated (optimally, more knowledgeable young people). Central to Black and Wiliam's (1998a, 1998b) argument was an understanding that learning outcomes, including accountability, could only be improved when the specific nature of what was happening in the classroom was clearly understood and strategically addressed. By prioritizing open scrutiny of classroom practice, the classroom teacher could become better informed about their actual practice and adopt effective strategies for subsequent implementation to improve student learning. That is, teachers' insights into learning, and more specifically, how and what learning was occurring in the classroom, would be significantly enhanced.

Assessment has long been understood as a process of collecting information or evidence of learning and inferring meaning from it. Linn (1992) made the point that no single assessment tool or approach can provide all the necessary information that teachers, parents and students themselves will need, and so there is a need for continuous assessment strategies and multiple indicators that allow those 'who are disadvantaged on one assessment to have an opportunity to offer alternative evidence of their expertise' (1992: 44). Teachers routinely face the need to provide multiple sources of evidence and opportunities for a mix of new and more traditional forms of assessment, including information on judgements about student performance:

> Decisions that affect individual students' life chances or educational opportunities should not be made on the basis of test scores alone. Other

relevant information should be taken into account to enhance the overall validity of such decisions ... More importantly, when there is credible evidence that a test score may not adequately reflect a student's true proficiency, alternative acceptable means should be provided by which to demonstrate attainment of the tested standards. (American Educational Research Association, 2000)

As Shepard (2000: 12) reminded us, teachers will 'need help in learning to use assessment in new ways'. Teachers will need opportunities to reflect on their own beliefs and gain deep understanding of what is involved in designing tasks that promote learning and that engage the students themselves in various methods of assessment. This chapter is about the field of alternative new forms of assessment reform that centre on teachers' work. There is no doubt that the success of the broadening of assessment approaches will require skilled teachers who are prepared in sufficient numbers to sustain complex forms of teaching that are aligned with assessment.

This chapter starts with the notions that validity is central, that assessment is always and inevitably social, cultural and contextual, and that effective assessment is vital in promoting learning. Broadly speaking, 'a test is valid if it really does measure what it purports to measure' (Scriven, 1980: 40). It is now widely recognized that assessments, including tests, should be valid in order for the results to be accurately applied and interpreted. While pencil-and-paper examinations have been influential for many years in classroom assessment, especially for reporting purposes, there is now also widespread recognition that validity is not determined by a single statistic or test result, but rather by a body of information that demonstrates the relationship between the test and the behaviour it is intended to measure. From this vantage point, the effectiveness and quality of assessment is vital. Further, assessment is taken to entail

> the relationship between the learner, the teacher and the assessment task in the social, historical and cultural context in which it is carried out ... the learner and the teacher are entangled ... learning cannot be viewed in isolation, only in relationship between the learner and the teacher. (Elwood, 2006: 230)

Here, assessment 'is integral to the teaching process and embedded in the social and cultural life of the classroom' (Gipps, 1999: 378; Black et al., 2003).

While insights into assessment from a sociocultural perspective are still developing, Gipps (1999: 377) went on to suggest that the 'requirement, in the sociocultural perspective, to assess learning in the social setting can be met in a number of ways. Portfolios can be used to reflect the processes of learning and their development over time' and ideally should reflect or in some way articulate the social setting in which learning took place. So, what and how students learn in the classroom relies in large part on the effectiveness of teacher-designed activities, including assessment tasks that students are asked to undertake. The teacher's repertoire of knowledge and skills for teaching and assessment is taken here to include a range of design decisions, and systematic new ways of thinking about task design. It is through this approach that teachers are able to connect assessment with planning for learning and teaching. As used here, the term 'task' is taken to refer to assignments or pieces of work that are intended to be cumulative; that is to say, that build upon and extend student learning. They include, for example, projects or assignments to be completed by students individually or in pairs and teams. They also include ways of working online and in the preparation of some form of demonstration or production. They are routinely completed over time and so are distinguished from, say, short-answer and more limited activities that could be completed within a section of a lesson.

An extension of the focus on task design is for teachers to use official statements of standards relevant to their phase of schooling and jurisdiction, where available, and consider the demands of their classroom assessment activities in relation to these. In many standards-referenced assessment systems, efforts to develop teachers' efficacy with the use of stated standards involve focusing teacher attention on the features of quality in classroom tasks and the features evident in official statements of standards. How teachers can develop their own task-based criteria and standards and incorporate them into their teaching is discussed elsewhere in this book. Our aim here is to recast assessment and the act of arriving at a judgement of quality as a *process*, not just the award of a final grade by an individual teacher. The start, therefore, is with teachers' own assessment literacies and the professional capabilities and dispositions needed to connect or align assessment, the intended curriculum and student learning.

Assessment literacies and professional capabilities in aligning curriculum and assessment

This section presents the idea that quality assessment processes begin concurrently with planning for teaching and learning, with teachers focusing attention on their assessment plans and, more specifically, on the main activities or tasks that students are to complete. This timing means that teachers can ensure assessment tasks are designed to support and extend, as well as validly assess student learning. This is in keeping with the view of assessment 'as a decision-making, not a measurement, process' (Pitman et al., 1999). Our interest here is in the professional capabilities and attributes involved in *front-ending assessment* (Wyatt-Smith and Bridges, 2007), taken as a verb signalling deliberate action on the part of the teacher. That is, directly connecting the intended curriculum with decisions about the information to be collected in order to know what learning is occurring in the classroom and how best to tailor teaching and learning opportunities to enable success for all learners.

Broadly speaking, there are eight key professional capabilities and attributes that form part of teachers' assessment literacies. These are essential for teachers as they undertake reviews of assessment plans, checking to see that the assessment is aligned with and validly assesses the intended curriculum and course or programme learning objectives, as well as achieving clear task specifications.

In order to support and validly assess student learning, teachers need a repertoire of knowledge, capabilities and dispositions. Specifically, they need:

1 Well-developed knowledge of the curriculum domain. This is foundational for effective assessment and curriculum planning and task design.

2 To be able to self-identify and verify the suitability of their assumptions about students' prior knowledges and capabilities as these relate to curriculum and cross-disciplinary priorities such as literacy and numeracy. Effective teachers reported reviewing their earlier assumptions about student readiness to proceed to new learning, as well as assumptions about the prior learning that students have undertaken.

3 To be able to connect or align the assessment evidence to be collected in the classroom with educational intentions or learning objectives. Such alignment means that teachers are in tune with the interactivity of assessment, teaching and learning and can inform students about the intention and requirements of tasks, in relation to the learning in which they are engaged.

4 To consider the intellectual challenge, range and balance of the tasks set for students. This involves teachers in examining depth of knowledge, skills, concepts and attributes called forth by the tasks and which students will need in order to achieve success. Also relevant here are the opportunities for students to work in a range of contexts (alone and unaided, in small groups or pairs, with expert 'others' outside the classroom) and with a range of resources (traditional print forms and design and communication using new technologies).

5 To take account of student diversity and ensure the curriculum and assessment plan is appropriate for diverse learners. This involves consideration of the range of opportunities for students to demonstrate their learning.

6 To develop skills in identifying and clearly communicating to students and parents the intended cognitive expectations of tasks and the purpose and relevance of set tasks. This includes the rationale for the tasks used, including their type, purpose, timing, sequence and weighting. Such explicitness of assessment has a focusing effect on pedagogy.

7 To develop skills in communicating to and with students the desired features or characteristics of quality in set tasks. This extends to discussing how students themselves can use stated criteria and standards to review the quality of their work in development and upon its completion. Such discussions can have a focusing effect for students as they engage in self-assessment and peer assessment.

8 A willingness to reflect upon and open up or deprivatize their own judgements and share discussions about the qualities or features of work samples, assessed against stated standards. This can be achieved when teachers come together in professional conversations about planning and actual classroom assessment samples (built on ideas presented in Wyatt-Smith and Bridges, 2007, pp. 44–58, copyright Commonwealth of Australia, reproduced by permission).

In the next section these ideas are explored further and the reader will 'hear' comments from teachers themselves as they reflect on their experiences of front-ending assessment and aligning curriculum, learning and teaching and assessment. The talk segments are drawn from teachers and leaders of local teacher networks, referred to as 'clusters'. Readers interested in the project report are advised to see DEEWR and DETA (2007), and Wyatt-Smith and Bridges (2007), the source material from which these talk segments are drawn (copyright Commonwealth of Australia, reproduced by permission). There were 15 clusters, 107 schools, 273 teachers and approximately 5000 students involved in this project. The relevant page numbers in Wyatt-Smith and Bridges (2007) from which the teacher talk is drawn are provided after each segment.

Hearing what teachers have to say: Teachers' knowledge of the curriculum and learners

Deep knowledge of the domain or discipline and the expected outcomes in the intended curriculum are foundational to professional practice.

Individual and group teacher planning is far from a new idea. Also well recognized is the importance of teacher knowledge of the domain or discipline and official materials that present the intended curriculum. So, routinely, teacher planning could be expected to entail a close revisiting of syllabus documents as well as shared clarifications of curriculum intent. Such shared and individual planning stimulates how teachers, other curriculum leaders and school principals establish and maintain a quality assessment culture within the school. This includes teachers sharing curriculum knowledge, both at and across year levels. In several studies (Harlen, 1994; Murphy and Hall, 2008) there is a recurring observation: teachers' own clarity about the nature of the knowledge and capabilities that are to be learnt and assessed is critical for student success. Such knowledge is foundational to planning and effective practice. Optimally, capacity building in how to 'front-end' assessment and achieve alignment, as outlined above, involves teachers working together in a team or a supportive learning community of teachers within and even across schools, as indicated below in the comments about sharing expertise:

> ... So there's a much better knowledge of the syllabus, at least in terms of the units – the two units that were developed and other needs that we might have had like making things authentic ... the planning process ... [has] ... been a very genuine learning process for everybody and we've learnt things from Year seven teachers and Year seven admin-primary administrators and vice versa and we've got some expertise in Science in our school, which I know the primary school teachers have welcomed and they've got some expertise in literacy which we have welcomed. (Advocate, Cluster 11; Wyatt-Smith and Bridges, 2007: 44)

In the segment above, the teacher identified how professional learning can occur as a truly collaborative enterprise across the years of schooling, across areas of expertise and across leadership roles. Such professional conversations, where they have a focus on 'front-ending' and 'alignment', can also unearth a range of other teacher learning, and below one teacher talks about assessment tasks and the realization of their size and complexity. In this case, what emerges is how assessment activities can have powerful, built-in barriers to student success:

> ... probably the biggest learning for a lot of our teachers was the scope of the task that they were asking their kids to do and just understanding the burrowing down, the drilling down of that was what the biggest learning I think for a lot of our teachers, what they were asking for their kids to do, from the beginning was just miles too big, we were trying to achieve too much and for some of our teachers that was the biggest learning they had, the expectations that they had, their awareness of what the kids knew before they came. (Advocate, Cluster 6; 2007: 45)

Teachers need to verify the suitability of their assumptions about students' prior knowledges and capabilities: curriculum, literacy and numeracy

There is ample evidence in the literature that teachers make assumptions about students' prior knowledges and capabilities. Also clear is how such assumptions can build in barriers to student success where they are not checked against information about student readiness to proceed with new learning. Carefully designed assessment early on in a teaching programme gives teachers an opportunity both to check the suitability of their assumptions about students' prior learning and to establish a basis for establishing realistically attainable goals for learning for all students. One Australian teacher talks below about how in her school assessment community teachers came together to establish the curriculum and literacy demands of assessment tasks. She talked of how they:

> ... actually determined what the knowledge and the skills are that's ... needed and our teachers have actually had a real problem doing that because so much of it is implicit sort of knowledge ... The other thing that they've found hard is ... the idea of determining what the strengths are that the kids bring and also what the knowledge gaps are. It's got to do with many of our teachers coming from that sort of white, middle-class background that doesn't really understand that there are kids who have homes without newspapers or have homes where they haven't been embedded within a ... you know we talk about it, we know it at a head level but we don't really know it ... our teachers have really had to come to terms with [student difference]. (Teacher, Cluster 15; 2007: 45)

While it is widely recognized that teachers' carry with them evaluative experience that they have accrued over time, they also bring what the teacher above refers to as an *implicit sort of knowledge* to curriculum planning. For a quality assessment school culture, it is beneficial for such knowledge be shared and made explicit. Then conversations can take into consideration what teachers know about students' prior knowledge, the physical and cultural resources of the community in which the school is located and how this can inform efforts to connect students' in-school learning to their out-of-school learning. One teacher talks about how such an approach marks a difference in how she and her school engaged in 'front-ending' assessment to make explicit what was previously implicit:

> ... being aware of your own preconceptions and assumptions so they are just so critical to any assessment task that you develop and I think one of the major learnings is that in the past we've always said 'well we've got to know our content and we've got to know where we're going and we've got to know what outcomes we want but we have left out this major critical thing about knowing our kids and knowing ourself' ... (Teacher, Cluster 15; 2007: 45–6)

The following segment also makes evident how teachers confronted their assumptions about students' prior knowledges, becoming aware of how they had in some cases 'mis-read' students' entry knowledges. This positive application of formative assessment – assessment for diagnostic purposes – is introduced early in the teaching and learning plan, to enable the teacher to 'tune into' what is involved in progressing learning.

> ... you would assume that [students] knew certain things like ... one was I assumed one day about drawing mud maps and assumed being country students that they actually knew what a mud map was and when I asked them to draw that they had no idea what a mud map was so I had to spend half a lesson explaining what a mud map was and how to draw mud maps and go back through that sort of explanation so yeah going through the formative assessment sort of practice highlighted some flaws in my assumptions basically of what students' prior knowledge was. (Teacher, Cluster 5; 2007: 46)

As used here as part of front-ending assessment, *entry knowledge* is a broad concept. It is taken to include not only curricular skills and knowledges but also the sociocultural skills and knowledges that students bring with them into the classroom. There are, of course, key transitions or stages in schooling, and teachers' efforts in achieving clarity about students' entry knowledge can be difficult when the students come from a range of different schools. One teacher talks about this below and how she also is aware of students' knowledge as being influenced by a range of factors, including parental engagement, in students' learning:

> ... in year eight [the first year of high school] we don't know, we have a general idea of what our feeder schools are teaching but ... a major learning curve for us ... some of our kids know a lot more than they've ever been taught at school but they know a lot more from their parents and especially a lot more of racial issues from their parents ... (Teacher, Cluster 9; 2007: 46)

So when teachers front-end assessment, they not only collect information useful for knowing the prior knowledge that students bring with them into the classroom, but also have the opportunity to consider their own sociocultural assumptions. From this vantage point, diversity can be seen as a classroom resource, with the teacher attending to children's in-school and out-of-school knowledges: when planning, in the words of the teacher below:

> *T*: It's the sorts of knowledge and skills that we expect the kids to have when they're moving into a new unit of work or a new task. So part of that …

> *T*: … the entry knowledge, the prior learnings but also too … some of my kids in my class for example are very instinctive in their knowledge of how for example (a map) works while some of the other kids are less so. So it's just determining what their knowledge, what their skill levels are at, what they're bringing with them from home, from watching the television, reading newspapers if that's what they're doing or just what their background knowledge is and where they're acquiring that knowledge from. So those were the sorts of things that we'd used our formative assessment to determine … (Teacher, Cluster 15; 2007: 47)

> So basically once you have the assessment firmly in place the pedagogy became really clear because your pedagogy has to support that – that sort of quality assessment task … that was a bit of a shift from what's usually done, usually assessment is that thing that you attach on the end of the unit whereas as opposed to sort of being the driver which it has now become … (Facilitator, Cluster 1; 2007: 48)

Being explicit about assessment expectations can have a focusing effect on pedagogy and facilitate deeper learning

As mentioned earlier, setting assessment tasks can be treated as an endpoint or terminal activity. In this section the focus is on how being explicit about assessment expectations from the outset can have a focusing effect on pedagogy and can facilitate deeper learning. One way to achieve this is for teachers to analyse the culminating or summative assessment tasks that students will be required to complete, and to identify the explicit skills and knowledges that students will need for academic success. These can include curriculum or content knowledge as well as literacy and numeracy skills, depending on whether the tasks are traditional pencil-and-paper in nature, or involve demonstrations or online activities. One teacher talks about what 'being explicit' meant for a team of teachers with whom she was working:

> … we started off talking about quality assessment and the first thing that came up was the need to be explicit when designing the assessment task and that's both in terms of the expectations of the kids and the required schooling to prepare … From that stems a number of things such as the inclusion of step by step checklists for students to follow when they've completed their task – when they were completing their tasks and also it allowed the kids to become very, very familiar with the [assessment] criteria … When we looked at the quality of pedagogy again we talked about the modelling of expectations with students and that again coming back to students becoming familiar with the criteria by actually using the criteria. Sort of said that

pedagogy became clear after the assessment task was created ... (Facilitator, Cluster 1; 2007: 51)

The intention here is not to suggest that teachers should try to pre-specify all aspects of tasks or assessment criteria. For teaching and learning purposes they necessarily represent provision of indicators of quality – an anticipated set. Teachers are familiar with the experience of the surprises that sometimes come in students' work. That is, when a student takes an unanticipated approach and produces high-quality work, deserving of recognition. The interest in pre-specifying criteria is, however, to highlight how typically, assessment, and in particular the design of assessment tasks, tends to be tied to the teachers' authority and, in turn, how assessment expectations can remain in the black box. This could occur when teachers do not include in their classroom practice opportunities for students to see and discuss samples of quality student work, and other discussions about the desired features or characteristics of performance. Here, we suggest that teachers and students can both benefit from talking about quality in the classroom. It is through such talk that students can be inducted into knowledge about what counts as quality and develop their own evaluative experience by applying assessment criteria to samples of others' work and, in turn, their own, under the expert guidance of the teacher.

Such talk and actions contribute towards demystifying assessment as a whole, and make available for students vital information about how they can improve their learning. The benefits of this approach can be seen in the extract below, where a teacher describes specific strategies she employs in her classroom to link pedagogy and assessment, and the positive effects not only on disengaged students but on other class members:

> What I did in particular with my guys, we did a unit on Space and as our assessment task it was to design a Space board game and what we actually did was create a task booklet with all the steps that were involved, all the teaching activities in order to produce the final product and so what in particular with the disengaged kids, what it meant was that they could see what was coming ahead of them, they could flip forward and go 'oh, when are we doing this activity' so I found personally it was a great way of getting them engaged and motivated. Not just the disengaged kids but the ones that maybe just wanted to have a bit more ownership in their task so I'd definitely be using that again in future assessment tasks. (Teacher, Cluster 12; 2007: 51)

Another strategy is to provide students with stated criteria or to generate features of quality with them through a whole-of-class discussion. One teacher talks about the benefit of distributing an assessment rubric and how it served to enhance student engagement:

> Y: ... giving the explicit rubric to the students actually stimulated them to really try and achieve a lot more than we previously expected them to. So it made them more motivated and quite keen, having in front of them: what it was to achieve a high (A). We didn't call it (A) but that's

how the children referred to it so that was a really interesting and exciting thing that we [learnt from it].

> ... we actually gave them a copy which they've glued in their book which they could refer back to and they kept saying, for example when doing surveys 'okay how many surveys do I need to get that top mark' so they were – we referred them back, have a look at your rubric to see what you need if that's what you're aiming for, that was – a lot of students, even the at-risk kids were asking us such questions which was great to see. (Teacher, Cluster 6; 2007: 51)

As mentioned already, another focusing strategy to open the black box of assessment for and with students is to supply them with previously completed work samples and to ask them to discuss it in relation to relevant criteria and any other features that they choose to identify:

> No, I've never tried that [*students using criteria to judge past samples before beginning their own assessment piece*] before and I would try it for every unit of work in the future. It was very, very powerful to do that ... We don't often give – well I believe we don't often give the students the same opportunity to see what other people have done and learn from that, sort of say well right, well this is what they got, they got a beginning for that, why did they receive that result and then they can grow from that. Some of our disengaged students were coming up with terms like, you know I can see why they got a beginning and I will do better now as a result of that, with that statement in itself I felt was very, very powerful indeed to have disengaged students saying, I will do better as a result of seeing these samples of work and they now are displayed quite prominently on a back wall in our classroom linked to all of the areas of the rubric and actually picking out key points and, I guess focus words, for instance we're doing a point of view so the genre of point of view was also discussed with the rubric and they could actually sort of say well this is what we understand the word thesis means, etc. (Teacher, Cluster 12; 2007: 51–2)

Some teachers may feel uneasy about involving students so directly in classroom discussions about assessment and quality. We are not suggesting here that teachers pass over to students their proper role as the knowledgeable assessor in the classroom. Instead, the notion is that student learning and achievement can improve when students are given a role in assessment. This could start early in a programme of study to establish what students will be assessed on and what particular features of quality will be salient in judging quality. It could also extend to students using this information and, in particular, stated assessment criteria and relevant examples to undertake self-assessment and peer assessment to support their learning. The challenge is for teachers to enable students to monitor their own learning and, in the absence of specific information about quality, the query remains: what are students expected to look for as indicators of quality in reviewing their work in progress? How can they close the gap between their current level of performance and the desired level, without explicit information about the features of that level?

Further, clarity about assessment expectations in task design can be used to facilitate teacher/student/parent conversations about quality and learning and streamline home–school communications. One teacher in a course drawing on both history and geography reported that she was surprised by the level of engagement that her students displayed when they could contribute to discussions about expected quality:

> U: I've been working with my year nine SOSE class and they are in the middle of an assessment task on a unit of work we're doing on South-East Asia at the moment and a couple of days ago in class we drew up a criteria grid and I gave them the strands that they are assessed on through the SOSE work program which are basic – the knowledge, the processes they have to go through to acquire that knowledge, and communication, and I said to kids 'okay what do you expect that an A is going to look like' and I said 'what sort of words do we use to describe an A' and we went through and we brainstormed a whole list of words and we did that for each of the strands … and then we had this huge round table conference going in the classroom where the kids were saying 'well this is what we think a B should be getting, and a B task would look like and what a C task would look like' … (Teacher, Cluster 15; 2007: 53)

Teacher–student conversations in both sharing and negotiating the criteria may require further professional learning, if it is not an expected or routine part of classroom practice. However, once students are given the opportunity to have some agency in discussions, such as those mentioned above, the benefits for learning can extend to possibilities for students to lessen their dependence on the teacher as the sole source of feedback. Additionally, the benefits of pedagogy changed in this way extend to students who may previously have been disengaged and those who may be at educational risk. One teacher talks about her classroom when she 'tried on' these ideas:

> I: … the biggest learning I encountered was having a task that I could change to accommodate the needs of students as the task was in progress. So when we went through the criteria in the beginning and we looked at the A, what you need to do to achieve an A, well in order for those lower level kids to be able to aspire to that we had to change things (along the way) so that we could – instead of going from an individual task then go to a small team task so they could pair up with or match up with higher achieving students so we've got more peer support or student support and we work with more of an expert jigsaw model. So that's the way we tried to get those more at risk kids to be able to achieve to that high level based on what was written in the criteria by having their peers model for them and work with them and for them to get greater self-esteem by tapping into whatever skills they had to offer the group rather than having to tackle the whole thing by themselves.

> G: And how did that work? Did you get any student feedback from that informally?

I: I could see they were operating better rather than sitting there lonely and disheartened, they would try – they even tried and changed [beeps occlude voice] work more effectively so I could see that. The whole flexibility thing was really playing a significant role and to [them] wanting to work better and knowing how to work better by changing the different groups they were with or even making that move to work in a group rather than working in isolation as they originally had chosen so there was fluidity within the process. (Teacher, Cluster 6; 2007: 53)

Uncovering and teaching the literacy and numeracy demands of assessment calls for different ways of working in the classroom

Here, we focus attention on how literacy and numeracy demands that tend to remain unstated or implicit can present powerful barriers to student academic success. We draw on a new conceptualization of the literacy curriculum interface that has emerged from a national study of the literacy demands of curriculum in senior schooling (Cumming et al., 1998; Wyatt-Smith and Cumming, 2000, 2003). A key finding of that study was that it was 'no longer appropriate to talk about literacy across the curriculum or even literacy and curriculum' (Cumming et al., 1998: 12). Instead, the researchers developed the term *curriculum literacies*, whereby 'curriculum' is deliberately used as a noun, rather than the adjectival 'curricular', to demonstrate that this conjunction represents the interface between a specific curriculum and its literacies, rather than literacies related to curriculum in a generic sense, or a single literacy that can be spread homogeneously across the curriculum. By way of example, the writers referred to 'science literacies' to describe the science–literacy interface, and more specifically, perhaps 'physics literacies', 'English literacies' or 'food technology literacies' (Cumming et al., 1998: 12).

Specifically, the notion of 'curriculum literacies' allows a shift away from the profligate use of the term 'literacy' as synonymous with 'fluency' or 'a knowledgeable state' to the conceptualization of literacies in terms of the integrating of reading, writing, listening, speaking, viewing and critical thinking practices in recognizably appropriate, subject-specific ways (Cumming et al., 1998: 12).

Of relevance here is that the literacy demands of curriculum typically remain unstated or implicit in both pedagogy and assessment, including assessment for formative (diagnostic and improvement) and summative (reporting) purposes (Wyatt-Smith and Cumming, 2000, 2003). A range of studies shows that students can be expected to manage these demands, in the main without explicit instruction, and the demands themselves can then become powerful barriers to student learning and academic success.

Three questions can be asked when teachers wish to review the literacy demands of curriculum:

1 What literate capabilities do students need to enable them to access and participate in learning opportunities?

2 What literate capabilities do students need to enable them to complete assessment activities successfully?

3 How do the literate demands that students face in their classroom learning align with the literate demands they face when being assessed?

Such questions support teachers as they progress their thinking about how to align assessment with learning and teaching. Specifically, alignment can become a means of informing and directing teacher and student efforts in learning and learning improvement. Using a sporting analogy, this involves shifting attention away from a view of assessment as being about checking how action is occurring on the playing field to actually knowing and naming what is involved in playing: where the goal posts are, what is high-performance play and how high (or low) the bar is placed.

Design decisions

The next section of this chapter presents a set of features (Wyatt-Smith and Bridges, 2007, Appendix 1: 77–9) that represents points of decision making for teachers in developing quality tasks that form part of how they align curriculum, teaching and learning, and assessment. For each feature there are several questions that can guide teacher decision making in designing quality assessment tasks. These stimuli are intended to centre on actions and thinking for developing quality assessment tasks for learning purposes.

Teachers could use these to explore how they progress assessment for success and engage learners in self-assessment and peer assessment. There is also opportunity to consider the collection of evidence of learning and achievement: documentation that could, for example, take the form of assessment portfolios that can be far more than a collection of assignments.

Feature 1: Alignment

- How is the assessment opportunity or task aligned with the formal curriculum and intended learning?
- Is the task to be designed for a single learning area or is it transdisciplinary, drawing on two or more learning areas?
- When is the assessment opportunity best scheduled in the teaching–learning year?
- How does the assessment require students to carry forward and build on prior learning? Does it enable students to demonstrate how they are carrying forward and connecting their prior learning to what they are currently learning?

Feature 2: Intellectual challenge and engagement

- What knowledges (from a field of knowledge/learning area or across fields/ learning areas) will students be involved in accessing, using and creating?
- What prior knowledges, skills and strategies are necessary for students to engage with the task? (In the absence of this, the assessment may build in student failure from the beginning.)

- What are the dimensions or aspects of the task? Does it involve students in: locating, retrieving and re-presenting information, problem-solving, taking action, making a presentation to an audience? What are the cognitive, aesthetic, creative and critical aspects?

- Will students see the assessment task as worthwhile and as having relevance to them? For example, does the task connect to the communities of practice that students identify with outside school? These could be actual communities, as well as virtual communities, including those participating in certain blogs, online chat rooms and game playing, for example.

- What outside-school knowledge and experiences may influence how boys and girls engage with the task?

Feature 3: Assessment scope and demand

- What is the level of demand of the task? Is the task designed in such a way as to enable a heterogeneous group of students to achieve success at different levels? Is the task to be designed to meet a minimum requirement for success?

- Does the task build in the opportunity for the teacher to discriminate among performances at different levels?

Feature 4: Language used to communicate the task

- Is the task to be written or presented in ways that draw appropriately on the accepted terminology of the learning area/s?

- Is the wording of the task free of bias (gender, racial)?

- Is the language (be it written, spoken, visual) clear and accessible to all students, taking account of students' cultural and linguistic backgrounds?

- What, if any, prerequisite cultural and linguistic knowledges are called upon to access the intended meaning of the task?

Feature 5: Literate capabilities involved in doing and completing the task

- What curriculum literacies are required for successful completion of the task, and what literacies are being assessed? (How can these be made explicit for students, and taught to them?)

- What are the modes that students need to use to engage with the task? For example, will students be accessing and using written, visual, auditory language as they progress through the task?

- Will tasks involve students in working in one mode (writing, for example), or will they be working multi-modally, both within and across modes (for example, combining written, visual and auditory language)?

- Will they need to use any digital technologies to be able to succeed at the task (for example, searching the internet, software programmes, online communications)?

Feature 6: Performance contexts

- Does the task have any connection to students' outside-school experiences? If so, are the conditions for doing the school task simulating the conditions that students experience outside of school in a similar or related activity?
- Will students be working individually, in pairs or in small groups? (Monitoring of how students work with peers can be an important part of formative assessment.)
- What resources, human and material, will they need to access in order to do the task? Will feedback be provided by parties other than the teacher?
- Will these resources be available and accessed at school, during school time?
- Will some additional resources need to be accessed outside school?
- How much time is needed to complete the task successfully?
- Will work-in-progress be shared with the teacher and/or with peers, for feedback purposes?

Feature 7: Knowing what is expected both during and on completion of the task

- What information is provided to students about how to progress through the task, checking, for example, on use of resources and time?
- What access do students have to information about how the quality of what they do is to be judged? *Standards descriptions,* as discussed next, as well as *exemplars* showing how the requirements of standards have been met are both useful to convey to students information about the desired features of performance.

Feature 8: Student self-assessment for improvement

- How are expectations of quality communicated to students?
- How are students enabled to monitor their progress – including time management and resource management?
- How are students enabled to monitor the quality of their work during production? (By what means will students know i) what and ii) how to improve?)
- Taking account of age and year level, what practices will be put in place to enable students to determine the overall quality of their work once completed? (For example, with students in the early years, standards can be communicated orally as part of teacher-led classroom conversations about quality, with authentic student-generated exemplars showing the type of work students are to produce, being useful. For students beyond the early years, explicitly defined or stated standards are informing, especially when students play an active role in developing these.)

Feature 9: Intended purposes of assessment information

- What is the intended use of the assessment information generated by the task? Is it:
    - i primarily for formative purposes (to improve student learning)
    - ii primarily for summative purposes (to report student achievement) or
    - iii is it possible that the information may serve both formative and summative purposes?

This suite of features involves teachers considering the cognitive expectations built into the task: is it intellectually challenging as suited to the level of education? Also called for is consideration of whether and how the task draws in sufficient depth and breadth on the targeted knowledges, concepts and skills of the domains. In such discussions teachers could canvas the range of thinking skills and understanding called for by the task calls and whether there is opportunity in the task design for the student to demonstrate critical analysis of a type suited to the year level.

Consistent with a futures-oriented approach to curriculum, learning, teaching and assessment, teachers could review, individually and in school teams, how assessment tasks offer opportunities for students to demonstrate expected valued attributes and attitudes, as well as cross-curricular priorities informed by education policy and expected practice in jurisdictions.

Finally, teachers could then return to the matter of what emerges from the discussion about what counts as evidence, and whether they wish to involve students in monitoring their own learning and achievement through assessment portfolios. This is taken up again in Chapter 6.

Conclusion

In this chapter we presented ideas about aligning assessment with teaching and learning. We also presented some insights into teachers' own experiences of achieving alignment, focusing in particular on front-ending assessment and quality task design.

Teaching and learning can be fused with assessment in classroom practice – both formative and summative – as a dynamic process of engaged inquiry. The potential for this approach lies in what it offers for assessment to become a tool for critical inquiry into the learning process, working to sharpen both the assessment and teaching focus.

Review questions

How has assessment served to support learning in my experiences as a student, at school and in post-school settings?

What do I expect planning to include?

What decisions would I need to take in front-ending assessment in my practice?

Are there risks involved in making assessment expectations explicit for students and for parents?

What knowledge would teachers need to be able to co-develop task-specific criteria and standards with students?

At what age could students begin having classroom discussions about expected features of quality in work they are undertaking?

References

American Educational Research Association (AERA) (2000) *Protection Against High-Stakes Decisions Based on a Single Test*. Available at: www.aera.net.

Black, P. and Wiliam, D. (1998a) *Inside the Black Box*. London: King's College.

Black, P. and Wiliam, D. (1998b) 'Assessment and classroom learning', *Assessment in Education*, 5 (1): 7–73.

Black, P., Harrison, C., Lee, C., Marshall, B. and William, D. (2003) *Assessment for Learning: Putting it into Practice*. New York: Open University Press.

Broadfoot, P. and Black, P. (2004) 'Redefining assessment? The first ten years of Assessment in Education', *Assessment in Education: Principles, Policy & Practice*, 11 (1): 7–26.

Cole, N.S. (1988) 'A realist's appraisal of the prospects for unifying instruction and assessment', in C.V. Bunderson (ed.), *Assessment in the Service of Learning*. Princeton, NJ: Educational Testing Service.

Cronbach, L.J. and Meehl, P.E. (1955) 'Construct validity in psychological tests', *Psychological Bulletin*, 52: 281–302.

Cumming, J., Wyatt-Smith, C., Ryan, J. and Doig, S.M. (1998) *The literacy-curriculum interface: The literacy demands of the curriculum in post-compulsory schooling*. Final report. Brisbane: Centre for Literacy Education Research, Griffith University and Department of Employment, Education, Training and Youth Affairs.

DEEWR, Department of Education, Employment and Workplace Relations and DETA, Queensland Department of Education, Training and the Arts (2007) *Meeting in the Middle – Assessment, Pedagogy, Learning and Educational Disadvantage. Literacy and Numeracy in the Middle Years of Schooling Initiative – Strand A, Project Report*. Canberra: Commonwealth of Australia. Available at: http://education.qld.gov.au/literacy/docs/deewr-myp-final-report.pdf.

Elwood, J. (2006) 'Formative assessment: possibilities, boundaries and limitations', *Assessment in Education: Principles, Policy and Practice*, 13 (2): 215–32.

Gipps, C. (1999) 'Socio-cultural aspects of assessment', *Review of Research in Education*, 24: 357–92.

Glaser, R. (1963) 'Instructional technology and the measurement of learning outcomes: Some questions', *American Psychologist*, 18: 519–21.

Glaser, R. (1976) 'Components of a psychology of instruction: Toward a science of design', *Review of Educational Research*, 46: 1–24.

Glaser, R. (1986) 'The integration of instruction and testing', in Proceedings of the 1985 ETC invitational conference, *The redesign of testing for the twenty-first century*. Princeton, NJ: Educational Testing Service. pp. 45–58.

Glaser, R. and Nitko, A.J. (1971) 'Measurement in learning and instruction', in R.L. Thorndike (ed.), *Educational Measurement*. Washington: American Council on Education.

Harlen, W. (1994) 'Towards quality in assessment', in W. Harlen (ed.), *Enhancing Quality in Assessment*. London: Paul Chapman.

Linn, M.C. (1992) 'Gender differences in educational achievement', in J. Pfleiderer (ed.), *Sex Equity in Educational Opportunity, Achievement and Testing*. Princeton, NJ: Educational Testing Service.

Linn, R.L. (ed.) (1989) *Educational Measurement* (3rd edn). Washington, DC: The American Council on Education and The National Council on Measurement in Education.

Matters, G.N. (2006) 'Using data to support learning in schools: Students, teachers, systems', Australian Council for Educational Research: Camberwell, Victoria. Available at: www.acer.edu.au/documents/AER_49-UsingDatatoSupportLearninginSchools.pdf.

Matters, G., Pitman, J. and O'Brien, J. (1998) 'Validity and reliability in educational assessment and testing: A matter of judgment', *Queensland Journal of Educational Research*, 14: 57–88.

Messick, S. (1989) 'Validity', in R.L. Linn (ed.), *Educational Measurement* (3rd edn). London: Collier Macmillan. pp. 12–104.

Moss, P.A. (1994) 'Can there be validity without reliability?', *Educational Researcher*, 23 (2): 5–12.

Murphy, P. and Hall, K. (eds) (2008) *Learning and Practice: Agency and Identities*. London: Sage.

Newton, P. (2012) 'We need to talk about validity'. Paper presented to the National Council for Measurement in Education Annual Meeting, Vancouver, Canada.

Pitman, J.A., O'Brien, J.E. and McCollow, J.E. (1999) 'High-quality assessment: We are what we believe we do'. Paper presented at the IAEA Conference, Bled, Slovenia.

Sadler, D.R. (1989) 'Formative assessment: Revisiting the territory', *Assessment in Education: Principles, Policy and Practice*, 5: 77–85.

Schön, D. (1983) *The Reflective Practitioner: How Professionals Think in Action*. London: Maurice Temple Smith.

Scriven, M. (1980) 'Prescriptive and descriptive approaches to problem solving', in D.T. Tuma, *Problem Solving and Education*. Hillsdale, NJ: Lawrence Erlbaum. pp. 127–35.

Shepard, L. (2000) 'The role of assessment in a learning culture', *Educational Researcher*, 29 (7): 4–14.

Stenhouse, L. (1975) *An introduction to Curriculum Research and Development*. London: Heineman.

Torrance, H. (1997) 'Assessment, accountability and standards: Using assessment to control the reform of schooling', in A.H. Halsey, H. Lauder, P. Brown and A.S. Wells (eds), *Education, Culture, Economy and Society*. Oxford: Oxford University Press.

Wilson, M. (ed.) (2004) *Towards Coherence between Classroom Assessment and Accountability*. Chicago: University of Chicago Press.

Wyatt-Smith, C.M. (2000) 'Exploring the relationship between large-scale literacy testing programs and classroom-based assessment: a focus on teachers' accounts', *Australian Journal of Language and Literacy*, 23 (2): 109–27.

Wyatt-Smith, C.M. and Bridges, S. (2007) 'Evaluation study report', in DEEWR and DETA, *Meeting in the Middle – Assessment, Pedagogy, Learning and Educational Disadvantage. Literacy and Numeracy in the Middle Years of Schooling Initiative – Strand A, Project Report*. Canberra: Commonwealth of Australia. Available at: http://education.qld.gov.au/literacy/docs/deewr-myp-final-report.pdf.

Wyatt-Smith, C.M. and Cumming, J.J. (2000) 'The literacy demands of assessment practices in post-compulsory schooling', *Literacy Learning: The Middle Years*, 8 (1): 21–32.

Wyatt-Smith, C.M. and Cumming, J.J. (2003) 'Curriculum literacies: Expanding domains of assessment', *Assessment in Education: Principles, Policy and Practice*, 10 (1): 47–59.

Web extras

Moss, P.A. (1994) 'Can there be validity without reliability?', *Educational Researcher*, 23 (2): 5–12.

Rust, C. (2002) 'The impact of assessment on student learning: How can the research literature practically help to inform the development of departmental assessment strategies and learner-centred assessment practices?' *Active Learning in Higher Education*, 3 (2): 145–58.

5

Moderation and the use of standards

Overview

In this chapter we will define moderation and the use of standards and present the main purposes and processes involved. We explain the different modes and models of moderation and their use at the different levels of education, from early years through to higher education.

We will provide illustrative examples of systems and school-level moderation, to demonstrate how the processes of consistency, comparability, use of standards, evidence and exemplars come together in practice. In conclusion, we will discuss the potential of online moderation practice and the use of standards.

Introduction

What are the purposes of moderation, and how does its practice attend to the purposes of accountability and improvement? In this chapter we address these major questions underpinning this book. We consider ways in which moderation practice serves to achieve reliable and valid judgements with high levels of inter-rater reliability. We discuss the ways in which moderated judgements support teachers' use of standards that link to systems-level reporting, with reference to different moderation systems, from the phases of primary and secondary schooling through to higher education. We also discuss ways in which moderation assists teachers to improve their teaching of the curriculum and informs their assessment practices. We conclude with an examination of the potential for evidence-based teacher judgement, using standards that can be facilitated through the use of information and communications technologies (ICTs).

To begin with, we consider some systems-level purposes and procedures in how moderation is enacted, and present different ways in which education systems establish practices to achieve consistency and reliability of teachers' standards-referenced judgements. We analyse and discuss ways in which moderation can be used to support and improve teacher quality, as this relates to the design and enactment of assessment practice. In fulfilling this purpose, moderation practice actively engages teachers in critically reflecting upon what and how they teach and assess the curriculum, including their design of assessment tasks. Engagement in these activities helps teachers to address the priorities of quality and equity in assessment, by examining the opportunities afforded to students in order that they might reach high standards in their learning outcomes. The relationship of assessment with curriculum, teaching and learning are made explicit by reference to research evidence and drawing on exemplary moderation processes to illustrate established systems and practices.

Moderation practice

Moderation is practised through different modes: face-to-face meetings, gatherings facilitated by ICTs (ICT-mediated moderation or e-moderation) or a combination of these. This variety of approaches to moderation enables the practice to be conducted in a diverse range of contexts. For example, moderation can take place within an institution or within a school – that is, intra-school or intra-institution moderation – or between institutions or schools, as in inter-university or inter-school moderation, extending the practice from a particular context or region. ICT-mediated moderation broadens the reach of the practice beyond the local context to include different regions, states or territories of a nation. A tension that emerges from this is that variations and differences emerge in the understanding of what moderation means, its purposes and how it is practised.

Purposes of moderation

Moderation is conducted at all levels of education, from the early years (Woods and Amorsen, 2011) through to higher education (Sadler, 2009), and is defined differently in these contexts. However, similarities are apparent in the discourse used to define and articulate the purposes of moderation. For example, moderation has been described as a:

- quality review and quality assurance process
- quality control process
- procedure to promote consistency of teacher judgement and comparability of results across different assessors, programmes and contexts
- process to inform curriculum, teaching and learning areas for improvement
- method to inform and support expected performances or standards
- support for teacher assessment design and marking of student work
- peer review through explanations of what is valued and how judgements are made about student work.

When analysed, these common definitions and purposes can be classified into two main categories. The first relates to the desire to achieve consistency in interpretation of the standards or related qualities of the assessed work, together with the comparability of the professional judgements made; that is, valid and reliable judgements that are consistent with one another and with official achievement or performance standards. This function of moderation involves judgements that are consistent, reliable and based on evidence within the student response. These aims relate to the accountability functions of moderation practice of quality assurance and quality review.

The second related category is the goal of quality control to improve teachers' assessment and pedagogic practice for enhanced learning purposes. It is anticipated that through participation in regular moderation discussions at different stages of a teaching period, teaching practices and thus student learning will improve. In short, moderation becomes integral to the entire process of effective teaching and learning.

What is moderation?

Moderation, or 'social moderation' (Linn, 1993), is a process involving teachers in discussion and debate about their interpretations of the quality of assessed work. This practice involves teachers expressing their interpretations of assessment criteria and standards with the aim of reaching agreement on the award of the grade or standard assigned to the student work or portfolio of evidence being scrutinized. The expectation in moderation practice is that teachers will explicate their interpretations of the quality of the work.

'Consensus moderation' is a term that has been used to describe this form of social moderation. While consensus is emphasized, dissent can occur as different interpretations of the criteria and standards emerge when teachers begin to share their judgement practices or when their interpretations are made public. It is from such instances of disagreement, or dissent, that new knowledge or understanding is generated regarding the interpretation of the standards. This sociocultural view of assessment practice aligns with an interpretivist, as opposed to a positivist, theoretical paradigm. From an interpretivist perspective, assessment is viewed as a social practice, such that the cultural context, beliefs and values mediate our judgements. These ideas and arguments were pursued further in Chapter 3.

Background

Many writers have referred to the work of Linn (1993) in their articulation of the definitions, the practices and the purposes of moderation. In the 1990s, at a time when there were demands for a variety of assessment types, Linn referred to moderation as a form of linking, and he identified five examples to illustrate the variety of circumstances under which comparisons of results from different assessment types were required (Linn, 1993: 83): equating, calibration, statistical moderation, prediction and social moderation. Linn claimed that these types signified a continuum of statistical rigour, with equating, at one end, being representative of the highest degree and social moderation, at the other end, being reliant exclusively upon professional judgement.

Since the time that Linn developed his categorization, there has been more research and theorization of professional judgement. This increase in the use of professional judgement for assessment purposes is due to the increased use of performance-based assessment, or 'rich' tasks, which take the form of more open-ended questions or problems requiring solutions. This type of assessment is reliant upon teacher judgement and contrasts sharply with standardized assessments and multiple-choice or short-answer responses.

Linn (1993) referred to social moderation as 'consensus moderation, auditing and verification'. He distinguished between the statistical approaches that he had categorized as equating, calibration, statistical moderation and predictions, and 'approaches that rely primarily on judgement' (Linn, 1993: 97). Linn described this type of moderation as 'performances on distinct tasks ... rated using a common framework and interpreted in terms of a common standard.' He gave the example of essays written in different regions or states using different prompts in each state but 'interpreted in terms of the same national standards' (Linn, 1993: 87). The requirements of social moderation were specified as follows:

- development of consensus on the meaning of the standards and on the performances that meet those standards
- development and review by staff of discrepancies in ratings
- assignment by local teachers of ratings, compared to independently assigned ratings from other raters and the latter used to adjust local scores
- provision of documentation regarding the degree to which different sets of judges agree that given responses to different tasks meet common standards. (Linn, 1993: 87)

Social moderation, according to Linn, involves states, or groups of states, participating in the development of performance-based assessments, with reference to a common curriculum or content framework. Teachers' professional judgement is central to the assessment of student performance and work. Checks and verification of professional judgements are made with the expectation 'that the performance of individual students, schools, districts and states are compared to a single set of national standards' (Linn, 1993: 87).

In social moderation practice, then, teachers from different schools or institutions meet with samples of student work that have been assessed using teacher judgement. It is at this meeting, through discussion and debate, that a shared understanding of the standards is negotiated. As a consequence of the meeting there may be a need to moderate or amend some of the previous judgements (Newton, 2007).

Three elements that make up teacher judgement of student work include: the teacher attending to the learner's production; appraising this against some background, or reference framework; and making an explicit response, such as assigning the learner's work to a class (as in grading) (Sadler, 1998). Some of the intellectual and experiential resources that teachers must be able to draw upon when making a judgement of student work are:

- superior knowledge about the content or substance of what is to be learned
- deep knowledge of criteria and standards (or performance expectations) appropriate to the assessment task
- evaluative skill or expertise in having made judgements about students' efforts on similar tasks in the past
- a set of attitudes or dispositions towards teaching, as an activity, and towards learners, including their own ability to empathize with students who are learning, their desire to help students develop, improve and do better, their personal concern for the feedback and veracity of their own judgements, and their patterns in offering help. (Sadler, 1998: 80–2)

From this perspective, teachers are viewed as the primary change agents who, through judgement practices that are integral to the requirements of assessment tasks and expectations of quality performance (Sadler, 1998), are best placed to identify important steps for students to take in order to improve in their learning, and to develop useful insights about how best to change pedagogy to meet students' particular learning needs. Such classroom assessment to promote learning requires the use of assessment data by the teacher to inform teaching and to facilitate students' learning (Hattie, 2005). Fundamental to attaining greater coherence between systems-level accountability and local-level practice are teachers' judgements and informed interpretations of assessment data.

Further, it is widely recognized that standards written as verbal descriptors necessarily remain open to interpretation and call for qualitative judgements. To address this, Sadler (1987) argued that exemplars or samples of student work provide concrete referents to illustrate standards that otherwise remain tacit knowledge. He made the point that the stated standards and exemplars work together to show different ways of satisfying the requirements for the award of a standard or a grade such as A–E.

The twenty-first century saw the global development of national curricula and assessment systems that were increasingly futures-oriented and called for student development of sophisticated knowledge, skills and understandings. The consequence of such reforms has been the introduction of performance-oriented assessment incorporating rich tasks. This type of assessment is increasing and by its very nature is reliant upon standards, teacher judgement and moderation. The processes involved in the practice of teacher judgement in the context of moderation are complex and interrelated. So the role of each of the essential resources used in each of the processes, and the processes themselves, are now described independently; in practice they are interconnected, interrelated and overlapping.

Processes of moderation

School-based and teacher-based assessments are usually considered valid forms of assessment, but the reliability of such practices are dependent upon processes such as moderation to ensure both consistency and comparability in judgements. Moderation processes are a means by which comparability can be achieved in assessment practice when needed. The processes to ensure a common understanding of the standards and to establish that there is similar recognition of performances that demonstrate the standards (Maxwell, 2009) is a process that entails reaching agreement, comparability, consistency and learning improvement. Given their importance in achieving dependable and reliable judgements, these processes are discussed in the following section. To begin, we present the role of each of the various resources (standards, evidence and exemplars) that are drawn upon in this process of achieving agreement, comparability, consistency and learning improvement.

Standards

What is the role of standards in the processes of moderation?

Standards describe the expected features or characteristics of quality at various levels of performance. The role of standards is to assist teachers' decision making in assessing the quality of student work at various levels. Standards provide a common set of stated reference points for teacher use, and acquire meaning through use over time. This is because standards, written as verbal descriptors, require interpretation and application within a community of practice. Standards are important in informing teaching and learning in terms of the development of assessment tasks. In the teaching–learning cycle, teachers share the standards with students, in order to provide information about the expected qualities to which they should aim. In this way standards are linked to teacher feedback and student self-assessment and peer assessment.

Evidence

What is the role of evidence in the processes of moderation?

Evidence used to make a judgement can take a range of forms: print, multi-modal, spoken, performance and digital. Teachers decide upon the evidence that is relevant for the learning, teaching, judgement and reporting. Fitness-for-purpose is integral to these decisions, whether they are for formative or diagnostic assessment, or for summative assessment and reporting. Evidence is related to learning and teaching activities and should also reflect the qualities represented in the standards. The connection between the evidence and the standards must be articulated. Evidence of the characteristics or traits of performance should be apparent in the student work sample, in order to make a judgement about a grade or mark. Evidence should be explicit and available for scrutiny by others. Consistency of judgement is possible through the direct links that can be made between the identified evidence of quality and the stated standards. In this way, judgements are made defensible.

Exemplars

What is the role of exemplars in the processes of moderation?

Exemplars are useful in illustrating the requirements of standards. A range of exemplars to illustrate each grade helps teachers understand the application of standards to achieve that grade or mark. Exemplars are developed by teachers or supplied by the system. They are useful for both teachers and students, in informing teaching and learning, and are a vital support to illustrate the range of standards. Where exemplars are of optimal use they include a commentary addressing how the standards have been applied. This involves making explicit the match between the evidence of the qualities in the work and the standards. In addition, the commentary explains the compensations or trade-offs that teachers considered in arriving at the final judgement.

Consistency

What is consistency of teacher judgement?

Consistency in the context of moderation and teacher's professional judgement is achieved when two or more teachers assess a student's work and at the end of the judgement process reach agreement regarding the grade or mark to be awarded. Achieving a 'like' judgement, expressed as a grade or mark, involves teachers applying a shared understanding of those qualities that characterize the standards as they apply at different levels. If there is consistency in judgement, it will be evident in the comparability of teachers' grading decisions. The term 'consistency' does not apply directly to the processes that teachers rely upon to arrive at a judgement. It is accepted that these processes will vary from teacher to teacher and context to context. As is argued throughout this book, assessment and moderation are social processes that are based on an interpretive perspective. To emphasize: consistency is the outcome of informed use of the stated standards.

Comparability

How can moderation ensure comparability of teachers' judgements?

Moderation involves teachers meeting within their own school/institution, between schools/institutions or in clusters of schools/institutions to discuss how they apply the standards in relation to student work. Such meetings can occur face-to-face and/or be technologically mediated. Generally, teachers assess and grade student work prior to the moderation meeting. Central to moderation is the matching exercise of the evidence and the standards through discussion of work samples, which helps to make the linking explicit.

Moderation that focuses on the application of standards to student work is integral to systems and local efforts to achieve consistency and comparability of judgement. In the process, direct inter-student comparison plays no part. The focus is on the matching of evidence in the work to the standards. It is through moderation practice over time that teachers develop a community of shared understanding regarding the application of the standards to student work in a range of contexts. This helps teachers develop their confidence in applying the standards to arrive at judgements that are dependable and in which they can have confidence. Moderation opportunities provide teachers with the context for reviewing the quality of the assessment tasks and the extent to which these tasks enable the students to demonstrate achievement across the full range of the standards.

Moderation can function as part of system quality assurance. Essentially, it provides a mechanism to demonstrate accountability in terms of comparability of individual teachers' judgements. In this accountability context, the focus is on how consistently the standards have been applied within and across school contexts. The judgements are scrutinized for their comparability. This is taken to include the reliability of teachers' judgements and the application of the standards over time. Considerations or evidence that are not apparent in the student work should not influence the judgement.

Agreement

How is agreement reached in the processes of moderation?

Agreement is possible when teachers concur on the match between the evidence and the standards, which implies that the teachers share a common interpretation of the standards. This can only be developed with use over time. Discussion among teachers regarding the evidence depicting the qualities of the standards is fundamental. Teachers therefore need to make explicit how the qualities of the standards are met in the student work. This reflects the various ways in which the requirements of the standards can be met. An on-balance judgement is reached when teachers consider the overall qualities of performance, as evidenced in the work being assessed. Teachers attend to the overall judgement of the qualities to assess the best fit between the work and the stated standards in order to reach a final grade.

What if agreement cannot be reached?

When teachers disagree about a grade, this usually reflects differing interpretations of the criteria and the standards. Teachers are advised to talk about how they applied the criteria and standards to the particular student work. In this discussion it is vital that teachers focus on the evidence and how it matches the standard. Sometimes the disagreement can be an indication that teachers are drawing on considerations other than those evident in the work. Where this occurs, discussion should focus on the impact of these considerations on the overall judgement and the resulting effect upon fairness or biased decisions.

Learning improvement

How do the processes of moderation inform learning improvement?

When teachers work with standards in their school communities in the context of moderation they share their understanding of those standards and how they apply them in developing assessment tasks or opportunities. As teachers become confident in their knowledge and application of the standards, they integrate their use in their own teaching and learning. They attend to the assessment demands that students are expected to meet and design learning that enables student success. This involves the alignment of their teaching with assessment, including opportunities for students to use the standards to review and improve the quality of their work. Teachers' work extends to the induction of students into knowledge of the standards and their use in feedback for learning, self-monitoring over time, peer-assessment and self-assessment.

Models of moderation

Several different models of moderation have been developed in varying contexts for the different purposes of promoting consistency and developing teachers' confidence in their judgement practice. Some of these are discussed here to illustrate the range of approaches.

Calibration

The *calibration model* involves the selection of a range of samples of student responses, which teachers assess and grade individually. A process of calibration then follows, whereby teachers consider the grades awarded for the selected sample. They compare the grades awarded by other teachers with their own judgements. In their discussions about the quality of the evidence identified in the student responses to justify their judgements, teachers make reference to the standards. Through engaging in this form of professional interaction, teachers may adjust their interpretation of the standards to reach consensus about the quality of the assessed work samples and, in so doing, develop a common understanding of the standards. Reaching this understanding occurs prior to the teachers grading the remaining work samples from their own classes. At this point, teachers are applying the interpretation of the standard as calibrated. This model is time-efficient, in that a common understanding of the standards in context is established at the outset, before the teachers proceed with the marking of the remainder of the student responses. However, it can be difficult to make a quality judgement in isolation.

Conferencing

In the conferencing approach to moderation, teachers grade student responses individually and then select student samples representative of their application or understanding of the A–E qualities. A meeting is convened, during which a conferencing process is employed to enable teachers to share samples and discuss their judgements. Teachers refer to the standards during discussions about the quality of student performance. These discussions are based on the evidence identified in the students' responses. Teachers aim to reach consensus on the interpretation and application of the standards by engaging in professional dialogue using a common language. Teachers review the judgements they have made on the student work graded previously. At this point, teachers are applying the shared understanding achieved through the conferencing process. Teachers are involved in professional dialogue with other teachers in order to reach consensus; however, the development of a common interpretation and application of the standards occurs after student work has been allocated a grade. Teachers may therefore need to regrade some of their students' work.

Expert

As the name suggests, this approach to moderation involves an expert who considers a representative sample of teachers' graded work samples and then provides advice regarding their application or understanding of the qualities of the standards (A–E). The advice of the expert confirms whether there is consistency in the way in which the standards are interpreted and applied, or whether teachers need to adjust their understanding, and why. When reviewing judgements about their previously graded student work, teachers will use this advice. This approach necessitates a common, school-based view of the interpretation and application of the standards. However, teachers do not benefit from the professional dialogue of reaching consensus with other teachers. This approach can be used to reach consistency within a school, rather than to support consistency of teacher judgements across a state or region (QSA, 2010).

Moderation systems

In some states of Australia and Canada there is a long history of moderation practice. In these states, moderation has served to fulfil both an accountability function and the purposes of improved teaching and learning. Meaningful opportunities for teachers to be reflexive in their teaching practice and to identify changes for improvement derive from participation in moderation practice. A detailed discussion of the case of Queensland, Australia, where moderation has been practised for the past 40 years, is included here. We describe the Queensland system, which comprises externally moderated, school-based assessment with the use of a standardized test – the Queensland Core Skills Test – as a method for deriving tertiary entrance ranks using the test results to scale the grades from school-based assessment.

The Queensland system

The enactment of the purposes, processes and models of moderation are described with reference to the particular case of the Queensland system. This externally moderated, standards-referenced assessment system for senior school (Years 11 and 12) is unique within Australia and internationally. In 1972, the wholly school-based assessment system was introduced in Queensland to replace the external examinations held at the end of Year 12 (age 16–17 years). In this state teachers are responsible for the teaching, assessment and reporting of student achievement from Preparatory year, or Kindergarten, to the senior students. In the senior years students are taught and assessed by their schools within a rigorous, statewide quality assurance framework. School-based curriculum development and assessment distributes the responsibility for quality assurance to the system as a whole.

The Queensland Studies Authority (QSA) is an independent statutory body of the Queensland government, responsible for managing Queensland's system of externally moderated school-based assessment and senior secondary certification. QSA provides senior syllabuses that prescribe the expected content and that specify the criteria and achievement standards teachers use to make judgements about student achievement. The syllabuses 'are based on the principles of informed prescription and informed professionalism' (QSA, 2010: 12). Queensland teachers use the syllabuses and guidelines provided to design continuous school-based programmes and to make judgements about standards achieved by their students, including summative judgements for reporting purposes. They also make informed professional judgements about how to shape the curriculum to best meet the needs of their students. A handbook details the operational policies, protocols, procedures and strategies that underpin the system (QSA, 2010). This handbook is especially useful for those teachers who are new to the state or who are working with this system for the first time. This school-based assessment system positions the teacher as central in developing assessment and linking assessment to learning.

Each senior syllabus aims to establish alignment of teaching, learning, assessment and reporting through the provision of important information relating to general objectives, standards, subject content and assessment requirements. The general objectives make explicit what students should achieve by the end of the course of study. These objectives are categorized into dimensions considered to be key characteristics of the subject. For each dimension there is an exit standard that aims to give an indicator for judging how well students have achieved the general objectives. Subject matter to be taught, inclusive of core and mandatory requirements, is detailed and assessment requirements and advice about achieving the general objectives, and demonstrating exit standards, are also included.

Standards-based assessment

The assessment system is standards-based, which means that teachers have an important role in using professional judgement to assess student work and in making decisions about levels of achievement. The senior syllabuses are designed such that teacher judgements about the quality of the student achievements are to be made using the pre-stated standards to describe how well students have achieved the general objectives of the syllabus. The standards are developed from student work and describe the characteristics of that work. Specifically, the exit standards:

- state what students are expected to know and be able to do at each exit level of achievement
- describe the qualities that teachers should look for in student responses and use to make judgements about each exit level of achievement
- provide a meaningful way for teachers to report on student learning and achievement to parents and carers

- provide students with guidance for their learning and allow them to monitor their progress

- provide transparency so that students, parents and carers understand how teacher judgements are made. (QSA, 2010: 13)

In this system it is understood that teachers who are informed by the syllabus principles of exit assessment and who use evidence collected over time across a range of formats and contexts are in the best position to judge students' levels of achievement.

Professional judgement using standards

Teacher judgement is central to assessment, and it is the teacher's role to collect evidence of student achievement as part of the teaching, learning and approved assessment programme. From the evidence collected the teacher makes a judgement about the match between the qualities in the student work and standards as described in the syllabus. Teachers in this system also make an on-balance judgement about a student's achievement across a folio of work. To ensure consistency, objectivity and transparency regarding the judgements of student achievement, both within and across schools, teachers are required to:

- select the general objectives to be assessed

- design assessment instruments to allow students to demonstrate the range of relevant standards

- develop instrument-specific criteria sheets as a tool for making judgements about the quality of students' responses to assessment instruments

- provide students with criteria sheets for the assessment instruments. (QSA, 2010: 13–14)

Teacher judgements of the standards achieved on the assessments are recorded. In matching student work to the standards, teachers can use numbers, alpha codes or other symbols to record judgements over time, but all must clearly show the match between the standards descriptors in the syllabus and the students' responses. In the professional judgement the teacher must make explicit the identified standard demonstrated and how the qualities in the student responses match the standards described in the syllabus. In this system it is expected that teachers will, at the senior secondary level, inform students, parents/carers and other teachers who participate on review panels about what is expected, how judgements are made and how they are justified.

Decisions about the levels of achievement

The teachers make decisions about the levels of achievement and the standard achieved in each dimension, by reviewing the students' folios of responses to several assessment types that are completed under a range of conditions over the course of study. Teachers are informed that '[s]imply adding up marks to arrive at a level of achievement, does not allow for consideration of the standards achieved in each of the dimensions' (QSA, 2010: 14) across the assessments.

In order to ensure that consistent and comparable judgements about students' achievements within and between schools occur, moderation meetings are organized whereby teachers engage in professional dialogue to discuss and evaluate judgements based on the match between the syllabus standards and the qualities in the student work. 'The exit standards in the syllabus provide a common language for this dialogue within and across schools' (QSA, 2010: 14).

Consistency and comparability at school and system levels

At the school level, in moderation meetings teachers consider the alignment between syllabus standards and student work to ensure that there is consistency in the application of standards and comparability of judgements about the standards achieved by students in different classes. Student folios of work are reviewed for the purposes of:

- analysing whether there is an appropriate match of student achievement with the exit standard descriptors
- evaluating whether the judgements match the syllabus requirements for exit level of achievement.

At the system level, the teachers choose a sample of folios to demonstrate how the school has matched the student achievement with the relevant syllabus exit standards. The folios are submitted to the QSA review panels for monitoring and verification. The folios of student work are scrutinized by review panels for evidence of school judgements about standards and school decisions about levels of achievement (QSA, 2010: 15). The panels provide feedback in terms of advice and recommendations to the schools about:

- the coverage of the mandatory aspects of the syllabus
- the effectiveness of assessment in providing students opportunities to demonstrate the achievement of the general objectives and the range of standards
- the use of standards to make judgements and decisions about levels of achievement. (QSA, 2010: 15)

Distinctive features of the Queensland system

There are eight key features involved in the Queensland system, which are now summarized. First, syllabuses that prescribe the objectives and the core content to be taught, the standards for the award of the five levels of achievement and the stipulation of the contents of the folios of assessed student work by the end of Year 12 are developed and approved by the QSA.

Second are the work programmes that are developed by the schools and involve the approval of panels of teachers (from other schools) trained by QSA. In each district of the Queensland education system a subject review panel of experienced, practising teachers exists to provide advice. There are approximately 393 subject review panels of experienced practising teachers in 13 districts, and there are also 51 state review panels. The subject panels review the work programmes that include prescribed parts of a syllabus including additional content, consistent with the syllabus and learning experiences selected by a school in alignment with the school's and students' particular needs. The assessment programme and examples of assessment instruments to be administered are also included in the review to establish whether the requirements of the corresponding syllabuses have been met.

The third feature of this system is that at the end of Year 11, standards are monitored. Each school sends sample folios of assessed student work for each subject in Year 11 to QSA subject review panels, for advice to the school's principal regarding whether the approved work programme has been followed, the assessment instruments developed by the school are effective and the teachers at the school are making valid and reliable judgements about the standards being achieved by the students. This occurs prior to the provision of advice and recommendations for Year 12 by the review panel. If a school is identified as in need of assistance, QSA staff members provide training and examples of best practice.

The fourth feature of this system is the verification of the Year 12 standards. At the end of term three, each school sends a carefully prescribed sample of student folios to the QSA, where trained district panels of teachers from other schools examine sample student folios from each subject at each school, in order to check schools' judgements about students' interim achievements and to establish whether the samples meet the standards prescribed in the syllabus. The confirmation of Year 12 results involves the district review panel chairs, state review panel chairs and the QSA standards and assessment officers, who examine the accuracy of student exit levels of achievement that are proposed by the schools. QSA staff members negotiate the final distribution of levels of achievement with the principal of each school, based on written advice of the panel and, if required, additional folios of student work are selected by QSA staff.

The fifth feature relates to the Queensland Core Skills (QCS) test, which assesses the Common Core Elements (CCEs) that students experience in studying their respective combinations of subjects during Years 11 and 12. This test of two multiple-choice papers, a short-response paper and a writing task involves a total of 7 hours of testing taken by eligible students over two consecutive days in August of Year 12. Students receive an A–E grade on this test.

In Queensland, a profile of tertiary entrance ranks is used with the main rank on a 1–25 point scale, called an Overall Position, and five subsidiary ranks on 1–10 point scales called Field Positions. The ranks are constructed by using group results on the QCS test to scale the externally moderated, school-based assessments. This constitutes the sixth feature of the system.

The next feature involves a comparison of moderated standards with standards on the QCS test. In this phase, the QSA compares the students' distribution of results on the QCS test with the distribution of results from externally moderated, school-based assessment. Where mismatches occur, the QSA reduces the effect of the mismatch for the calculation of the tertiary entrance rank. If the mismatch is traced to an issue with a school's assessment programme, QSA staff members provide training to the relevant staff of the school.

In the final phase, the QSA selects a stratified random sample of Year 12 folios from schools across the state. Different panels from different districts review the folios. This is part of the quality assurance process after the awarding of the Senior Certificates. If problems or concerns emerge from review of the school-based assessment, staff of the QSA contact the school and advise the principal of the appropriate action to be taken.

The Ontario system

In the Canadian state of Ontario, as in the Australian state of Queensland, the teacher is recognized as the one who is best placed to identify important steps for students to improve in their learning and to develop useful insights about how best to change pedagogy to meet a student's particular learning needs. Teachers in Ontario are therefore supported with the provision of resources designed to foster collaborative assessment of student work through teacher moderation. A multimedia package, which includes print, video and Microsoft PowerPoint™ resources, is available from Curriculum Services Canada. Teachers are encouraged to follow a step-by-step procedure in enacting the teacher moderation process. This approach to moderation is aimed at the school level and differs to the senior school Queensland model, which is for certification purposes and operates at a systems level.

In the Ontario system, teachers are encouraged to meet prior to the moderation meeting to decide collaboratively on an assessment task based on identified curricular expectations that may be used to assess students' understandings and areas for improvement. At this point teachers are also expected to determine the assessment tools and resources that they will use to conduct the assessment. These are suggested to include: rubrics, checklists, school-based or district-based assessments, anchors, rationales and Ontario Curriculum Guides to Effective Instruction (The Literacy and Numeracy Secretariat, 2007).

A time for teachers to conduct the moderation session is determined immediately after the assessment has been completed. It is recommended that feedback be given to the students soon after completion of the assessment, to make a positive impact on their learning. Teachers are advised to make copies of the student work for distribution to the group members. Once a location has been arranged and the resources for the session are set up the meeting is called. The first task is for the nomination of a facilitator to guide the process.

Guidance for the moderation process focuses on examples of student writing. It is recommended that the meeting commence with a teacher reading a student's work aloud to 'hear' the fluency and ease of writing. The student's work is then assessed using the pre-set criteria in conference with the group members. In order to assess the writing, teachers are reminded to consider the four categories of knowledge and skills using the four levels of achievement. They are also referred to the anchors, rationales, rubrics, curriculum documents and other support materials. If appropriate the student's teacher may provide the context of the work and more information about the student, although teachers are reminded that anonymity of students ensures that prejudgements and bias are eliminated from this process. Teachers engage in respectful dialogue to develop a common understanding of the levels of achievement and the assessment criteria. Teachers are encouraged to use the language from the achievement chart; that is, 'limited', 'some', 'considerable', 'high degree'. Collectively, the teachers engage in discussion regarding the students' strengths, gaps in their learning, patterns and trends in the data. Goals are set for student progress based on curriculum expectations and achievement categories and, together, teachers investigate and share key instructional strategies to plan their next steps.

After the moderation meeting it is expected that teachers will implement the steps for instruction and prepare to begin the cycle again. Student progress is again assessed and analysed to determine the effectiveness of identified teaching strategies. It is also at this stage that teachers set new goals for the student, the class and for school improvement (The Literacy and Numeracy Secretariat, 2007: 3).

A higher education system

Moderation is also increasingly important in higher education, with many systems currently developing or reviewing their moderation practices and policies. For example, Curtin University in Perth, Western Australia, has developed a draft policy to guide teachers. At this university, moderation is viewed as integral to quality assurance, to ensure that 'assessments are marked with accuracy, consistency and fairness' (Lawson et al., 2009: 21). Moderation is required for assessment that is reliant upon professional judgement, which involves a degree of subjectivity. In this particular university context, moderation is considered to be a part of the Quality Assessment Cycle and is enacted through different methods. Moderation begins with the design of the assessment task (or assessment event) and includes an analysis of the fitness of the assessment to the intended learning, after the assessment event has occurred or assessment task has been completed. The process of moderation, as outlined, can include the adjustment of student marks; however, it is recommended that such adjustments occur on the basis of the re-assessed student work. As part of the moderation process, the adjustments to student marks or grades take place before the script or the marks are communicated to the student.

Principles for the conduct of moderation are outlined as follows:

1 The front-end of the assessment process is key: that is, the design of assessments and their direct links to learning outcomes, as well as clear defensible marking criteria (also known as rubrics).

2 Review of assessments – their frequency and style and the relative success rate of students – must be a regular part of the unit improvement cycle.

3 Clear communication with assessors helps ensure clear understanding of the assessment task, the marking criteria, and expectations of students.

4 Pre-marking meetings with assessors to clarify marking criteria are essential and decrease post-marking issues.

5 Offshore and remote campuses and partnerships have specific needs and require constant and reliable communication between coordinators and markers: when things go wrong they are harder and more costly to fix. (Lawson et al., 2009: 17)

Scaling or statistical analysis for the adjustment of student grades 'without reference to the quality of student scripts, or after work has already been returned to students' is not recommended at this university (Lawson et al., 2009: 17).

There are five phases of assessment design, communication with markers, marking, moderation, feedback to students, including return of work, feedback to markers, assessment review and refinement. These are outlined below.

Assessment design

At this university, assessments are to be reviewed prior to student take-up, to ensure that the assessment is reflective of good practice. It is the unit coordinator who is responsible for the review, which may involve comment from colleagues within or outside of the university. The review is expected to consider the assessment in relation to:

- alignment with the intended learning outcomes
- consistency with the scope and level of the unit
- clarity of the task and assessment criteria
- equivalency when offered in multiple locations
- design that averts plagiarism
- appropriate weighting and scheduling across the period of study.

The process of assessment design occurs prior to the start of the unit or course.

Communication with markers

There is also an expectation that details of the assessment tasks, the weighting, due dates and marking criteria will be specified and made available to students in accordance with the unit outline. It is recommended that students are informed when their work will be assessed or marked, when feedback will be available, and are given written notification of any changes to the assessment as is necessary. This level of communication is expected to occur between the marking team to ensure that there is complete understanding.

Marking

In terms of the assessment of the student work, the assessors are to be provided with sufficient information to ensure comparability. In this context it is the unit coordinators who have the responsibility to provide clarification and/or guidance to other assessors if this is required during the marking or assessment process. A collaborative approach among the assessors is expected.

Moderation

The unit coordinator reviews the results, using one of the following methods:

- spot checking a random or selected sample of student work to check for consistent application of marking criteria and standards
- second-marking a random or selected sample of student work to compare marks awarded

- second-marking student work deemed to be at a borderline (pass/fail or between grade boundaries)
- statistical analysis of results for any potential variance between markers.

If any anomalies are found, it is recommended that student work be reassessed and marks adjusted accordingly prior to the release of grades or marks to the students. As this university has contracts in place with offshore campuses and partners, it is recommended that moderation should align with all contractual obligations. This phase of the moderation process involves post-marking by the coordinator, together with the team review, and that adjustments occur prior to the announcement of the results to the students.

Feedback

Students should receive all marks, assignments and feedback as soon as possible, to maximize their opportunity to improve performance in forthcoming assignments. Markers should be provided with feedback on the effectiveness and efficiency of the marking and moderation processes. Such feedback may include a review of the:

- assessment task, to establish whether it was set at an appropriate level
- assessment criteria, to establish whether they were easy for students and markers to use
- timing of the assessment, marking and the moderation processes employed
- feedback provided to students. (Lawson et al., 2009)

This final phase of this university's draft moderation policy involves feedback from the students and the team regarding the assessment design and the process for important feedback to the review process and the re-commencement of the cycle of the five phases.

Potential of online moderation practice and use of standards

Online moderation has the potential to promote the practice of developing a common understanding of the expected standards across a broader range of locations than is possible using face-to-face, paper-based moderation practice. For those teachers situated in remote or distant locations, it is also an opportunity, facilitated by technology, to develop confidence through practice and communication in working in a standards-referenced assessment system.

The ICT-mediated moderation process provides the capacity to extend practice to diverse locations and dispersed cohorts of teachers, as in countries such as Australia and Canada where there are vast distances between centres, and in New Zealand and Scotland, where there are many isolated and inaccessible regions. In standards-based education systems, where teachers are dispersed and work in such diverse areas, technology can facilitate their efforts of using moderation for both accountability and improvement of teaching and learning purposes.

Technology can be used to facilitate different levels of participation, to support and assist teachers' judgement practice. However, new and additional challenges arise to those identified in the face-to-face mode. To begin, it is essential to establish protocols for online moderation and to outline the procedures for conduct of the meetings. An example of guidelines that were developed for a study of an online, externally moderated assessment system (Connolly et al., 2011) is provided at the end of this chapter (see Figure 5.1, ICT Guidelines for Joining the WebEx Meeting). The teachers involved in this study were able synchronously to meet and moderate in an online situation, using a commercial web-conferencing software package. In these online meetings, an individual teacher's grades were moderated by a group of teachers in order to achieve consensus. The guidelines made explicit the preparation of equipment for the meeting, how to organize the meeting, how to join a meeting website and how to use the software.

From this study, there appeared to be no qualitative difference in participants' views about the use of standards in moderation and consistency of teachers' judgements between those who participated in ICT-mediated moderation and those who did not. Teachers' views are qualified by their attitudes, not by the mode of moderation. Teachers who have experienced ICT-mediated moderated exercises have responded positively to this mode, with most experiencing little or no difficulty using the system (Connolly et al., 2011). A process that provided teachers with the means to join an online group of peers and carry out moderation was seen as a valuable and productive exercise.

Advantages of using ICT-mediated, externally moderated assessment include the use of the software tools to highlight more explicitly the identified evidence in student work, in order to illustrate the qualities that the teacher has interpreted as significant for the award of the particular grade or standard. The electronic tools and facilities of conferencing software can assist teachers in demonstrating how in their understanding certain aspects of the student's response match the criteria and demonstrate the achievement of the standards. This is how the technology is used to mediate teachers' interpretations of the standards, which contribute to the development of a shared understanding of their meaning and the creation of a community in an otherwise isolated profession, particularly for those in remote locations.

The provision for other teachers, from one school or department, to take part as observers or panel members by simply being present at the time of the ICT-mediated moderation exercise appears to be another advantage of this form of moderation. This process enables several teachers to attend the moderation meeting by means of the one computer terminal and to observe or participate in the practice. This is seen as potentially a valuable tool for training and alignment of agreement in the interpretation of the standards between teachers within schools.

The main advantage of the ICT-mediated moderation process is the opportunity for those teachers who would normally never participate in moderation to do so with teachers from other schools. The realization that the process can take place in remote areas, or even in metropolitan areas, with a relatively small degree of organization, cost and time expenditure, is seen as highly beneficial for teachers.

While the technology can support and facilitate the practice of this form of external moderation, it can also present teachers with a number of challenges and constraints. For example, many teachers are apprehensive and, in some cases fearful of, the use of the technology. Such attitudes and responses present barriers to the fluency of the moderation processes and practices. The explicit demonstration of how the evidence identified in the student work matches the standards may not occur if the teachers are reluctant users of the technology and find the practice too time-consuming or burdensome. The main concerns related to the efficiency of the ICT-mediated moderation process relate to perceptions about the amount of preparation required for the meetings, use of technology, alignment of schools' schedules, time taken for scanning or photocopying requirements and the efficiency and reliability of the networking system (Connolly et al., 2011).

For many teachers, the use of technology for the purpose of moderating judgement practice, as a first-time user, means that they are novices and require assistance and practice to develop trust in the process and the necessary skills for using the technology. Additionally, as teachers may be meeting with colleagues whom they have not met before, and may not be able to see, it is important that protocols are established. A nominated facilitator usually guides the meeting and helps in the establishment of a sense of community. Online moderation does not allow for intimacy in discussions, as available in the face-to-face mode. The opportunity to observe body language and physically experience the meeting have been identified as integral to developing a community and to produce greater meaning and consistency between participant interaction. As participants join the meeting it is therefore helpful if they introduce themselves to begin this process of social interaction. Although these are not advantages of the online mode, this concern is limited given the benefits of ICT-mediated moderation.

Research suggests that teachers, by working with other experienced professionals in moderation practice in an online mode, can reach negotiation and agreement of their interpretations of the standards in relation to students' assessed work (Connolly et al., 2011). Novices to ICT-mediated moderation might need support in their use of the conferencing and annotation tools to identify the evidence in student work. It is anticipated, however, that with the aid of the technology more teachers will be able to develop confidence in their judgement practice in a standards-referenced assessment system that mediates their pedagogic practices and assessment practices in their own teaching and learning contexts.

Review questions

Why is the provision of standards and exemplars necessary but insufficient for achieving consistency and reliability of teachers' judgements?

What resources do teachers draw upon when judging the quality of student work?

What are the benefits for teachers of making their judgements explicit during moderation practice?

What system-level supports are necessary for teachers to be able to use moderation and standards effectively in their assessment practice?

How does online moderation practice contribute positively to education systems and teachers' assessment practice in particular?

ICT Guidelines for Joining the WebEx Meeting

Contents

ICT equipment needed for the meeting

You will require access to a computer with Internet capabilities and a phone. The WebEx meeting is held online through a website and you will talk to participants using a phone located near the computer. As you will be navigating the website during the meeting and referring to documents, you may find headphones or a handsfree/speaker phone function on your phone helpful.

Invitation to attend an ICT- mediated moderation meeting

You will receive an invitation to attend your ICT Mediated Moderation meeting through your email. The invitation will provide you with the details of the meeting and with a link to access the meeting's website.

The information about the meeting will look like the following:

> Topic: Moderation Meeting – Year 9 English
> Date: Wednesday, 19 September 2007
> Time: 1:30 pm, Australia Eastern Standard Time (GMT +10:00, Brisbane)
> Meeting Number: 123 456 789
> Meeting Password: elephant

Joining the meeting

How to join the meeting website

Approximately 10 minutes before the scheduled time for the meeting, refer to your email invitation for directions on joining the meeting. Begin by clicking on the link provided in Step 1 of your email and it will automatically take you to the meeting website. Continue to follow Steps 2–4 as detailed in your email. The following is an example of Steps 1–4 for joining a meeting:

> \---
> To join the online meeting
> \---
> 1. Go to https://griffith.webex.com/griffith/j.php?ED=92760777&UID=0
> 2. Enter your name and email address.
> 3. Enter the meeting password: elephant
> 4. Click 'Join'.

[Please note, the details specific to your meeting will be different to those that are in the above example. Print your meeting directions to refer to for joining your meeting.
Please refer to Step 1–4 contained in your email invitation.]

The following notification box will appear advising you on duration until the Meeting Manager is established. Please note that Time Remaining may at first display a lengthy period but it will reduce. This process usually takes about 2–5 minutes.

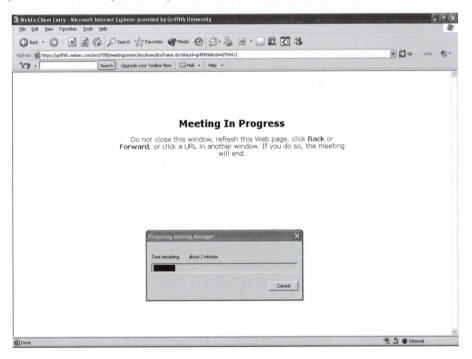

Appearing on your screen will be the following Internet Explorer notice. This screen needs to remain open for the duration of your meeting. A new screen will appear for the meeting.

Entering your details for call back

Once you have entered the meeting site the following box will appear asking for your phone details for an automatic call back. Please note:

1. Country/Region – this needs to be 61 for Australia. If it is not 61, click on the box on the right and select Australia. The field should automatically update to 61.

2. Enter your phone number beginning with your area code followed by your number without brackets or spaces. Please note, you will need to use a direct dial number that connects straight to your phone extension.

(Continued)

Figure 5.1 (Continued)

You will be called back by WebEx immediately if all details are correct. You will then be asked to 'Press 1 to enter the meeting.'

Additional information you may need for joining a meeting

The* meeting has not started *notice

If the meeting has not yet started you will receive a screen notifying you of this. Click *Ok*. This screen will then appear.

The meeting will not begin until the Host has opened the meeting. After a few minutes click the refresh button and when the status of the meeting changes, click *Join Now*.

It may be that a list of meetings available will appear; next to the meeting you are interested in click *Join Now*. You will then be asked to enter details about you and those provided in the email invitation:

1. Name
2. Email address
3. Meeting password

Now refer to the information on *Joining a Meeting* above.

First time load of the Meeting Centre software

The first time you visit the WebEx Meeting Centre you may be asked to load on the Meeting Centre software. You will be presented with this screen.

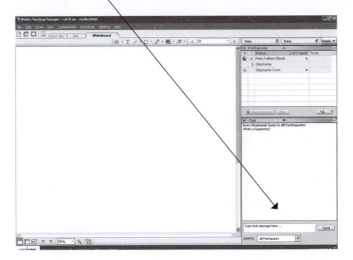

Follow Steps 1–3 in the first option presented to you. You will then be presented with a screen that details the meeting. Click *Join Now*.

Now refer to the information on *Joining a Meeting* above.

How to ring in if you do not receive a call back

If you experience difficulties and do not receive a call back within a few minutes please call the following toll-free number (expenses for the call are automatically charged to the project not the school) – 1800-093-897.

Follow the directions using information provided in your invitation email as requested. [Please note: when the pound button is referred to use the hash (#) key.]

How to let us know you are continuing to experience problems

If you continue to have problems joining the teleconference aspect of the meeting, please write a message in the chat box on the bottom right of the Meeting site. We will call you and join you in.

An overview of the Meeting Centre's functionality is provided in an easy to use and refer to A3 guide, sent to you in your package.

Figure 5.1   ICT guidelines for joining the WebEx meeting

References 📖

Connolly, S., Klenowski, V. and Wyatt-Smith, C. (2011) 'Moderation and consistency of teacher judgement: Teachers' views', *British Education Research Journal*, 38 (4): 593–614.

Hattie, J. (2005) 'What is the nature of evidence that makes a difference to learning?' Paper presented at the Australian Council for Educational Research Conference, Melbourne, Australia.

Lawson, K., Yorke, J. and Oliver, B. (2009) *Assessment and Moderation at Curtin Pilot Project: Final Report*. Perth: Curtin University, Office of Teaching and Learning.

Linn, R.L. (1993) 'Linking results of distinct assessments', *Applied Measurement in Education*, 6 (1): 83–102.

Maxwell, G.S. (2009) 'Defining standards for the 21st century', in C.M. Wyatt-Smith and J.J. Cumming (eds), *Educational Assessment in the 21st Century*. Springer. pp. 263–86.

Newton, P. (2007) 'Examination standards and the limits of linking', *Assessment in Education: Principles, Policy and Practice*, 12 (2): 105–23.

QSA, Queensland Studies Authority (2010) *A–Z of Senior Moderation*. Brisbane: QSA. Available at: www.qsa.edu.au.

Sadler, D.R. (1987) 'Specifying and promulgating achievement standards', *Oxford Review of Education*, 13 (2): 191–209.

Sadler, D.R. (1998) 'Formative assessment: Revisiting the territory', *Assessment in Education: Principles, Policy and Practice*, 5 (1): 77–84.

Sadler, D.R. (2009) 'Indeterminacy in the use of preset criteria for assessment and grading in higher education', *Assessment & Evaluation in Higher Education*, 34 (2): 159–79.

The Literacy and Numeracy Secretariat (2007) *Teacher Moderation: Collaborative Assessment of Student Work*. Ontario, Canada: Curriculum Services Canada. Available at: www.curriculum.org.

Woods, A. and Amorsen, A. (2011) *Evaluation of the Year 1 Literacy and Numeracy Checkpoints Assessments Trial – 2010*. Brisbane, Qld: Queensland University of Technology.

Web extras

Jessop, T., McNab, N. and Gubby, L. (2012) 'Mind the gap: An analysis of how quality assurance processes influence programme assessment patterns', *Active Learning in Higher Education*, 13 (2): 143–54.

McVee, M.B., Dunsmore, K. and Gavelek, J.R. (2005) 'Schema theory revisited', *Review of Educational Research*, 75 (4): 531–66.

6

How teachers can use standards to improve student learning

Overview

In this chapter we consider the constructive use of achievement standards for summative purposes in improving learning and teaching. We consider what is involved in a dialogic-inquiry approach to classroom assessment that has at its heart intentional and artful connections across curriculum, instruction and assessment. As central to a long-overdue focus on quality in the classroom, we present teacher judgement and standards as direct benefits for teachers and students seeking to improve student learning. At issue is the pedagogical utility of standards: how teachers and students can use standards to work purposefully toward the development of student knowledge about the expectations or characteristics of quality, as well as how to apply standards in improving performance.

This focus opens a space to consider approaches that support teachers in rethinking the traditional relationship between the teacher and student, and offers the possibility of including the learner's perspective in the use of assessment standards for improvement. The interest is not in standards for measurement and accountability – narrowly defined – but in standards as pedagogical tools for both teachers and students in a relationship in which assessment is a shared enterprise. Foundational to the ideas presented here is that assessment can be understood as generating an evidence base for decision making and action by teachers and students at the local or site level, as well as at system level, where issues of resourcing, for example, need decisions. Also at play is the understanding that assessment practices are inevitably social and cultural. As such, they are reflective of nested assumptions, often implicit, which affect and are reflected in what happens in classrooms. These assumptions constitute, in part, what teachers bring to acts of judgement: notions of what counts as valued curricular knowledge and skills; the relationship between learning, teaching and assessment; 'proper' teacher judgement practices; and understandings about the relationship between curriculum and cross-curricular priorities.

Assessment as decision making and judgement

Broadly speaking, it is accepted in several fields, including curriculum design, instructional design, assessment, and literacy and numeracy education, that the teacher is the central person in the assessment process, best placed to guide and monitor learning through direct or first-hand observations of student learning. Further, a key component of successful classroom assessment is teacher expertise.

Several kinds of teacher expertise and knowledge are required. There is, for example, teacher knowledge of the intended curriculum and what students are expected to learn, and knowledge of assessments for formative purposes, including diagnosis of difficulties and ways to improve learning, and summative purposes such as the reporting of student achievement and certification. These expectations are normally communicated in official curriculum and assessment policy documents as well as in a school's local materials. They may include publicly available curriculum and assessment documents, including those on the worldwide web, as well as a range of other documents, such as school statements of values and community relationships. The teacher also needs expertise in selecting and using a range of assessment techniques and modes to obtain useful information on student learning for monitoring and feedback purposes. The teacher's disposition towards students, and his or her expertise in the discriminating use of assessment purposes and tools are well recognized as part of the teacher's repertoire of assessment resources: the teacher's 'tool kit'. However, less attention has been given to teacher knowledge of, and expertise in, recognizing quality, and further, in how to focus this knowledge and expertise on how teaching occurs in the classroom. Kress (2001) made the point that learning to be literate involves learning 'how to see'. In this chapter our interest is in the transformative potential of assessment standards to provide the means for teachers and students to learn to 'see' and talk about quality in the classroom. As we discuss in the remainder of this chapter, our interest is in the pedagogic sharpening that can come from teacher and student dialogue about what counts as quality, and in using this shared knowledge to inform how learning occurs.

Accordingly, the chapter takes up Webb's (2009: 3) claim that

> facilitating change in teachers' assessment practice is not so much a resource problem as it is a problem of ... helping teachers develop a designer's eye for selecting, adapting and designing tasks to assess student understanding.

While Webb's reference to a designer's eye related to developing tasks, its application is broader here: how do teachers learn how to see – to develop a designer's perspective on learning opportunities – and, further, how do teachers and students develop perspectives on quality?

These questions resonate with the question Rowntree (1987) posed in his book title and provocation to readers, *How Shall We Know Them?* In addressing these questions we ask readers to consider a two-part answer: with the eye of the designer first, to regard assessment as decision making and, second, to appreciate the potential of assessment criteria and standards as pedagogical tools for improving both learning and learner engagement.

Understanding context

Assessment is always contextual: it occurs in settings that are cultural and historical in nature. As such, assessment can be thought of as *situated practice*. That is to say, over time, ways in which assessment occurs can become accepted, regarded as taken-for-granted, 'natural' activities in education. In practice, however, assessment is reflective of decisions and priorities at both local school level and at system or government level. There are, for example, resourcing decisions about print and online materials to be purchased, including standardized test materials; decisions about the types of activities or tasks students are required to undertake, and the performance contexts in which learning and assessment will occur. There are also other decisions about how teachers are expected to undertake curriculum planning; the nature, extent and timing of assessment information to be collected; those assessments, if any, that will be common across all students at a year level; the amount of class time to be given to test preparation; and whether assessments will include assignments or only student work completed under examination conditions, with restricted time and no access to resources.

How consequential are these decisions and how mindful does the teacher need to be about the consequences of such assessment decisions? Numerous writers (Messick, 1989) have reminded us of the effects of assessment on the lives of individuals. For example, Broadfoot and Black (2004) have declared that

> it is arguably as strong a moral imperative on educators to satisfy themselves that the [assessment] technologies being used are 'safe' and beneficial as there is on a nuclear scientist or on a biologist working on genetically modified crops. (2004: 13)

Ecclestone and Pryor (2003) similarly warn of the lack of knowledge about the effects of assessment on learners and on their identities and dispositions, and of assessment practices that ignore students' voices. They suggest that the effects of a system of assessment depend largely on its 'hegemony and room for manoeuvre by teachers and students' (2003: 477). This observation highlights issues of power in assessment and the control that can be exerted by an education system and by teachers directly through assessment requirements.

Two themes connect here: one related to equity and the other to the traditionally hierarchical student–teacher relationship in which, traditionally, assessment remains at the core of teacher authority in the classroom. As discussed elsewhere in this book (see Chapter 3), in regard to equity, the contents of the curriculum and assessment need to be evaluated in terms of fairness, bias and the inclusion (and omission) of minority group cultural knowledge. Gipps' (1999) observation that assessment of individual or group performance is culturally determined is relevant here. Gipps suggested that new approaches that rethink and open up the traditional relationship between the teacher and student offer the possibility of including the learner's perspective. Cumming and Wyatt-Smith (2001) aimed to create creative records of this perspective in the methodology they applied in a large-scale Australian study of the literacy demands of curriculum in senior schooling. Through the use of 'student-cam', screen records were made of classroom talk and interaction in all curriculum areas in senior schooling. Student-cam recorded the focus and line of sight of students during their classroom activities, with these records providing compelling evidence of the traditional patterns of interaction within classrooms, with the teacher exercising high authority over the learning agenda, and very limited student engagement with published assessment criteria and standards, where these were available. Also identified was how, typically in the observed senior schooling classrooms, the learners were 'allocated a strikingly subordinate position from which challenges to the learning [and assessment] agenda were not expected, and on the rare occasions when they did occur, they were not well received' (2001: 51–2).

Taking a focus on pupil voice, Ruddock has also advocated the changing of authority relations in schools, recognizing and acting on what she referred to as 'the huge potential contribution' students can make as active participants in the education system (Ruddock and Flutter, 2003; Ruddock, 2004; Flutter and Ruddock, 2004; Ruddock, n.d.). She sought to stimulate debate about the potential for gains in school improvement from student participation. Ruddock characterized students as the 'forgotten partners' in schooling who experienced complex situations and relationships and, at times, significant responsibilities outside of school while having less autonomy, responsibility and intellectual challenge in school.

There are, however, significant and entrenched barriers in allowing for 'pupil voice' and a new order of experience for students in schools. Further, while there can be no doubt about the potential for both students and teachers to experience anxiety about changes in the boundaries of teacher–student relationships in relation to learning and teaching, it is in the realm of assessment practice that change may well be more strongly resisted, even by students and parents. This is reflective of the traditional position that assessment is properly the solo business of teachers, lying at the heart of teacher authority in the classroom, and that student voice in this space is also properly to be limited.

Several writers have identified how, traditionally, the assessment relationship has been one of judgement or surveillance, foregrounding a need for teachers to reconstruct their relationships and the culture of the classroom to one whereby 'teachers share the power with students rather than exerting power over them' (Gipps, 1999: 386). This is not seen as teachers giving up responsibility for student learning but rather working towards a learning partnership in which assessment is shared among teachers and students. This returns the discussion to the issue of 'responsibility', raised earlier. Stiggins (2004) suggested that maximum learning comes from productive interactions between teachers and students, with both sharing the responsibility for making learning and assessment effective. So, recognition of assessment in a learning culture is not new (Shepard, 2000), just as it is not a new idea that teachers help students use continuous assessment to take responsibility for their own learning.

Here is the new space: What is involved in drawing on what the teacher brings to the assessment act so that it becomes a deliberate part of the curriculum? In opening this space we discuss three elements that are taken as complementary and foundational to realizing assessment as transformational: *conceptions of knowledge, values and understandings,* including as they relate to learners, and domain knowledge and the related capabilities to be assessed; *the conception of alignment,* in which assessment, learning and teaching are understood as dynamically interconnected and interdependent; and *the conception of standards as constructs of quality.*

The constant focus across the elements is on identifying and examining the suite of conceptions, values and assumptions that underpin teachers' decisions about classroom assessment practices. It is motivated by the general observation that while curriculum and instructional design matters are now well recognized as reflective of underpinning conceptions and assumptions, their influence over what is counted as assessment evidence, including for high-stakes purposes, is rarely acknowledged. It is as though, in order for assessment to be trusted, it is best understood to be value neutral. Of course, this can never be the case, though acts of assessment, including large-scale testing schemes, are rarely subjected to interrogation for the values that they reflect and for the underpinning assumptions they make about student learning and achievement.

Readers are asked to explore the set of elements as a way to open assessment practices to scrutiny, to reveal what would otherwise be taken for granted as 'normal'. The elements carry forward and build on an earlier conceptual framing of assessment as critical inquiry (Wyatt-Smith and Gunn, 2009), which drew on the work of Delandshere (2002) and was prompted by the lack of a general theoretical position that connects assessment to meaning making. The latter was taken to include concepts of knowledge, learning, language and context. In what follows, each of the elements is addressed in turn as a component of an approach for realizing the transformative potential of assessment. As a suite, they are offered for teachers in all phases of education, to tease out and examine 'the fit' or connections they could realize in practice across curriculum, teaching and learning and assessment.

Element 1: Knowledge and knowing

Some two decades ago, Gill (1993: 1) observed that:

> [a]mong the many and various articles and books on the quality and direction of American education, one searches in vain for an in-depth discussion of how knowing takes place, of who knowers are, and of what can be known.

Drawing on this observation, Delandshere (2002) asserted:

> Until we come to grips with, or at least frame the issue of, knowledge and knowing in ways that can guide education practices (including assessment), the enterprise of education runs the risk of being fruitless and counter productive. In its current state, assessment appears to be a process of collecting data about phenomena or constructs that we have not adequately defined, to answer questions that we have not articulated, and on the basis of which we draw inferences about the quality of the education system. (2002: 1462)

These observations are also evident in the work of several writers (James, 1998; Harlen, 2004) who concur with Delandshere's assertion about the need for a clearly defined and articulated domain of knowledge as the basis for teaching and assessment:

> The argument is that an assessment cannot require the use of the knowledge and skills or other constructs that are supposedly assessed unless there is clear definition of the domain being assessed, and evidence that in the assessment process the intended skills and knowledge are used by the learners. (Delandshere, 2002: 25)

This observation could be heard as calling for checks on validity and, in particular, construct validity, wherein the concern is with how assessment relates to what has been taught and learned. Validity of assessment remains a central concern, especially given the increasing numbers of classrooms in which student diversity (cultural, linguistic, ethnic and socioeconomic) is 'the norm'. This is where the issue of assessment validity intersects with the big questions, posed by Freebody (2006: 2), about 'what schooling is for, and about what kinds of futures individuals and communities can expect to be put on offer through schooling'. This includes consideration of 'the distinctive logical and content structures of particular bodies of human knowledge and understanding' (p. 8), or the epistemological domain, along with the connection of 'learning with the social, cultural, and economic elements of the surrounding community and "the world" outside the classroom' (p. 15), or pragmatic domain of curriculum. The world is a place of unprecedented change in communication practices, brought about in large part through developments in technologies. It is in taking account of this broader context that we argue the urgency in reconnecting assessment and, more generally, educational practices to theoretical considerations as a means of clarifying assumptions made about what is to be valued through to assessment. Rarely are these made explicit, and yet they are integral to how assessment actually occurs.

Knowing the learning domain

Knowing the learning domain and relevant syllabus materials are foundational to planning and effective teaching practice. More fundamentally, such knowledge is foundational to quality assessment. This may seem self-evident in good practice, but there is ample research on classroom practice to show that in periods of educational reform and change, especially when the pressure is more intensely focused on improving test scores, allocation of time for teachers to reflect critically on the knowledge demands of what they teach is often felt by teachers to be of secondary importance, even a luxury, when faced with the pressures of daily operation. The explicit provision of time for teachers to come together to meet in curriculum-specific or cross-curriculum groups within a school, or in collaborative networks of schools, is highly valuable. It is in such meetings that teachers can focus on planning for learning and for linking learning and assessment, both for diagnosis and improvement purposes. This is the opening through which we might take account of student perspective.

Specifically, teachers can take a deliberate focus on their knowledge of the assessment demands that students face in completing learning and assessment activities. This involves teachers 'tuning into' and verifying the assumptions they may hold about students' prior knowledges and capabilities and, more specifically, how these relate to what students are expected to learn next, and student readiness to proceed. Where this occurs, teachers can take account of student perspectives and check what they actually know about students as learners and what knowledge and experience students bring with them to school.

This orientation calls teachers to subject their own classroom practice to examination, by themselves or with colleagues. It invites teachers to discuss how they bring their personal, sociocultural backgrounds to classroom interactions and how, in the teaching and assessment decisions they take, they act to open up and close down different ways for students to demonstrate their learning and achievement. These discussions can also provide a forum in which to bring to the surface otherwise 'private' views about how social class, cultural and linguistic backgrounds and performance expectations may connect as influences on classroom assessment practice.

Element 2: Linking assessment, learning and teaching

In this section we focus on teachers' work in the artful linking or *aligning* of assessment to teaching and learning, through decisions that support the purposeful collection and interpretation of assessment evidence. We also consider what is involved in bringing the issue of quality into classroom talk and interactions, with a focus on the pedagogical utility of standards. In part, this extends to the use of carefully chosen exemplars of student work that illustrate different standards and opportunities for students to participate in self-assessment and peer-assessment for improving learning.

Broadly speaking, the characteristic of what is referred to here as 'linked-up planning' is that it connects assessment to how teaching and learning will occur. Efforts to realize such connections are evident in the published assessment literature, in which the focus is on assessment that the teacher undertakes. For example, some writers highlight the assessment-driven design process (Harris et al., 2003). In this process the intention is to place the purposeful collection of assessment information and the design of quality-assessment tasks or activities at the heart of planning.

As discussed in Chapter 1, historically, teaching, learning and assessment have been understood as a trilogy, whereby priority is given first to what should be taught, and therefore, what should be learned. In this trilogy, assessment can be relegated to third position, whereby key decisions about the assessment information to be collected are taken sometimes well into, or even at the end of, a teaching programme. That is, after teaching and learning are expected to have concluded. However, the notion of alignment as discussed here is that as teachers are planning and working with the curriculum, attention is given concurrently to planning for assessment. This involves deliberate linking or stitching together on the part of the teacher as a metacognitive activity that is a precondition for making assessment integral to teaching and learning.

Incorporating thinking about assessment into planning has a focusing or consciousness-raising effect on teaching. The benefits of such approaches have been shown in a range of studies in which assessment has been used as a driver for curriculum design (for example, Harris et al., 2006). When teachers deliberately build assessment into planning, they establish their own cognitive links between the official or intended curriculum, and planning for how teaching, learning and assessment are expected to take place. Further, in *front-ending assessment* into planning, the teachers' pedagogy is set up with a sharp focus on what will need to be taught and how to set students up for success on assessment tasks. This is not to be interpreted as restricting learning to what is assessed. Instead, it is to focus on student success and what students will need to know and to be able to demonstrate their learning. Such provision avoids the undesirable situation of a disjuncture between teaching and assessment, and where student failure can be a direct consequence of this disjuncture.

An important extension of this approach is for teachers to embed their assessment knowledge and expertise as students learn the curriculum. This approach can be applied in all phases of education, from kindergarten to postgraduate studies and higher education, across curriculum areas, and in units or courses designed as integrated or cross-disciplinary studies. It involves, in part, the teacher undertaking assessment as a shared enterprise whereby students are enabled to take a role in classroom assessment, and, more fundamentally, develop evaluative knowledge and expertise. In this view of assessment, the role of the teacher properly extends to inducting students into knowledge about expectations of quality; assisting them to learn how to recognize and talk about features of quality in their own and others' work (Elwood and Klenowski, 2002).

It also involves deliberate decision making about the information that is to be collected about what students are learning. That is to say, teachers take an approach to assessment as evidence-based practice and place the course or unit assessment activities at the heart of planning. This approach provides opportunities for teachers to decide early in a course of study the assessment information they want to collect for formative purposes and summative purposes. It also involves letting students know about these decisions so that they can be more 'knowing' about assessment expectations. In these ways, assessment becomes a shared or joint enterprise.

This thinking challenges traditional understandings of assessment as an endpoint activity, with attention given to the teacher's collection and interpretation of assessment evidence after teaching has been completed. For teachers who have traditionally thought of assessment as occurring at the end of a period of study, the notion of aligning teacher-generated assessment and learning may represent a shift in thinking, as can be read in the comments below of some middle-years teachers:

> So basically once you have the assessment firmly in place the pedagogy became really clear because your pedagogy has to support that – that sort of quality assessment task ... that was a bit of a shift from what's usually done, usually assessment is that thing that you attach on the end of the unit whereas as opposed to sort of being the driver which it has now become .... (Wyatt-Smith and Bridges, 2007 in DEEWR and DETA, 2007, Appendix 1: 48, copyright Commonwealth of Australia reproduced by permission)

In this segment we observe the teachers talking about assessment as motivating or driving certain teaching and learning approaches and activities. This is not to be misinterpreted as reductive or endorsing the idea of reducing teaching to the test. Similarly, it is not the case that by being explicit about assessment expectations, including the main assessment activities or tasks that students will undertake, teaching is taken to be giving students 'the answers'. Instead, the intention is to realize an active role for students in how assessment of their learning occurs, and for realizing the potential of assessment to engage learners in new ways as they themselves think about and learn how to talk about the quality of their learning. This calls teachers not only to see the interactivity of how assessment, teaching and learning occur within a dynamic process of inquiry, but also to extend practice to how assessment criteria and standards can function as pedagogic tools.

Element 3: Standards as constructs of quality

Sadler's (1989, 1998) work on 'formative assessment' provides a model for a teaching–learning–assessment nexus that shows how improvement follows when students are inducted into assessment knowledge and expertise. In this discussion, this induction is taken to extend to the teachers' knowledge of relevant criteria and standards, and, more specifically, how they can function for improvement purposes.

From this perspective, the teacher's ethical practice and, hence, authority as master, follows a guild model, reliant on a notion of connoisseurship (Sadler, 1989). In Sadler's characterizing of the teacher as expert and connoisseur and the student as apprentice, and drawing on the work of Ramaprasad, Sadler has proposed that the teacher must possess first, a concept of quality appropriate to the task and the student group; second, an ability to judge the student's work in relation to that concept and a desire to induct student-apprentices into the appraisal process; and third, a history of evaluative decision making developed over time.

Several writers (Black et al., 2003; Stiggins, 2004; Stiggins and Chappius, 2005), have similarly highlighted the importance of student involvement in assessment practices, suggesting that maximum learning comes from productive interactions between teachers and students, with both sharing the responsibility for making learning and assessment effective. In connecting a focus on feedback and standards, Sadler (1998: 82) argued that:

> if teacher-supplied feedback is to give way to self assessment and self monitoring, some of what the teacher brings to the assessment act must itself become part of the curriculum for the student, not an accidental or inconsequential adjunct to it.

These views are consistent with the numerous writers who have advocated for standards to be linked directly to learning and teaching, and directly integrated into classroom practice. For example, more than a decade ago Stigler and Hiebert (1997: 19–20) presented the cautionary note that a narrow focus on standards and accountability that ignores or short circuits teaching and learning processes in classrooms will fall short of providing the focus for teacher efforts to secure student improvement. We accept this position, and build on it to explore the conditions under which standards can be used as a pedagogical resource in the classroom. That is to say, the time is right for exploring, within the learning space of the classroom, what it means to say that assessment can be accomplished as a joint enterprise.

With this in mind, we now centre on the pedagogical use of summative assessment standards. Specifically, we explore the conditions under which teachers and students mutually can contribute towards and benefit from a dialogic approach to such standards, carrying direct relevance to classroom learning. First, however, we establish the intended meaning of the terms 'criteria' and 'standards'.

Distinguishing criteria and standards

Assessment can be called criteria-based when it focuses on the features or characteristics of a student's actual achievements in relation to specified criteria (rather than to an established norm or relative to other students). Standards-referenced assessment occurs when the primary focus is on standards rather than on criteria, although standards presuppose criteria.

The published literature offers a wide range of definitions of standards. In their purest form, standards are descriptions or other specifications of performance levels (that is, letter grades, numeric scores) that are free from any references to the performance of the typical student, the proportion or number of students expected to achieve a given level, or the particular age or stage of schooling at which a certain level of performance is thought to be acceptable.

In this chapter, standards-referenced assessment is taken to occur as part of qualitative judgements in classroom teaching. It can apply across a wide variety of subjects and curriculum areas, and in schooling and higher-education sectors: English and other languages, humanities and social sciences; mathematics, sciences and technical fields; the performing and creative arts, and manual and design technology areas. Furthermore, it can be applied to single tasks of different scope, including the single essay or dramatic performance (for formative purposes) to complete folios of work for final certification, and as Sadler (1987) has noted, does not require sophisticated mathematical modelling or external statistical interpretation of results.

Tognolini (2005) defines standards referencing as the process of giving meaning to marks assigned to student work by referencing the image of the work to predetermined standards of performance. Essentially, a standards descriptor is a statement or list of statements that aims succinctly to convey the required quality of, or features in, student work in order for it to be awarded the corresponding grade. Grades are linked to standards-referenced assessment and can operate as the subject or domain level, the task level or the examination level, or on exit from a course of study.

Typically, however, the features of student work required for the award of a given standard or grade cannot be fully described or comprehensively specified beforehand. Standards for assigning grades tend to provide an overall description for that grade level and can apply to a range of demonstrations of performance that all meet expected features or characteristics of quality, though in recognizably different ways.

There are many different views about the merits and limitations of criteria and standards that are specified beforehand, and we are not aiming to reconcile these viewpoints. Consistent with the direction highlighted by Broadfoot (2009), our interest is in the matter of *quality*. When teachers bring the notion of quality directly into how they work with students in the classroom, they can connect assessment not only to learning and teaching, but also and more fundamentally with standards, be they stated or unstated. It is by building into classroom talk and interactions explicit talk about standards and related criteria as quality indicators that students develop the skills to recognize and talk about what counts as quality and apply that recognition to their own work.

In this context the distinction between the terms 'criteria' and 'standards' in practice is relevant: it breaks the process of teacher judgement into two stages. First, the criteria are identified (what you are looking to be displayed in the student's response to the assessment); then the standards, which describe the level of the student's response identifying criteria representative of that level of performance, are specified (how well and to what depth it has been displayed).

For the student the highest standard (and related criteria) is a goal for which to aim. For the teacher, standards are used in assessing or describing the quality of student performance. It is the teacher who judges which standard best represents the characteristics of a student's performance; that is, what descriptor to attach to the performance, or what category (such as A–E) is most suitable. Readers are asked to see Chapter 7 for a discussion of how standards and judgement for the assigning of grades connect. Now, we consider professional judgement and standards within a dialogic inquiry approach to teaching and learning, through which assessment becomes a joint enterprise.

Introducing a dialogic inquiry approach to assessment with summative standards as pedagogical tools

Our aim in this section is to explore what is involved in a dialogic inquiry approach to assessment that takes account of the learner's perspective. The discussion is exploratory, and deliberately opens the space for thinking about approaches that could be applied by teachers in the classroom. It takes as its centrepiece standards and, in particular, the constructive use of summative standards for both learning improvement and accountability and reporting purposes. The case presented below is that a focus on summative standards in the hands of teachers is the next, necessary move in taking assessment forward.

Teacher judgement and achievement standards

As indicated earlier, we take a perspective on teachers' assessment in general and their professional judgement in particular as cognitive and socially situated. This stance is informed by work of Cobb and colleagues (1997), who considered social practices and individual psychological processes to be associated in a reflexive, mutually constitutive relationship. In our work, the relevant concept developed by Cobb et al. is that meaning, or more specifically in our area of interest the meaning of a stated standard or set of standards, is not necessarily self-evident or transparent to the parties expected to use them. Instead, standards written as verbal descriptors accrue meaning over time, through use, and through interactions among actors that allow the emergence of 'taken-as-shared-meaning' that informs their use. This perspective recognizes that the meaning of standards cannot be taken to be identical in the minds and practices of teachers and among students in a classroom. Instead, standards have meaning ascribed to them through use by teachers and students, not only over time but also in particular contexts of practice.

Here, we look to Wenger (1998) and his notion that meaning is continuously negotiated through participation in 'communities of practice'. Of particular relevance are the three dimensions that bring coherence to a community of practice: mutual engagement, joint enterprise and a shared repertoire of concepts, tools and terminology. In this section, we explore the notion of embedding summative assessment standards into classroom practice so that the standards function as a site for joint enterprise. According to Wenger (1998) joint enterprise occurs as

> a collective process of negotiation that reflects the full complexity of mutual engagement (and) is defined by the participants in the very process of pursuing it. It is their negotiated response to their situation and thus belongs to them in a profound sense, in spite of all the forces and influences that are beyond their control (and) creates among participants relations of mutual accountability that become an integral part of the practice. (1998: 78)

In classrooms, teachers and students work with summative assessment standards so that in processes of negotiation there is a development of practices through participation, both for individual members of the community and the collective.

According to Lave and Wenger (1991), learning takes place where knowledge occurs in action and where practice brings together that which is learnt through a dualistic process of participation and reification. Meaning in practice, Wenger (1998) argued, involves not only interaction, but more fundamentally negotiation of the interaction of two constituent processes, namely participation and reification. These work together to 'form a duality that is fundamental to the human experience of meaning and thus to the nature of practice' (p. 52). For students to develop practice in the use of standards requires them to observe carefully and be ready to adopt the practices they observe or those they have learnt to be formalized (reified) in the classroom context. Wenger (1998: 58) referred to reification as 'the process of giving form to our experience by producing objects that congeal this experience into "thingness"'. In broad terms, it refers to a shared understanding of meaning by participants in a community of practice. In reality, mutual engagement is an extremely complex form of participation in a community of practice that extends beyond a team or collective endeavour, with each community having its own way of engaging.

This notion is central to our proposal for the dialogic-inquiry approach to assessment and standards and their use in classrooms. Gordon Wells (1999) defined 'inquiry' not as a method but as a predisposition for questioning and for trying to understand situations by collaborating with others with the objective of finding answers. 'Dialogic inquiry' is an educational approach that acknowledges the dialectic relationship between the individual and the society, and an attitude for acquiring knowledge through communicative interactions. According to Wells, the predisposition for dialogic inquiry depends on the characteristics of the learning environments. From our vantage point, the interest is in how to constitute the classroom and standards as sites or contexts for collaborative action and interaction. According to Wells, dialogic inquiry not only enriches individuals' knowledge but also transforms it, ensuring the capacity for individuals and cultures to transform themselves according to the requirements of every social moment. So, to revisit the question posed earlier in this chapter: What is involved in using standards as pedagogical tools? Specifically, what practices would support teachers and students in using summative standards to inform improvement efforts in the classroom?

Central to this discussion are three assumptions, namely (a) a hallmark of an instructional system is the explicit provision it makes for students themselves to acquire evaluative expertise; (b) the best interests of students are not served when they remain dependent on evaluation judgements supplied by the teacher; and (c) teachers see it as integral in their professional role to develop their students as active participants in classroom assessment processes. These assumptions place the teacher, and more specifically professional judgement, at the heart of classroom assessment. They also call for an expanded repertoire of teaching–assessing practices that serve to develop students' evaluative experience and expertise and, in turn, lessen their dependence on the teacher as the sole or primary source of evaluative feedback.

The line of development taken here is that students benefit when standards are embedded in the talk and interactions of the classroom so that they function as long-term goals achievable over a year or phase of schooling. When teachers become main assessors in school-based assessment, one fundamental challenge is how to make the expectations of assessment transparent, known and understood by all participants, including students. This challenge is pressing in on all schools, but it is particularly the case with student cohorts characterized by diversity in all its forms, cultural, linguistic and socioeconomic.

The challenge for transparency in achieving an appropriate balance between explicit (stated) and tacit or latent (unstated) knowledge is well recognized. Here, explicit knowledge is viewed as 'conscious knowledge that can be put into words and can be expressed clearly and communicated openly in ways that are unambiguous for all concerned', while tacit knowledge is that 'which is learnt experientially or in terms of its incommunicability – knowledge that cannot be easily articulated and is elusive' (O'Donovan et al., 2004: 238). Polanyi (1998: 136) argued that 'we can know more than we can tell', and suggested that explicit and tacit knowledge are inseparably related, with all knowledge having a tacit dimension.

It is this relationship between explicit and tacit knowledge that provides fertile ground for rethinking how teachers can use summative standards as pedagogical tools. Specifically, it is in this space that the teacher can go beyond supplying students with stated standards to showing students what standards mean and how they can be applied in practice, both for judging quality and for improvement purposes. Drawing on Stake (2004: x), we are reminded that

> we need to take those early impressions [for example, of student work] and refine them, stretch them, challenge them, polish them – for the values of human encounter, however biased, reveal some deep and complex meanings that surface no other way. It is the message of listening to experience.

Standards as goals

By what means can teachers engage students in this 'listening' and tuning-in to quality? One answer is by enabling students to see standards as goals. In the preceding discussion, the term 'standard' has been used to refer to a specified level of attainment. However, a standard 'becomes a goal when it is desired, aimed for or aspired to' (Sadler, 1998: 18). Therefore, what distinguishes standards as levels of attainment from standards as goals is the student's personal response to the prescribed standards. Only when standards are accepted by students can they motivate their performance as goals. This clearly indicates that whereas standards can be prescribed within official curriculum documents, and used by systems and teachers to make judgements about student work, it is the opportunity to learn through the application of standards to one's own and peer work and the experience of benefiting from such opportunities that determine whether the standards can also function as goals.

Related to any discussion of standards as goals must be the means by which students can be given the necessary training opportunities to make qualitative judgements about their work in relation to the prescribed standards and then to act on these judgements in order to improve future performance. Sadler (1998) identified three conditions that must be satisfied if students are to be able to judge and improve the quality of their work during its production:

> The learner has to (a) possess a concept of the standard (or goals, or reference level) being aimed for, (b) be able to compare the actual (or current) level of performance with the standard, and (c) engage in appropriate action that leads to some closure of the gap. (1998: 6)

It is argued that if students do not possess a concept of the prescribed standard, then the two other conditions cannot be met. In this sense students' knowledge about standards can be regarded as a precondition for any improvement in performance.

Others (for example, Ahmann and Glock, 1971) have distinguished between prescribed standards or reference levels against which student achievement is judged, and standards to measure achievement in relation to an individual's learning ability and effort. Our interest is with teaching practices that allow students to develop and apply a concept of standards to their work, including during its production. Such practices involve teachers in sharing guild knowledge with students so they are able to acquire an understanding of standards and what counts as quality, both in school and beyond. As used here, the term 'guild knowledge' is taken to refer to the knowledge that experts rely on to recognize quality and to arrive at judgement of quality. Guild knowledge is, of course, susceptible to change over time as values and valuation practices change. However, it is fair to say that guild knowledge routinely goes beyond fixed rubrics of prior specified features, irrespective of the attempt of such rubrics to be comprehensive. The development of guild knowledge requires tutelage over time under an experienced other or master, much as a mentor who can develop in others through their own practice and modelling how to discern or recognize quality. The literature provides a clear case for the benefits of experienced or expert teachers sharing with students their guild knowledge and, for this to occur, teachers will need an expanded repertoire of resources and practices.

We argue that carefully chosen exemplars or actual samples of student work can illustrate the standards. They can provide concrete examples of what the features or expectations of performance look like. Further, a range of exemplars can show students different ways of satisfying the requirements of the stated standards. At another level, it is through such exemplars that teachers can talk about how standards apply in practice, modelling for students how they might apply them to their own work, both during production and on its completion. In this way, standards can be used to inform self-assessment and peer-assessment, developing in students the capacity to discern qualities in their own work and the work of others.

It is only through teacher and student talk and interactions around standards and exemplars that the teacher can induct students into what is involved in using standards to gauge quality, both on completion of the work and during its production. This practice goes beyond knowledge of stated criteria and standards to the ability to apply them. The view of guild knowledge and professional judgement taken here is that it involves the use of three categories of criteria that enable assessors to amend or focus expectations, even when they are engaged in the process of judgement making (Sadler, 1985; Wyatt-Smith and Klenowski, forthcoming). These are namely explicit (stated), latent (unstated or emergent) and meta-criteria.

Two points emerge here: first, that an experienced assessor is able to draw on not only stated criteria in discerning quality, but also in recognizing emergent or latent criteria that they discern in the piece being assessed. In effect, through knowledge of meta-criteria, the experienced assessor knows not only what criteria to apply, but also recognizes how previously unspecified criteria may need to be called into play to take account of the qualities of the work in front of them. This points to how professional judgement is a learned practice and, further, that experienced assessors know not only the criteria or features that apply, but also how and when to use them.

Experienced assessors also have experience of how the judgement of quality routinely involves seeing how strengths and limitations in a performance combine, with the former compensating for the latter in a decision about overall quality. As mentioned, it is not desirable for stated standards and criteria to be treated as rules for rigid application. They function as an anticipatory set of expected features of quality. As such, it is unreasonable to expect stated standards to capture the full range of qualities of performance and how these combine in all cases to be assessed.

Given this, students will not have access to insider knowledge of the complex decision making in applying standards, in the absence of discussion about how they apply to actual samples. The telling point is that a final grade recorded on a student's work may bear no trace of, or resemblance to, the decision making involved in arriving at a grading decision. The optimal approach therefore is to combine standards with exemplars chosen to illustrate quality, and accompanying commentaries that show how standards have been applied, including the operation of trade-offs or compensations in judgement practice.

Exemplars to demonstrate quality

Exemplars can be generated from the work of students in prior years or from publicly available professional materials. They can take the form of a task or set of tasks of different types. Alternatively, exemplar portfolios can be compiled to be illustrative of a particular standard or achievement level (say, A–E). While these could be located as within-band level, they could be more usefully chosen to illustrate the absolute minimum requirements for work judged to be a particular level. Such threshold-level exemplars would be particularly useful to illustrate the minimum requirements for a particular level, such as a C level. The role of these materials is to illustrate different ways of satisfying the stated requirements of the standards.

Once the features of quality are agreed, they can be published on the school intranet or the classroom wall for whole-class and individual use. Students could then take up the role of assessor and apply the criteria to their own work or the work of their peers. It may be that the criteria remain open to review, so that additional criteria can be added in the course of the unit of study and as other examples of quality work become available. The criteria can then also be used to inform student efforts at self-assessment and peer-assessment, both during the course of a unit and on completion of activities. The key point here is that when students can refer to stated criteria and standards as the point of reference for judging quality, they do not need to rely on direct inter-student comparisons as the basis for discerning quality.

The role of cognitive commentaries to show the application of standards in judgement

Carefully chosen exemplars that illustrate different ways of satisfying the requirements of standards and teacher-generated commentaries that accompany the exemplars are particularly relevant to student learning. Descriptive reports or cognitive commentaries such as the one shown below (see Figure 6.1) give insight into how tacit knowledge or emergent criteria can legitimately influence the teacher's view of the quality of the piece of work to be assessed. That is to say, the teacher can show how stated criteria and standards can be considered, in conjunction with features in the piece and that have not previously been specified, to arrive at a fulsome view of quality. This stance recognizes that while criteria and standards specified beforehand can be provisional markers of quality, they may not capture all features of quality in the work completed by students. Experienced teachers will recognize this, talking about it as being ready for 'the unexpected' in approaches to a topic or task, or the 'surprises' in student work.

Year 5 Studies of Society – Overall Teacher Commentary

Overall, this Student A's work sample is best matched with a 'Developing +' standard. This student generally expressed a point of view, used the exposition framework, provided some supporting evidence for the viewpoint and included some relevant details to provide information about life in the gold fields, which are matched with the 'Consolidating' standard. However the student needed to have written a final statement that referred to the viewpoint, explained the reason for her point of view in the thesis and made use of more specific conjunctions to strengthen the argument to achieve an overall 'Consolidating' standard. Because this student did not offer a conclusion but demonstrated a 'Consolidating' standard against 4 criteria, on balance, this work has been rated at no more or no less than a 'Developing +' standard.

Source: Wyatt-Smith and Bridges, 2007, in DEEWR and DETA (2007), Appendix 9: 295, copyright Commonwealth of Australia reproduced by permission.

Figure 6.1   Teacher commentary on sample A student in Year 5 Studies of Society

We describe a statement such as in Figure 6.1 as a *cognitive commentary*. While it may be unreasonable to expect a teacher to generate these for all major assessment pieces, illustrative examples compiled over a year in a student portfolio could support teachers and students in reflecting on how aspects of a performance or piece of work can combine. There is a strong case that this approach, when used in conjunction with actual student work and accompanying statements of standards, has the potential to show how standards apply in practice. More specifically, it can show how particular strengths and weaknesses in performance can be thought of as compensatory, functioning as 'trade-offs'. This gives students insight into how standards and standards-informed judgements are not rigid, mathematical formulae to be applied in a mechanistic, rule-governed way. In the commentary in Figure 6.1, for example, the teacher has recorded how she has considered both the strengths of the piece, as well as the limitations, trading them off to arrive at an overall judgement. This gives a window on the decision-making processes of the teacher in how she arrived at an overall judgement, including specifics about how compensations or trade-offs occur in judgement. Further, it is in this context that the legitimacy of the mix of factors impacting judgement can be opened for scrutiny by teachers working individually and in teams, and that students can learn to discriminate performances of different quality in ways otherwise not possible.

Conclusion

O'Donovan et al. (2004) have suggested that knowledge of criteria and standards and a deep understanding of performance expectations require a combination of methods that are:

> mutually complementary and interdependent ... practices range from those that are principally explicit and transferred through articulation, and principally tacit that can only be transferred through social processes involving the sharing of experience through methods such as practice, [verbal feedback] imitation, and observation. (2004: 330)

In exploring assessment as a joint enterprise, with a focus on the constructive use of standards to support learning, this chapter has opened a space for both teachers and students to share assessment experience. It has proposed a range of ways in which criteria and standards can be embedded in pedagogy to improve learning. This stance is consistent with what Lesley and Nelson (2004) have referred to as a 'new rubric of professionalism' that supports the time and space for teacher and student inquiry into and reflection on practice.

Review questions

Drawing on your own experiences, how do you answer the question posed in the chapter: How mindful does the teacher need to be about the consequences of assessment decisions?

What assumptions do you think you make about the curriculum, what should be learned and how, and also how assessment should occur?

What are your views about particular modes of assessment? For example, how do you view the value of examinations in which essays and short-answer questions are set? What do you see to be the value of assessments as assignments completed over time and where access to resources is encouraged, including feedback from others in improving the quality of the work?

What is your response to the notion that it is the teacher's role to induct students into standards? Do you support the idea that teachers actively engage students with activities to develop their evaluative experience and expertise as part of class-room practice?

References

Ahmann, J.S. and Glock, M.D. (1971) *Measuring and Evaluating Educational Achievement.* Boston: Allyn and Bacon.

Black, P., Harrison, C., Lee, C., Marshall, B. and Wiliam, D. (2003) *Assessment for Learning.* Maidenhead: Open University Press.

Broadfoot, P. (2009) 'Signs of change: Assessment past, present and future', in C. Wyatt-Smith and J.J. Cumming (eds), *Educational Assessment in the 21st Century: Connecting theory and practice* (preface). Dordrecht: Springer International.

Broadfoot, P. and Black, P. (2004) 'Redefining assessment? The first ten years of Assessment in Education', *Assessment in Education: Principles, Policy & Practice*, 11 (1): 7–26.

Cobb, P., Gravemeijer, K., Yackel, E., McClain, K. and Whitenack, J. (1997) 'Mathematizing and symbolizing: The emergence of chains of signification in one first-grade classroom', in D. Kirshner and J.A. Whiston (eds), *Situated Cognition Theory: Social, semiotic, and neurological perspectives.* Hillsdale, NJ: Lawrence Erlbaum Associates. pp. 151–233.

Cumming, J. and Wyatt-Smith, C. (eds) (2001) *Literacy and the Curriculum: Success in Senior Secondary Schooling.* Melbourne: ACER Press.

DEEWR, Department of Education, Employment and Workplace Relations and DETA, Queensland Department of Education, Training and the Arts (2007) *Meeting in the Middle – Assessment, Pedagogy, Learning and Educational Disadvantage. Literacy and Numeracy in the Middle Years of Schooling Initiative – Strand A, Project Report.* Canberra: Commonwealth of Australia. Available at: http://education.qld.gov.au/literacy/docs/deewr-myp-final-report.pdf.

Delandshere, G. (2002) 'Assessment as inquiry', *Teachers' College Record*, 104 (7): 1461–84.

Ecclestone, K. and Pryor, J. (2003) '"Learning careers" or "Assessment Careers"? The impact of assessment systems on learning', *British Educational Research Journal*, 29 (4): 471–88.

Elwood, J. and Klenowski, V. (2002) 'Creating communities of shared practice: Assessment use in learning and teaching', *Assessment and Evaluation in Higher Education*, 27 (3): 243–56.

Flutter, J. and Ruddock, J. (2004) *Students as Researchers: Making a Difference.* Cambridge: Pearson.

Freebody, P. (2006) 'Knowledge, skill and disposition in the organisation of senior schooling'. A discussion paper prepared for the Queensland Studies Authority (QSA). Queensland, Australia: QSA.

Gill, J.H. (1993) *Learning to Learn: Towards a Philosophy of Education.* NJ: Humanities Press.

Gipps, C. (1999) 'Socio-cultural aspects of assessment', *Review of Research in Education*, 24: 357–92.

Harlen, W. (2004) 'Can assessment by teachers be a dependable option for summative purposes?' Paper presented at General Teaching Council for England Conference, London.

Harris, C.J., McNeill, K.L., Lizotte, D.J., Marx, R.W. and Krajcik, J. (2003) 'Usable assessments for teaching science content and inquiry standards', *Peers Matter*, 1 (1).

Harris, C.J., McNeill, K.L., Lizotte, D.J., Marx, R.W. and Krajcik, J. (2006) 'Usable assessments for teaching science content and inquiry standards', in M. McMahon, P. Simmons, R. Sommers, D. DeBaets and F. Crowley (eds), *Assessment in Science: Practical Experiences and Education Research*. Arlington, VA: National Science Teachers Association Press. pp. 67–88.

James, M. (1998) *Using Assessment for School Improvement*. Oxford: Heinemann Educational.

Kress, G.R. (2001) *Early Spelling: Between creativity and convention*. London: Routledge.

Lave, J. and Wenger, E. (1991) *Situated Learning: Legitimate peripheral participation*. Cambridge, UK: Cambridge University Press.

Lesley, A.R. and Nelson, M. (2004) 'How teachers' professional identities position high-stakes test preparation in their classrooms', *Teachers College Record*, 106 (6): 1288–331.

Messick, S. (1989) 'Validity', in R.L. Linn (ed.), *Educational Measurement* (3rd edn). London: Collier Macmillan. pp. 12–104.

O'Donovan, B., Price, M. and Rust, C. (2004) 'Know what I mean? Enhancing student understanding of assessment standards and criteria', *Teaching in Higher Education*, 9 (3): 325–35.

Polanyi, M. (1998) 'The tacit dimension', in C. Rust (ed.), *Improving Student Learning: Improving Student Learning Strategically*. Boston: Butterworth Heinemann.

Rowntree, D. (1987) *Assessing Students: How Shall We Know Them?* London: Kogan Page.

Ruddock, J. (2004) 'The innovation bazaar: Determining priorities, building coherence: The case of student voice'. Paper presented at the WCET Annual Conference, Hanover.

Ruddock, J. (n.d.) 'Pupil voice is here to stay!' Qualifications and Curriculum Authority. Available at: www.qca.org.uk/futures/.

Ruddock, J. and Flutter, J. (2003) *How to Improve Your School: Listening to Pupils*. London: Continuum Press.

Sadler, D.R. (1985) 'The origins and functions of evaluative criteria', *Educational Theory*, 35: 285–97.

Sadler, D.R. (1987) 'Specifying and promulgating achievement standards', *Oxford Review of Education*, 13: 191–209.

Sadler, D.R. (1989) 'Formative assessment and the design of instructional systems', *Instructional Science*, 18: 119–44. Republished in W. Haren (ed.) (2008) *Student Assessment and Testing*. London: SAGE. pp. 3–28.

Sadler, D.R. (1998) 'Formative assessment: Revisiting the territory', *Assessment in Education*, 5 (1): 77–84.

Shepard, L.A. (2000) 'The role of assessment in a learning culture', *Educational Researcher*, 29 (7): 4–14.

Stake, R. (2004) *Standards-based Responsive Evaluation*. Thousand Oaks: Sage.

Stiggins, R. (2004) 'New assessment beliefs for a new school mission', *Phi Delta Kappan*, 86 (1): 22–8.

Stiggins, R. and Chappius, J. (2005) 'Using student-involved classroom assessment to close achievement gaps', *Theory Into Practice*, 44 (1): 11–18.

Stigler, J.W. and Hiebert, J. (1997) 'Understanding and improving classroom mathematics instruction: An overview of the TIMSS video study', *Phi Delta Kappan*, 78 (1): 14–21.

Tognolini, J. (2005) 'Measurement', unpublished manuscript. Sydney: Australian Council for Educational Research.

Webb, D.C. (2009) 'Designing professional development for assessment', *Educational Designer*, 1 (2): 1–26.

Wells, G. (1999) *Dialogic Inquiry: Toward a Sociocultural Practice and Theory of Education*. Cambridge, UK: Cambridge University Press.

Wenger, E. (1998) *Communities of Practice: Learning, Meaning, and Identity*. Cambridge, UK: Cambridge University Press.

Wyatt-Smith, C.M. and Bridges, S. (2007) 'Meeting in the middle – Assessment, pedagogy, learning and students at educational disadvantage'. Final evaluation report for the Department of Education, Science and Training on Literacy and Numeracy in the Middle Years of Schooling. Available at: http://education.qld.gov.au/literacy/docs/deewr-myp-final-report.pdf.

Wyatt-Smith, C.M. and Gunn, S. (2009) 'Towards theorising assessment as critical inquiry' in C. Wyatt-Smith and J. Cumming (eds), *Educational Assessment in the 21st Century: Connecting Theory and Practice*. Dordrecht: Springer International. pp. 83–102.

Wyatt-Smith, C.M. and Klenowski, V. (forthcoming) 'Standards, judgement and moderation: Communities of practice', in C. Wyatt-Smith, V. Klenowski and P. Colbert (eds), *The Enabling Power of Assessment: Quality, Ethics and Equity*. Dordrecht, The Netherlands: Springer International.

Web extras

Hall, J.N. and Ryan, K.E. (2011) 'Educational accountability: A qualitatively driven mixed-methods approach', *Qualitative Inquiry*, 17 (1): 105–59.

Seashore Louis, K., Febey, K. and Schroeder, R. (2005) 'State-mandated accountability in high schools: Teachers' interpretations of a new era', *Educational Evaluation and Policy Analysis*, 27 (2): 177–204.

7

Sustainable assessment cultures

Overview

In this chapter we discuss how intelligent accountability systems give greater recognition and support to the professionalism of teachers, particularly in times of major assessment and curriculum reform. We explain how teachers use standards, judgement practice and achievement data to make decisions appropriate for formative and summative purposes. We use case-study material of exemplar pedagogic and classroom assessment to illustrate the concept of front-ending assessment at the local professional level in order to achieve coherence with system-level curriculum and accountability demands. We explain how teachers engage students in judgement practice using achievement standards in classroom assessment practice that is explicit, defensible and aligned to their pedagogy. In our analysis we focus on teachers' use of exemplars in classroom teaching to engage students in the assessment process and, in so doing, enhance students' understanding of the standards and quality learning required. We identify strategies for achieving equity, to ensure that assessment is valid and reliable, and that judgement practice is both rigorous and responsive to the diversity of students in the classroom.

Introduction

A recent review of curriculum specification in seven countries (Australia, Canada (the provinces of Alberta and Ontario), Finland, New Zealand, Scotland, Singapore and South Africa) revealed that each country specified curriculum content and provided some indication of levels of achievement (INCA, 2011). While the terminology may differ, 'achievement standards' (Australia), 'learner expectations' (Canada), 'descriptions of performance expressed as levels' (Finland), 'national standards' (New Zealand), 'levels of learning' (Scotland), 'desired outcomes of learning' (Singapore) and 'assessment standards' (South Africa) were specified to some extent in each case. Not only was subject content outlined but 'general capabilities' and 'cross-curriculum priorities' (as in Australia) were also made explicit for the public, teachers and students; these were described as critical/creative thinking skills, planning, communication and application in Canada, ethics in Finland, and in New Zealand as competencies of thinking, using language, symbols and texts, managing self, relating to others, participating and contributing. These developments in curriculum and assessment have major implications for teachers' classroom practice. The move to more future-oriented curricula with the introduction of twenty-first-century skills requires teachers to adjust their assessment practices and pedagogy. Such curriculum reform requires teachers to provide students with opportunities at appropriate levels to learn, demonstrate and apply new knowledge and skills. The associated standards-referenced reforms bring to the fore of teachers' classroom practice their competence and skills in assessment.

In this chapter we make illustrative use of case-study material to show how the teachers' skills in assessment may be used to tackle the challenges experienced by classroom teachers worldwide. A shift to more intelligent accountability systems, as discussed following, acknowledges the value of quality of teaching in developing the role of the learner through mutual engagement in a community of practice. How such practice is enacted in classrooms is demonstrated through analysis of how front-ending assessment, the use of exemplars and application of principles for effective assessment are brought together pedagogically to educate the student about the changing curriculum and assessment demands, and to achieve coherence with system-level accountability demands. First, however, we discuss intelligent accountability to highlight the importance of support for teachers' professionalism and judgement. Next, we offer an explanation of recent international reforms and the associated demands that they place on teachers at the site level. We conclude the chapter with a discussion of assessment and principles by which to enact effective practice.

Intelligent accountability

Fundamental curriculum changes, including the development and application of skills, bring parallel changes to teachers' pedagogic and assessment practices. System-level support in terms of resources, allocation of time for teacher professional development and helpful policies are needed. In some countries such support is provided through promulgation of principles for effective assessment, development of resources such as assessment tools to demonstrate good assessment design and practice, availability of curriculum materials to illustrate how teachers can design assessment tasks to align with new curriculum demands and provision of professional opportunities to develop teacher learning and to also improve teaching using standards. A system's policy context that supports teachers to develop the necessary capabilities and provides resources to facilitate the implementation and development of the reform is demonstrative of intelligent accountability. This is what O'Neill (2002: 58) called for in her claim that if 'we want greater accountability without damaging professional performance we need *intelligent accountability'*. O'Neill explained that regulating performance through standardization and provision of detailed regulation for total control are damaging. Intelligent accountability, she claimed:

> ... requires more attention to good governance and fewer fantasies about total control. Good governance is possible only if institutions are allowed some margin for self-governance of a form appropriate to their particular tasks, within a framework of financial and other reporting. Such reporting ... is not improved by being wholly standardised or relentlessly detailed, and since much that has to be accounted for is not easily measured it cannot be boiled down to a set of stock performance indicators. Those who are called to account should give an account of what they have done and of their successes or failures to others who have sufficient time and experience to assess the evidence and report on it. Real accountability provides substantive and knowledgeable independent judgement of an institution's or professional's work. (O'Neill, 2002: 58)

One state in Australia has applied an intelligent accountability approach in the context of major curriculum and assessment reform by valuing the professionalism of teachers and by supporting their curriculum and assessment decision making at the local level to meet system-level accountability demands. Teachers are accountable to one another and to parents, the public and their students through the use of evidence-based assessment practices. Teachers also hold students to account and provide the necessary supports and development of skills. In this chapter, case-study material of one teacher's assessment practice in a regional school is analysed to show how in this policy context she used assessment tools and resources designed to support adjustments to assessment practices and curriculum design, to align with local contexts and to be responsive to the diversity of the student cohort. In this state system, the professionalism of teachers is supported, trusted and encouraged through evidence-based assessment practice, whereby teachers defend their judgement practices by accounting to their peers through moderation. In this way, teachers' professional judgements and decisions at the site level are quality assured through the system-level provision of necessary and sufficient supports of assessment tasks, curriculum materials and moderation practice.

Contemporary curriculum reforms and demands

From the review of curriculum specification in seven countries (INCA, 2011) it is apparent that in some of these countries it is a requirement of the national curriculum for teachers to assess students' application of their understanding and their development of skills such as inquiry, analysis, investigation, critical and creative thinking and reflection. Such reforms have implications for how teachers make their judgements of student work and how they develop and provide assessment tasks and opportunities designed to support the development and application of such content knowledge and skills. As identified by Sadler (1998: 80–2), teachers need to draw on the following intellectual and experiential resources when making those judgements:

- superior knowledge about the content or substance of what is to be learned
- sound knowledge of criteria and standards (or performance expectations) appropriate to the assessment task
- evaluative skill or expertise in having made judgements about students' efforts on similar tasks in the past
- a set of attitudes or dispositions towards teaching, as an activity, and towards learners, including their own ability to empathize with students who are learning, their desire to help students develop, improve and do better, their personal concern for the feedback and veracity of their own judgements, and their patterns in offering help.

In the example that follows the teacher's assessment practice is analysed to provide some insight into how teachers might respond in order to develop their own assessment and pedagogic practices and, in so doing, support students to improve in their learning, with the aim of achieving higher standards. Teachers' classroom teaching practice in the subject of English, applicable to students in the age range of 12–14 years is analysed to demonstrate how teachers at a government school in regional Australia have pedagogically incorporated into their classroom teaching practice some of the identified skills or 'general capabilities' and a cross-curriculum priority of 'Aboriginal and Torres Strait Islander histories and cultures'. It is interesting to note that in countries such as New Zealand, Finland and provinces in Canada (Alberta, British Columbia, Manitoba and Saskatchewan), cross-curriculum themes and/or instruction of cultural and language groups are included. The implication is that teachers' assessment practice should be reliable and valid, with attention paid in particular to diversity for the achievement of equity.

Assessment practice

In this section we discuss the message system of assessment. For, as indicated, the changes brought about by the curriculum reform have implications for the way in which teachers use assessment, both for summative or 'endpoint' testing and for formative means for improving learning and teaching. We have defined assessment as the purposeful collection of information and data about students' learning using a range of means by systems and teachers. At the site level, teachers' assessment helps them to identify and attend to students' learning needs by monitoring their progress and identifying the implications for how they can modify their teaching and learning strategies.

For intelligent accountability purposes it is useful to provide principles to guide assessment practice and to inform policy development. Such assessment principles are valuable in assisting in the design of assessment for classroom practice and school systems, as well as for policy and accountability purposes. These principles can help to continue to improve on practice that currently exists, to ensure that common achievement standards are supported by examples of excellence in assessment practice and to support the use of assessment for a range of summative and formative purposes. Internationally, different approaches to assessment have been adopted, with students assessed at different times and in different ways to address principles of equity and excellence.

Principles of assessment

The following principles of assessment were developed to be useful for teachers, schools and systems in order to: plan assessment programmes; review current assessment practice(s) and programmes; and inform and develop teachers' professional learning to ensure teachers have assessment capability.

1 The main purposes of assessment are to inform teaching, improve learning and report on the achievement of standards.

2 Assessment is underpinned by principles of equity and excellence. It takes account of the diverse needs of students and contexts of education, and the goal of promoting equity and excellence in Australian schooling.

3 Assessment is aligned with curriculum, pedagogy and reporting. Quality assessment has curricular and instructional validity – what is taught informs what is assessed, and what is assessed informs what is reported.

4 Assessment aligned with curriculum, pedagogy and reporting includes assessment of deep knowledge of core concepts within and across the disciplines, problem solving, collaboration, analysis, synthesis and critical thinking.

5 Assessment involves collecting evidence about expected learning as the basis for judgements about the achieved quality of that learning. Quality is judged with reference to published standards and is based on evidence.

6 Assessment evidence should come from a range of assessment activities. The assessment activity is selected because of its relevance to the knowledge, skills and understanding to be assessed, and the purpose of the assessment.

7 Information collected through assessment activities is sufficient and suitable to enable defensible judgements to be made. To show the depth and breadth of the student learning, evidence of student learning is compiled over time. Standards are reviewed periodically and adjusted according to evidence to facilitate continuous improvement.

8 Approaches to assessment are consistent with and responsive to local and jurisdictional policies, priorities and contexts. It is important that schools have the freedom and support that enables them to develop quality assessment practices and programmes that suit their particular circumstances and those of the students they are assessing.

9 Assessment practices and reporting are transparent. It is important that there is professional and public confidence in the processes used, the information obtained and the decisions made. (ACACA, 2012: 5–6)

These principles are applied to the following analysis of the assessment and pedagogic practices of a teacher seeking to meet the challenge of teaching curriculum that requires change in standards-referenced assessment practice, to include opportunities for students to develop skills and capabilities and to learn about cultural awareness through cross-curricular themes and priorities.

Analysis of classroom practice

In this particular school context, National Curriculum and Achievement Standards were accessed and curriculum materials from the state Education Department provided. These resources included: planning documents providing details about what students need to learn – a template for a whole-school plan, year-level plans, unit plans, lesson overviews, assessments and marking guides (where applicable); materials (lesson plans and resources) on how to support student learning; multi-year level materials, conceptual maps, unit plans, lesson overviews, assessments and marking guides (where applicable); and lesson resources and planning materials for differentiation of students with diverse learning needs, including a model unit plan and an example lesson.

The Achievement Standard that provides information about the expectations of student achievement in English at the end of Year 8 is as shown in Figure 7.1.

Receptive modes (listening, reading and viewing)

By the end of Year 8, students understand how the selection of text structures is influenced by the selection of language mode and how this varies for different purposes and audiences. Students explain how language features, images and vocabulary are used to represent different ideas and issues in texts.

Students interpret texts, questioning the reliability of sources of ideas and information. They select evidence from the text to show how events, situations and people can be represented from different viewpoints. They listen for and identify different emphases in texts, using that understanding to elaborate upon discussions.

Productive modes (speaking, writing and creating)

Students understand how the selection of language features can be used for particular purposes and effects. They explain the effectiveness of language choices they use to influence the audience. Through combining ideas, images and language features from other texts, students show how ideas can be expressed in new ways.

Students create texts for different purposes, selecting language to influence audience response. They make presentations and contribute actively to class and group discussions, using language patterns for effect. When creating and editing texts to create specific effects, they take into account intended purposes and the needs and interests of audiences. They demonstrate understanding of grammar, select vocabulary for effect and use accurate spelling and punctuation. (ACARA, 2012)

Figure 7.1 Year 8 Achievement Standard for English

The Australian English curriculum stipulates that students in upper primary and middle school learn about how language, poetry and stories are central to the ways in which people represent their experiences, identities, points of view and feelings. This was the focus of the teacher's lessons observed for the following analysis, in which students had been taught how the choices made by text producers such as authors, scriptwriters and poets can influence, and position, the audience to think, feel and respond in particular ways. The class had read and interpreted a variety of literary texts in which Indigenous producers explored issues of identity and history. The students also had been given the opportunity to consider the use of the language of affect and how this influences the ways in which sense is made of the stories being shared.

The assessment task, which had curricular and instructional validity (assessment principle 3), included an oral, multi-modal presentation. The teacher had adjusted the task to suit the needs and interests of the students and their unique history and cultural context (assessment principle 2 and assessment principle 8) as shown in Figure 7.2.

The library has decided to make a collection of important stories from our area that helps to share and celebrate the many experiences of being Australian. The stories will be available to any member in our community who wants to share these stories, but the library thinks they will be of particular interest to school students, historians and tourists to the area.

This chapter of the collection is focused on the stories and experiences of Aboriginal and Torres Strait Islander histories and cultures. You have been invited to participate in this exciting project with a multi-modal presentation.

There are two stages involved in this submission:

Part A: An emotive reading of your selected text.

Part B: An analysis of your selected text, demonstrating the language of affect and how you constructed your reading to have an emotive response with your audience.

Figure 7.2 Assessment task as adjusted to student and local contexts

This modified assessment task for students in Year 8 (13 years of age) focused on the representations of Aboriginal and Torres Strait Islander perspectives in texts and was designed to help develop students' capabilities in literacy, competence in information and communications technologies (ICT), ethical behaviour and intercultural understanding. The teacher explained:

> The assessment was an adaptation of the task provided ... the [name of state education programme] tasks feel like they lack a context or real life/life-like purpose to their descriptions, so this is an element we were looking to add. It lets students identify the role they are taking on in the presentation, and focus in on the way they want to use language to establish the relationship, I think.

To illustrate the teacher's point about the assessment task provided by the state curriculum programme, the example of the task is shown in Figure 7.3.

> Students find a literary text or text excerpts (poetry of prose) relating to representations of Aboriginal and Torres Strait Islander histories and cultures. They record an oral presentation that includes:
>
> - a reading of the texts and a speech explaining how the texts use language to influence how a listener feels and thinks about different perspectives on the human experience.

Figure 7.3 Task as set by state curriculum programme

The cross-curriculum priority of raising awareness of 'Aboriginal and Torres Strait Islander histories and cultures' is intended to provide all young Australians with the opportunity to gain greater understanding and appreciation of Aboriginal and Torres Strait Islander histories and cultures, their significance for Australia and the effects of these on our world, past, present and future. Such cross-curriculum priorities are incorporated into learning areas or subjects (of English, as in this analysis) where appropriate and have either a strong or varying presence.

In addition to the task, the state curriculum programme includes information regarding making judgements and the achievement standard. The information is shown in Figure 7. 4.

> **Making judgements**
>
> Achievement standard
>
> In this unit [Reading and interpreting literary texts about Aboriginal and Torres Strait Islander People's histories and cultures], assessment of student learning aligns to the following components of the achievement standard.
>
> By the end of Year 8 students listen to, read and view a range of spoken, written and multi-modal texts interpreting key information, concepts and issues, and evaluating the effectiveness of language choices used to influence readers, viewers and listeners. They summarise and synthesise the main ideas and viewpoints in texts and evaluate the supporting evidence. They support their own opinions with specific textual evidence, and evaluate evidence used by others. They explain ways in which different groups in society are represented in literary, persuasive and informative texts drawn from a range of social and historical contexts. They compare and describe text structures and language features in texts, and explain how these are designed for a variety of purposes and audiences.
>
> Students create sustained and coherent written, spoken and multi-modal texts in a variety of forms to explore significant ideas, report events, express opinions, and respond to others' views. They interact confidently with others in a variety of contexts and deliver presentations to report researched information, share opinions, debate issues, present imaginative interpretations, and evaluate differing perspectives. They select elements from different literary genres to create informative, imaginative and persuasive texts. In constructing texts, they take account of intended purposes, the needs and interests of audiences, selecting vocabulary and appropriate text structures and language features to clarify intended meanings and to create specific effects. They select language devices to build cohesion in texts, clearly showing connections between ideas and information. (Australian Curriculum: English for Prep (F0–10 Version 1.2))

Figure 7.4 Making judgements and the achievement standard

Title: Grading Scale for Year 8 English Task

		A	B	C	D	E
Understanding and skill	**Receptive modes**	Discerning analysis and explanation of **how the text positions audiences** to view Indigenous representations and perspectives.	Effective analysis and explanation of how the text positions audiences to view Indigenous representatives and perspectives.	Analysis and explanation of how the text positions audiences to view Indigenous representatives and perspectives.	Identifies how the text positions audiences to view Indigenous representations and perspectives.	Inappropriate explanation of representations and perspectives in text.
		Comprehensive explanation of how a **variety of language features, images and vocabulary are used to represent different ideas and issues.**	Effective explanation of how a variety of language features, images and vocabulary are used to represent different ideas and issues.	Explanation of how a variety of language features, images and vocabulary are used to represent different ideas and issues.	Description of language features and images are used for a purpose.	Identification of language features and images.
	Productive modes	Discriminating explanation of the effectiveness of **language and image choices used to influence the audience in own text production.** (Part B)	Effective explanation of the language and image choices used to influence the audience in own text production. (Part B)	Explanation of how a variety of language features and images are used for desired purposes in own text production.	Statement of language features and images used for purposes in own text.	Identification and description of language features and images.
		Discerning use of features of a **multimodal presentation:** • Spoken features[1] • Non-verbal features • Visual features[3] (Parts A and B)	Effective use of features of a multimodal presentation: • Spoken features[1] • Non-verbal features[2] • Visual features[3] (Parts A and B)	Use of features of a multimodal presentation: • Spoken features[1] • Non-verbal features[2] • Visual features[3] (Parts A and B)	Limited use of features of a multimodal presentation: • Spoken features[1] • Non-verbal features[2] • Visual features[3] (Parts A and B)	Some features of a multimodal presentation: • Spoken features[1] • Non-verbal features[2] • Visual features[3] (Parts A and B)

Feedback:

_____

_____

_____

_____

[1]For example: pronunciation; pace, phrasing and pausing; audibility and clarity
[2]For example: facial expressions, gestures, proximity, stance, movement
[3]For example: graphics, still and moving images

SIGNATURE: OVERALL GRADE: A   B   C   D   E

Figure 7.5 Grading Scale - A to E

Figure 7.5   Grading scale for Year 8 English task

The assessment criteria for knowledge and understanding for this task relate to how well the students can identify and articulate the 'language of affect' in other people's work, particularly in Aboriginal and Torres Strait Islander texts. The standards, which incorporate the criteria to be used to assess the understanding and skill from both the productive and receptive modes as represented in the student's task are given and discussed with the students at the outset (see Figure 7.5). These descriptors of the standards are also incorporated into the teaching and learning activities so that assessment becomes an integral part of the teaching–learning cycle.

The teacher explained the demands of the task in this way: 'This is pretty abstract and tough! NANBERRY was one of the texts the [state Education Department] used, but again I had to make adaptations and links for my own context and learners'. The novel *Nanberry: Black Brother White* by Jackie French describes a clash of cultures and the consequences for both. It is a narrative set in early colonial Australia, offering insights into the travails of the early settlers, of the contributions of women in this era, and above all, into the tragic displacement of Indigenous people during that time.

The teacher identified the necessary steps for the students to ensure that they addressed both Part A and Part B of the assessment task. The explicitness of the

Have I understood the task?
Year 8 Oral multi modal task sheet

YOUR TASK: The Library has decided to make a collection of important stories from our area that help to share and celebrate the many experiences of being Australian. The stories will be available to any members of our community who want to share these stories, but the library thinks they will be of particular interest to school students, historians and tourists to the area.

> **Comment [q1]:** This is the CONTEXT – it gives our reason for organising our text, and what we want it to achieve.

> **Comment [q2]:** This is our AUDIENCE to consider – how will we appeal to, and communicate our understandings, to them?

This chapter of the collection is focussed on **the stories and experiences of Aboriginal and Torres Strait Islander histories and cultures.** You have been invited to participate in this exciting project with a multi-modal presentation.
There are two stages involved in this submission:

> **Comment [q3]:** SO we need to make sure that the story we select is appropriate to this category.

PART A: An emotive reading of your selected text

> **Comment [q4]:** This can be my multi-modal movie or powerpoint

PART B: An analysis of your selected text, demonstrating the language of affect and how you constructed your reading to have an emotive response with your audience.

> **Comment [q5]:** This is the part I need to present in class.

PART A – USE YOUR HIGHLIGHTER FUNCTION TO HELP YOU IDENTIFY YOUR TASK AND TOPIC WORDS
Find a literary text or text excerpts (poetry or prose) relating to representations of Aboriginal and Torres Strait Islander histories and cultures. Use the library and the websites provided to select your text(s). Check with your teacher that your text will be suitable for the task

> **Comment [q6]:** TASK/PROCESS word

> **Comment [q7]:** TOPIC/PARTICIPANT – who, what

> **Comment [q8]:** CIRCUMSTANCE – some information about when, where, why, with , about

Make sure you **read and understand this text** – What is it telling and sharing in its representation? Are there any historical or contextual references that you will need to find out more about?
Practise your **presenting techniques** for this task – Think about the kind of MOOD you want to create with your words and how you will represent this story with your story telling elements.
Prepare and present your multi-modal elements that includes:
– 	Your **presentation** of the text(s). This can be presented "**live**" during our lesson OR you can choose to **record your presentation at home** and screen it to the audience.

Figure 7.6 Planning my multi-modal presentation: Year 8 English task

instructions to the students is highlighted as the teacher has annotated the task sheet to draw the students' attention to the important elements for their consideration (see Figure 7.6). It is in this way that the teacher ensures that all students have access to the literacy demands of the task and can interpret what is needed to complete all aspects of the carefully planned and designed task.

Further, the teacher provides comprehensive instructions to the students regarding Part B of the task. She reiterates how the task is designed to assess whether the student has understood the English lessons related to language of affect and how language is used to communicate human experience. This, too, is part of front-ending assessment so that in:

> … pursuing the goals of effective assessment for learning … teachers and students … grow in a community of practice where nothing in the assessment process is hidden and all hurdles are understood clearly and explicitly. It is only then that assessment will be fully understood as the most important tool for effective learning. (Elwood and Klenowski, 2002: 255)

Additional teacher support is apparent in the explicitness of the instructions to the students concerning Part B, as evident in Figure 7.7.

PART B – this part is your analysis of CHOICES – by the writer AND you. How you have understood the LANGUAGE OF AFFECT in the author's work? THIS PART NEEDS TO BE PRESENTED IN CLASS IN FRONT OF YOUR AUDIENCE.

Your speech is explaining how your text(s) uses language to influence how a listener feels and thinks about different perspectives on the human experience. It includes evidence selected from the text(s).

UNDER EACH OF THESE POINTS, PUT DOWN YOUR NOTES THAT WILL HELP FORM THE BASIS OF YOUR ANALYSIS

- Plan and prepare your paragraphs using Statement Expand Evidence Comment (S.E.E.C.) Structure.

  1. Introduce the text you are sharing in your reading – Tell the audience who you are and your purpose. Next tell us the name and the text producer of the text you are sharing. You might want to introduce us to the reason WHY you selected this text, and something you want to draw the audience's attention to.

  2. Give an overview of the **ideas and viewpoints** in the text, how these connect with the values and identity of Indigenous Australians represented by the text and our unit.

  3. WHAT is the subject of this text? What is the VIEW it is presenting about its subject or focus?

  4. Explain how **language choices of your selected text** position audiences to think and feel in a particular way. THIS IS WHERE YOU NEED TO IDENTIFY YOUR LANGUAGE OF AFFECT – think about the examples we worked on in class.

  5. NANBERRY

  6. RABBIT PROOF FENCE

  7. MY SITTING DOWN PLACE

  8. Explain the **choices that you made in your multi modal presentation – what did you want the audience to understand through your representation? Why did you select to use particular images, or ways of reading, in telling this text?**

  9. Conference and draft with your teacher.

  10. Prepare and present final copy.

  11. Examples of AFFECTIVE READING for My Sitting Down Place (website provided) and further resources or web pages provided for student use.

You can choose to represent your selected text PART A through a variety of multi-modal elements including PowerPoint, Movie Maker, including music or illustrations. You might like to film your representation of the story outside of school but this is your own responsibility.

Figure 7.7 Instructions for Part B

Scaffolding to guide the students in their preparation of Part A of the assessment task is given in the form of the planning sheet (shown in Figure 7.8) devised by the teacher, which students are encouraged to use to plan their oral presentation. This, too, forms part of front-ending assessment in that the teacher is carefully ensuring that all aspects of the task are fulfilled and draws the students' attention to the key expectations and requirements of the assessment task. The teacher also provides students with an expectation of the quality of what is expected in the task demands.

NAME: _____

WHO is my audience?	WHAT is my purpose?	HOW do I need to communicate my ideas?

Details about my selected text – TITLE, TEXT PRODUCER, SOURCE, YEAR	
Subject matter – what is it about?	
How does this invite us to see and understand a human experience? What kind of mood does it have?	

LANGUAGE OF AFFECT – As you read through your selected text, think about how it positions us to FEEL and how it expresses emotions

Whose perspective is this text told from?	
What is the overall FEELING or MOOD?	

Happiness	Unhappiness
Security	Insecurity
Satisfaction	Dissatisfaction

VOCABULARY – Using my EXPERT WORDS

Representation	Audience	Text producer	

Figure 7.8 Organizing my analysis for my oral task – Year 8 English

To accompany the annotated task instructions and the planning guidelines, the teacher also provides her own exemplar of the task to the class, for as she explains:

… [in] my assessment, I always aim to make explicit the language features so I do the task myself as my exemplar. The 'Good Morning Invited Guests' work is my unpacking of the task. Then, in class as part of our joint deconstruction and construction phase, we went through our copies to identify what is going on to drive the text. I can see the students in this class picking upon the establishment of a clear role, language choices as experts and expanded nominal groups, for example, because they are elements we learnt to do in class.

This is a further aspect of front-ending assessment by the teacher. She has thought carefully about the task, modified it to fit the local context and her students, aligned the task to the curriculum and her teaching of the language elements. Further, she has clearly articulated the task in steps and has presented this using a slideshow presentation to define the task and ensure that the students have access to the literacy demands of the task. In addition, she demonstrates to students through her presentation of her own exemplar the expectations and requirements to complete the task. Through her modelling of the task and her presentation she also illustrates the standard for which they should aim. Finally, she invites the class to assess her example and to focus on whether her response addresses both parts of the task and whether she has clearly demonstrated how text communicates human experience. She writes to them as shown in Figure 7.9.

In this letter the teacher draws the students' attention to the key questions that they will need to attend to in their own presentation and respond to both parts of the assessment task. She highlights the criteria by which the student's product (Part B) will be assessed. In addition the students use the assessment criteria as represented in the A to E standards descriptors (see Figure 7.5) and which have been discussed at the outset of the teaching and learning activities that have been associated with the teaching of this aspect of the curriculum.

Dear class,

This is my draft [Figure 7.10] of my speech for you to consider and mark.

What do you think I am doing well?

Is it how you expected the PART B to be organized?

Can you identify my expert language?

How am I organizing my S.E.E.C (Statement Expand Evidence Comment) paragraphs?

HAVE I EXPLAINED HOW LANGUAGE IS USED TO REPRESENT A HUMAN EXPERIENCE?

Figure 7.9   Articulating the task instructions

Good morning invited guests and welcome to the launch of the latest chapter in The Tablelands Library collection – My Stories My Home. My name is [name provided], and although I am a new member to this region, I am very excited to contribute a story to this project. I think it is important to have stories about our experiences in Australia because it helps us all feel connected as a community. The story I have selected to represent is an extract from the historical fiction NANBERRY. In this opening chapter, the reader is invited by award winning Australian author Jackie French to consider the perspective of Nanberry and his family as they witness the colonists arrive from England. Although Nanberry has never seen anything like these people before, the language choices are not all about **threat and insecurity**. I think people who listen to this story will have a new perspective on the experience of contact between the First Australians and the Europeans who came to Australia to start a new life.

In this short extract, the author is representing Nanberry's life and family. The choices emphasize that, for Nanberry, his home is not a house or structure, but a connection to his place. The language choices focus on Nanberry's **happiness and security**. This is then challenged by the **possible threat** with the arrival of the European ships.

I hope you enjoyed this short extract from the prologue of NANBERRY. (READ MY PART A)

This representation invites the audience to see the world through the protagonist Nanberry's eyes. Jackie French represents Nanberry as **curious** and this section of the story **predicts the changes that are going to occur**. As he watches the arrival of the strange canoes, Nanberry is both **wary** of the strangers and **fascinated** by the ships and the possibilities they present to slip between the sea and the sky.

To represent this, Jackie French has used the language of affect to influence us, the audience, to view this moment as a mixture of emotions. She wants us to read this experience as being a **life changing moment** for all the stakeholders but it is not all negative. Initially, Nanberry's world is represented as being **happy and safe**. French uses the simile, 'Wriggles like a fish' to show Nanberry is enjoying being young and care free. Even when the girls tease him about not having fish, it is represented as loving because the girls **laugh** and Nanberry **grins** in response.

Next, when the boats are spotted, there is a change in language and the writer highlights that something **potentially dangerous** is coming. The vocative of '**maigul' or 'strangers'** indicates that these people are unfamiliar and to be treated with caution. French uses the metaphor '**white ghosts'** to emphasize these new people are unfamiliar and strange, not like the Cadigal. The girls go back into the trees and Nanberry is told to **come away** from the sea. There is the indication that the safety and known way of life for Nanberry and his Cadigal family will change forever with this contact. Nanberry considers the confident actions of the new arrivals, and thinks they behave '**As though they expected us to fade away**.'

While there is a **challenge to security**, the author emphasizes the potential for **positives and possibilities** with her language choices. French uses the simile, '**like the sea eagle controlled the wind**' to create a strong visual image of how Nanberry desires to slip between two worlds, and how the new boats could provide this feeling.

To invite my viewers to understand that this experience is through the curious and inquiring perspective of Nanberry, I selected the close up **image of a child's eye** to be my final image. I felt this connected with the action processes for Nanberry like '**peering**' and '**lingered**'. I also selected visual images that made a connection with the places that were important to Nanberry and the Cadigal, like the beach. My fonts are in **green** to emphasis the connection to the trees surrounding Nanberry's home and I used a font that flowed across the screen, like the waves that are important to connecting Nanberry's worlds of sky and sea, and also the connections between family.

In conclusion, I hope my selection will help people from all backgrounds know and understand more about Aboriginal and Torres Strait Islander perspectives relating to the changing history of Australia, and also encourage all Australians to understand that change and migration is part of our shared history.

Figure 7.10 Teacher's exemplar for Part B

In providing her own exemplar (Figure 7.10) the teacher demonstrates the standard of work that is expected and sets the level to which the students can aspire. She acknowledges the agency of her students by valuing their active engagement in the assessment process. The students are given the opportunity to assess her exemplar using the A to E standards. In this way the teacher informs them about the standards and about the quality of the work that is expected for each level.

Once the students have familiarized themselves with the expectations, the standards and the demands of the task through the various planning resources and related activities, including the assessment of the teacher's exemplar, they are then instructed to complete a first draft of the task. The completed draft is then submitted to the teacher for formative assessment purposes. The teacher gives feedback as in the example in Figure 7.11. This is how formative assessment fulfils the important function of supporting student learning and provides important information to the teacher regarding how well the students have understood the requirements

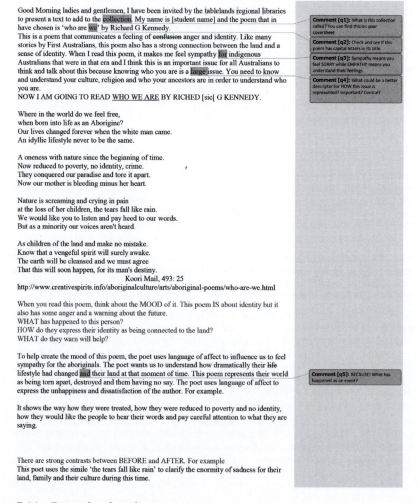

Figure 7.11 Example of student responses

of the task and learnt the skills of analysis through the related teaching and learning activities.

The teacher's presentation of the exemplar is later reflected in the students' attempts, as evident from the example in Figure 7.11. This student's response depicts how she completed the task using a poem of her choice to demonstrate and identify the language of affect and to illustrate her understanding of how language has been used in the poem to represent human experience. The teacher has provided helpful feedback, as evident in the track changes and inserted comments, to identify how the student can improve on this draft version of the task.

Figure 7.12 is the student's final improved response. It was this response to the task that was summatively assessed by the teacher and was awarded a B grade.

Good Morning ladies and gentlemen, My name is [name given] and the poem that I have chosen is 'Who Are We' by Richard G Kennedy. I have been invited by the Tablelands Regional Libraries to present a text to add to the collection of important stories from our area that help to share and celebrate the many experiences of being Australian.

This is a poem that communicates a feeling of anger and identity. Like many stories by First Australians, this poem also has a strong connection between the land and a sense of identity. I think identity is an important topic for all Australians to think and talk about this because knowing who you are is a central issue for today's society. You need to know and understand your culture, religion and who your ancestors are in order to understand who you are as an individual.

I HOPE YOU ENJOY THE POEM 'WHO WE ARE' BY RICHED [sic] G KENNEDY.

[Here the student recites the poem.]

The poet wants us to understand how dramatically their lifestyle and land since the arrival of the Europeans. In the poets opinion in this he represents their world as being torn apart, destroyed and them having no say in their past circumstances. The poet uses language of affect to express the unhappiness and dissatisfaction of the aboriginals, for example.

The poem shows how they were treated, how they were reduced to poverty and no identity, how they would like the people to hear their words and pay careful attention to what they are saying.

The poet uses the words 'Nature is screaming and crying in pain at the loss of her children' to represent the connection between nature and the Indigenous Australians, it demonstrates how strong they believe in the land and the way of their people but when the British settlers landed in Australia that connection was taken from them. A major part of how they lost that connection was through the stolen generation, when the colonists took custody over the Aboriginal children, they told not to speak their original language or do anything that related to their culture. Culture is an invisible bond that ties people of a community together, it displays itself through the lifestyles of individuals. Culture plays an important role in shaping the persons principles of life. If this was taken away from the children then how would they know who they are, how would they have an individuality?

In conclusion I hope that people from any race, religion and culture will take into consideration how the first Australian's world has been turned upside down since the first fleet has arrived to Australia. Also for people today to understand their culture and to encourage all Australians today, to find who you are and the only way to that is by knowing your culture and past.

Figure 7.12   Student's improved (final) response

Discussion

It is apparent from this example of teacher assessment practice that the assessment principles have been applied successfully. The assessment task and related activities are clearly designed to inform teaching and improve learning, which is reported using a grade of A–E (assessment principle 1). The different needs of the class are considered by tailoring the task to the range of needs of the diverse student cohort and the context to promote equity (assessment principle 2).

Teachers in 'successful' schools devote more time to the development of their own teaching materials than those in 'less successful' schools, and they change the content of the prescribed syllabus to make the programme more interesting and meaningful to their students (Ramsay, 1985). This established research finding is an important factor in improving student learning, clearly understood by this teacher. Attention to context and the need for change to curriculum and assessment design is particularly appropriate for students from different cultures including those from Indigenous communities. In this school, teachers were required to make use of the curriculum materials, provided by the state Education and Training Department. Teachers could use each lesson and associated resources provided by the department without modification. This was not the case in this teacher's practice.

The assessment task was adjusted to make it authentic and more realistic for the students of this regional school, together with the features of the completed work to be assessed made explicit at the very outset (assessment principle 5). It is often the case that an assessment task set by the teacher is given to the students with limited explication of the criteria and standards to illustrate how the task will be assessed and the expectations of quality. The students in such instances are deprived of an understanding of what is required and the particular qualities the teacher is seeking in assessing the completed work. This was not the approach adopted by this teacher as the oral presentation required students to demonstrate skills in analysis, research, critical inquiry, use of technology and presentation, and to illustrate an understanding of how the text positions audiences. The students were required to show their understanding of the variety of language, images and vocabulary that are used to represent different ideas and issues. This is how the teacher applied assessment principle 4, with the focus held firmly on assessment of substantive knowledge of how language is used to position the audience as well as skills of problem solving, analysis, synthesis and critical thinking. At the outset the teacher provided the students with a package of information to guide and support them in the completion of the task. The package incorporated:

- a comprehensive outline of the task (Parts A and B as described above)
- a planning document to scaffold the students' planning and organization of the task
- an annotated commentary to further help scaffold the students' responses
- an exemplar that has been completed by the teacher
- an annotated version of the exemplar to highlight how the teacher has addressed the key requirements of the task
- a rubric that outlines the criteria and standards by which the task will be assessed.

This teacher understands that the provision of this level of detail is necessary. Further, she illustrates how she is also addressing assessment principles 6, 7, 8 and 9: as the assessment task is inclusive of a range of activities that focus on knowledge, skills and understanding (principle 6), the students have an exemplar to guide them in the completion of their own efforts and the teacher provides feedback to the students on their draft work so that evidence of improvement is compiled over time (principle 7). The assessment task meets the state requirements and has been adapted to meet the particular circumstances of these students in regional Australia (principle 8) with the assessment processes made transparent (principle 9).

Conclusion

This pedagogic analysis of one teacher's assessment practice illustrates the nature of the task required, given the curriculum reform, and the degree of support provided to enable teacher and students to engage in substantive conversation, with connections to the world beyond the classroom, pertinent to the region and local circumstances. These conditions are more likely to support standards that move beyond the acquisition of 'reproductive knowledge' to opportunities for the development of more generative knowledge and understanding (Anyon, 1981). As teachers are confronted with increasing pressure to focus on the improvement of standardized test scores, it is feasible that they pursue 'the basics', to the neglect of intellectual demand and development. Such enacted curriculum is insufficient (Anyon, 1981). Four standards associated with quality and authentic pedagogy include higher-order thinking, deep knowledge, substantive conversation and connections to the real world beyond the classroom (Anyon, 1981). These four standards provide a framework for understanding pedagogical and assessment practices in schools.

For curriculum that is 'futures oriented', and for a more sustainable and generative future for the next generation, teachers cannot afford to focus only on the basics and reproductive knowledge. With adequate system-level resources and support, together with teacher professionalism and commitment to the improvement of learning for all students, exemplary enacted pedagogic and assessment practices can provide a level of coherence between system-level accountability demands and site-level practice, as exemplified, to develop sustainable assessment cultures.

Review questions

What developments have occurred in recent curriculum reform that have implications for teachers' assessment and pedagogic practice?

Why is it important to modify the learning and assessment tasks to meet the particular circumstances of the student cohort?

How can exemplars be used to inform students of the expectations of the standards and learning demands of the curriculum?

What are the expected benefits of providing students with detailed explanations and descriptions of the assessment tasks?

How can site and system coherence be achieved in contexts of curriculum and assessment reform?

References

ACACA, Australasian Curriculum, Assessment and Certification Authorities (2012) *Principles of Assessment F1–12*. Available at: http://acaca.bos.nsw.edu.au/.

ACARA, Australian Curriculum, Assessment and Reporting Authority (2012) *The Australian Curriculum, Foundation to Year 12*. Available at: www.acara.edu.au/curriculum. html.

Anyon, J. (1981) 'Social class and school knowledge', *Curriculum Inquiry*, 11 (1): 3–42.

Elwood, J. and Klenowski, V. (2002) 'Creating Communities of Shared Practice: the challenges of assessment use in learning and teaching', *Assessment & Evaluation in Higher Education*, 27 (3): 243–56.

French, J. (2011) *Nanberry: Black Brother White*. Sydney: HarperCollins Australia.

INCA, International Review of Curriculum and Assessment (2011) *International Review of Curriculum and Assessment Frameworks: Curriculum specification in seven countries*. Commissioned by the National Council for Curriculum and Assessment for the Republic of Ireland. Available at: www.inca.org.uk/thematic_probes.html.

O'Neill, O. (2002) *A Question of Trust: The BBC Reith Lectures 2002*. Cambridge: Cambridge University Press.

Ramsay, P.D.K. (1985) 'Social class and school knowledge: A rejoinder to Jean Anyon', *Curriculum Inquiry*, 15 (2): 215–22.

Sadler, D.R. (1998) 'Formative assessment: Revisiting the territory', *Assessment in Education: Principles, Policy & Practice*, 5 (11): 77–84.

Web extras

Jacobs, G.M. and Farrell, T.S.C. (2003) 'Understanding and implementing the CLT (Communicative Language Teaching) paradigm', *RELC Journal*, 34 (1): 5–30.

McVee, M.B., Dunsmore, K. and Gavelek, J.R. (2005) 'Schema theory revisited', *Review of Educational Research*, 75 (4): 531–66.

8

Assessment and digital literacies

Overview

In this chapter we will explore what assessment is about from a digital vantage point, consider priorities for learners, changes in literacy and efforts at leveraging technology to provide a broadened landscape for assessment. We will also highlight how multi-modal performances call for moves away from print-dependent criteria and standards, and provide opportunities for digital exemplars to show quality in ways not previously possible.

In the twenty-first century, statements of criteria and standards continue to have a key role to play in promoting quality and more effective learning. Also of continuing relevance is the value of students applying skills of self-monitoring and self-regulation (for example, by assessing their own work against defined criteria and standards). Today, however, daily life and learning are occurring in a digitally enhanced landscape. This calls for rethinking:

- the terms used to capture criteria and standards
- the place of digital exemplars to show quality/standards in ways not previously possible
- how student e-portfolios could support students to 'see' achievement over time and reflect on learning in ways that are more generative than using outmoded technologies.

Introduction

The fundamental differences between the educational needs of young people today and those of earlier generations are widely recognized, with the rapidity of change through new technologies having profound effects on communication and the ways in which people make meaning. Just as humanity is shaping new possibilities for the design and use of technologies, so, too, present generations and the new ways of thinking and being are shaped in cultural contexts by those technologies. One obvious result is that governments, commercial and educational institutions are increasingly interested in the use of technology-mediated curriculum delivery and assessment, sometimes referred to as 'e-assessment'. Progress in classroom practice in the use of technologies in the classroom has been slow to date, even though outside the classroom there are high levels of engagement with new and emerging technologies in many aspects of life.

The irrefutable fact is that education models that have served society well in the past and that have been in place for more than 200 years are clearly inadequate for current needs, including preparing young people for digitally driven futures. New priorities to meet those needs include the development of skills and capabilities associated with reading and writing online, creativity, problem-solving, productive collaboration and effective communication. These all draw on a far wider range of modes of representation and channels of communication than were available in the past.

These priorities reflect how the development of new technologies has led to previously unimagined speed and ease of access to enormous amounts of information from different sources and, beyond this, to new possibilities for online interactions, sharing and creating of information and collaborative actions. New and emerging forms of connectedness to other people, ideas and cultures by means of convergent, miniaturized technologies and social media networks are routine in the everyday lives of many people around the world, across age groups. Notions of responsible citizenship, and the separation of public and private lives, are among those values being challenged, even as new technologies are emerging.

Since new literacies continue to defy precise definition and we cannot accurately define the nature of technologies and the literacy/social practices that they will involve in the future, we open the discussion by positing some priorities for learners. The focus is primarily on learning *with and through* the use of technologies taken to be new tools, just as the teacher's slate and lead pencils were stock-in-trade tools used in schools in past decades. The starting proposition is that new ways of using technology to assess learning will require a rethinking of the indicators of quality, with multi-modal assessment being of particular interest in this chapter. There is no attempt to standardize these, since such an attempt would be futile. At issue instead is progressing the conversation about an assessment meta-language that is in tune with digital multi-modal creation.

Priorities for twenty-first century learners

In research and education policy, creativity, innovation and connectivity have emerged as new priorities for schooling, higher education and workplaces. They have flowed from the contemporary working environment into education, prompting calls for universities and schools to build the creative capacities of graduates and to use the connectedness of networks to their utmost advantage. As noted by many writers, the creativity literature spotlights innovation, inventiveness and high levels of ingenuity, extending to design, problem solving and collaborating in teams. Further, creativity is a term that can extend to complex, higher-order thinking, unexpected juxtapositions of information, disciplinary concepts and materials, and new or different solutions to challenging problems.

Several governments have invested heavily in the development of basic literacy and numeracy skills in their education systems and further, in large-scale, standardized testing of these skills. Efforts at building young people's creative and problem-solving capacities are best understood as building upon basic skills. However, attributes associated with creativity are both distinguishable from and additional to basic or foundational literacy capabilities. One of the risks of government investment in prioritizing basic skills testing is that it can convey to teachers and the community more generally that quality in education is demonstrated publicly through high performance on tests. Developments in technology make clear that this is far from the case, with new digital literacies being the prerequisite for an informed citizenry and a well-prepared workforce.

Drawing on the work of Becker (2006) and McWilliam (2005), Kimber and Wyatt-Smith (2010) explored the notion of 'unlearning' as an essential skill for effective twenty-first-century learning. They stated that unlearning could be regarded as a precondition or prerequisite for creative thinking or action 'as it involves challenging accepted ways of doing something and opening the mind to other possibilities' (p. 610). They suggested how acceptance of this concept could support teachers and students to explore 'new approaches to technology mediated learning, fresh views on assessment and possibilities for co-creation of knowledge' (Kimber and Wyatt-Smith, 2010: 610). This is important for two reasons: first, it recognizes the radical changes facing the generation of teachers who are more likely to be comfortable with print-bound ways of thinking, and second, it positions teacher and student as co-learners in exploring how knowledge can be used, created, shared and assessed.

Interestingly, researchers' interest in the nature of creativity is evident in discussions about what have traditionally been taken as affective attributes or matters relating to attitudes and values. For example, Pink (2005) recommended that creativity be connected with empathy-building capacities and the demonstration of empathy in relationships with application to business through globalization as well as at personal, political and business levels. Just as Pink connected creativity with empathy-building capacities, so the obvious moves to globalization necessitate critical review of what it means to develop not only a competitive workforce, but also a workforce with well-developed intercultural sensitivities and communication skills.

This opens a space for considering the connectivity of formal and informal learning (Buckingham, 2007; Sefton-Green, 2003, 2008, 2009). While the physical boundaries between school and community are fixed, social networking and the advent of the internet mean that knowledge can be readily shared well beyond traditional boundaries. Just as connectivity underpins networked worlds, so rich learning and new assessment approaches call for connections to be made across aspects of curriculum and learning, inside and outside formal education sites. Drawing on a large and growing corpus of writing in several countries about the relationship of in-school and out-of-school learning, including literacy learning, practices that support such connections are those designed to:

- develop students' *deep knowledge and understanding* informed by learning within *disciplines* as well as learning across integrated and transdisciplinary themes. No longer can knowledge be taken as 'siloed' into discrete disciplines
- tap into and engage productively with those *community knowledges* that students bring with them into the classroom.

These knowledges can be traced to all learning spaces and physical places where young people learn and where the identities of young people (known as 'students' in schools and universities) may be quite other than those with whom teachers are more familiar. In these other spaces, young people can encounter new roles and new ways of knowing, being and doing that may have tenuous relationships, if any, with the official curriculum. This is not intended to diminish or call into question the value of these. Instead, it is to highlight the issue of relevance or fit: what do educators know about the relationship between the official curriculum as taught in classrooms, the students' informal learning outside school and the students' own aspirations or desired futures? If school-based assessment were to tap into these other realities, then it would need to recognize a wider range of interdisciplinary learning than has traditionally found a home in schooling. It would also include being playful with the affordances of the technologies themselves, with the value being in exploring the creative possibilities (as distinct from locating correct or sanctioned answers).

Practices that support connections are also those designed to:

- provide opportunities for students to learn basic literacy skills and to develop the *digital literacy capabilities* they need to be able to access and use existing knowledge, and beyond this, to interpret and use different channels and modes of communication to create new knowledge
- develop *evaluative (standards-informed), criterial knowledge and experience* in recognizing or discerning those features that constitute quality in a piece of work. (Note that the design of this suite builds on an earlier elaboration by Kimber and Wyatt-Smith (2009).)

This suite appears as four separate elements, though in operation they are understood as elements that are intrinsically related and interdependent in how learning and assessment occur. Taken as a connected set, they reflect the growing awareness of interdisciplinarity and how knowledge of different types can connect in practice. That is to say, while knowledge is typically 'siloed' in official curriculum documents or syllabi, it is rare for it to be separated in application. Only in schools do 'subjects' or 'disciplines' exist as largely separate areas of endeavour. This is not to argue for the blurring of disciplinary boundaries. Instead, it is to argue for students to develop deep knowledge of a given discipline and an awareness of interdisciplinary connections as they apply to the significant issues of our time.

From this position, assessment can be seen to be operating historically within a view of knowledge as being siloed, especially for summative assessment purposes. Students talk, for example, about doing assessments or examinations in English, science or agricultural studies. This is the case even though it is widely recognized that all curriculum areas bring with them intrinsic literacy demands. Further, we know that the literacy demands of curriculum, learning and assessment present powerful barriers to student success (Cumming and Wyatt-Smith, 2001; Wyatt-Smith and Cumming, 2003; Hipwell and Klenowski, 2011). The position we adopt in this chapter is that as the field of assessment engages with developments in technologies, and as the latter leverages change in ways not otherwise possible, it is timely to think about theorizing assessment in order to connect to what we know about learning in new times. Within such a theorizing, learners and learning are central.

Paavola and Hakkarainen's (2005) three metaphors of learning are helpful here. These are 'knowledge acquisition', 'knowledge participation' and 'knowledge creation'. Readers are encouraged to read the article by Paavola and Hakkarainen. In relation to these metaphors, assessment and, in particular, summative assessment, appears to remain grounded in knowledge acquisition. From this view of learning, the main focus is on a process of adopting or constructing subject-matter knowledge and mental representations. Traditional cognitivist theories provide the theoretical foundations and the unit of analysis is individuals. In the participation metaphor of learning, the main focus is on a process of participation in social communities and the theoretical foundations tend to be in situated and distributed cognition. Accordingly, the unit of analysis is groups, communities, networks and cultures. The move to the knowledge-creation metaphor involves taking a main focus on a process of creating and developing new material and conceptual artefacts. Here, the interest is in conscious knowledge advancement, discovery and innovation, and the theoretical foundations are activity theory, knowledge-building theory and epistemology of mediation.

In keeping with the focus of this chapter on assessment in the digital age, we have taken up a knowledge-creation focus in recognition of the affordances of technologies themselves and our own valuing of learner agency. In the assessment theory of meaning that we envisage, there is a clear need to move from the focus on assessing how well students have acquired knowledge to valuing the types of assessments that can tell us about how well individuals and groups are learning as they use and create knowledge, mindful of cultural contexts.

This repositioning of assessment has direct implications for the nature and function of standards and the types of exemplars that would provide concrete examples of what the standards look like in real 'student work'. Opening wide is the opportunity for assessment to incorporate technologies that could record students' learning progress and for this to be a resource for self-monitoring and feedback from others. A stance taken in the theorizing of formative assessment (Sadler, 1985, 1989) is that, through the use of standards and exemplars, and with regular practice and constructive feedback from the teacher (as more expert other), the learner is supported in developing evaluative expertise over time. Under these conditions they can close the gap between the current level of performance and the desired level. Through connecting assessment and understandings about digital literacies, we seek to extend this stance by opening the space to see how new technologies might widen the range of assessment tasks students undertake and engage experts outside of schooling (for example, on social networking sites) to support student learning.

What we mean by the term 'literacy'

Literacy has long been recognized as integral to learning and communication. In our current era of rapid and continuing technological change, literacy and, in turn literacy education, assumes heightened priority. According to Leu (2000), literacy is vital in enabling individuals, groups and societies

> to access the best information in the shortest time to identify and solve the most important problems and then communicate this information to others. Accessing information, evaluating information, solving problems, and communication solutions are essential to success in this new era. (2000: 1573)

Leu explicated how, within a period of some 15 years, we have seen the widespread appearance of, among others: word-processing technologies, electronic database technologies, CD-ROM technologies, multimedia/hypermedia technologies, email technologies and internet technologies. Currently, we are witnessing unprecedented further changes relating to the increasing convergence and miniaturization of technologies, all with high responsivity to user communication needs. Leu (2000) made clear how each of these developments has helped to redefine the nature of literacy and how each has seen new environments for the use of literacy to redefine or design anew the technology itself.

In reflecting on the general nature of literacy in these new communication contexts, there is a strong body of research indicating that reading and writing ability will become even more important in the future than they are today. Leu (2000) and colleagues (Leu et al., 2004), for example, argued that in an age when speed of access to information and communication are central to success, reading proficiency and writing will be even more critical to young people's futures. This valuing of reading and writing is complemented by the view put forward by many researchers, as we elaborate later in this chapter, that strategic knowledge will become even more important in successful literacy activities. Such knowledge includes new strategies for onscreen reading and writing, and searching and navigating complex information available in information networks and through choices of search engines, and for making discerning choices about credibility and relevance of located information to inform decisions and actions. Reading and writing online can involve different modes and channels of communication so that visual, verbal and kinaesthetic modes of representation, as well as different software applications, can combine in myriad ways for particular effect. So what is known about the desired features or elements for effective online use, creation and sharing of knowledge that will elevate the quality of thinking, evaluative practice and ethical actions?

Finding terms to capture learning in multi-modal facility

Ways to capture or talk about developmental changes in young people's multi-modal production is an emerging area of literacy education research. Two major projects were reported by Bearne (2009), the focus being on consensus of teachers in shaping a continuum of descriptors of multi-modal text creation – (a) in the early stages, (b) increasingly assured, (c) more experienced and often independent, or (d) assured, experienced, and independent multi-modal text makers. Her examples were not digital creations. Nevertheless, they were multi-modal, hand-drawn, image–text narratives, and the descriptors offered ways of talking about the capabilities of these primary school multi-modal creators. According to Bearne, progress was indicated by an increasing ability to attend to a series of specific aspects associated with matching mode and content to specific purposes and audiences, structuring texts, using technical features for effect, and reflecting.

Several literacy education researchers and writers have recognized progress in multi-modal text creation as a key issue for literacy teachers (Coiro et al., 2008). Sefton-Green (2009) argued that current school assessment systems operate as traditional and powerful gatekeepers and sorters of academic accomplishment, consistently requiring notions of failure or incompetence. From this perspective, Bearne's (2009) reference to 'in the early stages' of development could be read as signalling limited achievement or less-than-expected performance. This observation points to how assessment language is typically value-laden, carrying potent messages to the learner, parent and wider community, not only about what is valued but also about how successful (or otherwise) the learner is judged to be. These messages are conveyed from the first day of schooling, and through exposure over time students accrue these and they form much as sedimentary layers to constitute student identity as more or less successful. Such performance categories or labels as those mentioned here are in themselves limited. They give no real indication about learning processes and how assessment is enabling improvement in learner-focused curriculum.

Several projects have sought to foster teacher and student agency in assessment, drawing both into conversations about assessment criteria and standards as marking guides for assessing multi-modal learning. In an Australian study examining ways to cultivate and assess creativity with e-portfolios, Allen and Coleman (2011) argued for assessment practices to become more focused on the evaluation of generic graduate capabilities, additional to assessment of discipline-specific knowledge. Moreover, these researchers argued that it is time to move away from the assessment focus on products – summative assessment – to an holistic focus that connects process, produce, person and place. They offer a model of e-portfolio practice that engages various communities (for example, internet community, friends and colleagues, academic, professional practice), with the publishing and disseminating of work of customized selections for different audiences. In this approach, features of quality – criteria and standards – can be thought of as suited to the particular purposes and audiences for presenting the work.

With the increasing potential for collaborative interaction and feedback made possible by Web 2.0 technologies, both formative and summative feedback can be provided by a range of parties. Beyond this, Web 2.0 technologies are well suited to what Paavola and Hakkarainen (2005) proposed as the *knowledge creation metaphor of learning,* which builds on the elements of Bereiter's (2002) theory of knowledge building, Engestrom's (1987, 1999a, 1999b) theory of expansive learning, and Nonaka and Takeuchi's (1995) model of knowledge creation.

According to McLoughlin and Lee (2008), 'the knowledge creation metaphor mirrors the societal shift towards a networked knowledge age, in which creativity, originality and the capacity to gain knowledge from networks are highly valued' (p. 645). They went on to state that '[i]n line with the knowledge creation metaphor, learning is mediated by a range of digital tools and affordances that support networking, socialisation, communication and engagement with communities of learning' (p. 645).

A feature of new technologies and related software is that they permit the insertion of audio or video files, and multiple users' responses to online creations. Co-creation is readily accomplished, independent of the physical location of the parties. The dynamic impetus that this can give to feedback attempts go well beyond more traditional assessment practices in which the student typically remains dependent on the teacher as the primary or sole source of feedback. More fundamentally, Web 2.0 technologies call for patterns of interaction that are different from those in traditional classrooms in which the teacher's control over assessment lies at the heart of their authority in the classroom. The implications for formative assessment and summative assessment are significant. McClay and Mackey's (2009) research with Canadian teachers of English in the middle years highlighted the need for more innovative approaches to assessments and proposed the notion of 'distributed assessment' (p. 113), which could involve 'principled negotiations of purposes, tools, and appraisals' (p. 118) by teachers and students.

A further study of relevance here concerned the dynamic exchange or personal interactions on social networking sites. It involved the development of a framework for 'assessing rhetorical uses of multimodality' (Rowsell, 2009: 110, adapted from Selfe, 2007) in three individual social networking spaces. A series of questions unpacked the main criteria to describe the *Multimodal Impact/Statement, Organisation, Salience* and *Coherence* (p. 110). In evaluating the rhetorical devices used by the Facebook® site creators, comparisons were drawn in terms of (i) chosen modes, (ii) rhetorical effect, (iii) dominant mode and (iv) inventory of skills acquired through Facebook.

As reported by several researchers, while research on Web 2.0 technologies and multi-modality remain in their infancy, the dynamic nature of multi-modal assessment and opportunities for conversations about multi-modal text creation have already figured prominently. Several writers (Lee and McLaughlin, 2007; Beach et al., 2009), for example, investigated ways of attending to the dynamic nature of Web 2.0 technologies in assessment. They supported the use of digital tools embedded in the entire digital learning environment and process as a way of capturing the dynamic possibilities. Audio inserts, word-processed text boxes, blogs or wiki co-constructions, in single pieces or in e-portfolios in which reflection on continuing performance is prioritized, represent rich resources whereby the creator can review choices for mode, presentation or design with greater consciousness and support. According to these researchers, the benefits of such tools extend to raising metacognitive awareness and they argue that 'Having some formal mechanism for engaging in ongoing reflections fosters metacognitive awareness essential for learning' (p. 171), where self-assessment and design and redesign can be part of the learning and assessment process. From this vantage point, assessment is properly concerned as much with learning processes, including the making and reviewing of what have traditionally been considered 'mistakes' or 'errors', as it is with the quality of the completed piece of work. The developments in technology are such that today we can record and review development processes, as well as develop historical digital records of student products. We consider the implications of these developments for assessment next.

Attuning learning and assessment to digital worlds

Framework 1

The case for transforming student assessment as a means to free up or liberate teaching and learning has been made by several researchers. While the arguments put forward differ in terms of the specific details, common to all is the recognition that existing forms of assessment and, in particular, summative reporting of student achievement fall well short of providing information about the range of capabilities, attributes and dispositions required for today's workplaces, lifelong learning and changing communication practices. Bamford and Thompson (2005), for example, argued that assessment processes need to keep pace with the changes in learning and teaching, and beyond this to the innovations occurring within society and the workplace. They made the point that new approaches to assessment are needed, stating that 'if innovation, creativity and problem solving are endorsed as learning outcomes, they **must** become a valued and explicit part of the assessment process' (p. 18; bold and italics in the original). They argued that models of assessment based largely on recall and reproductive thinking, rote learning and individual performance are 'no longer of relevance to the sorts of qualities required into the future. Conversely, assessment needs to record creative, critical and reflective forms of learning' (p. 18). Their observations bring into stark relief how in the main, traditional assessments are insensitive to the processes that individuals and groups can engage in when they undertake projects over time, with access to a range of human and material resources.

Bamford and Thompson (2005) identified five categories or groups of criteria as part of an alternative online assessment system called ReView, with reported potential to accommodate learning across integrated and transdisciplinary themes. The ReView system incorporates five colour-coded categories of criteria presented below. The characterization of each descriptor relies on the terms used by the authors. (Readers are advised to see Bamford and Thompson (2005) for more detail.)

Creativity–innovation involves learning processes that encourage invention, risk-taking, imagining, problem-solving, playing, creating and originality.

The **communication** criteria explore the multi-modal nature of communication and the making of meaning. This involves speaking, writing, reading, mathematical literacies, gestural and non-verbal communication, visual literacy, multi-sensory communication (for example, sound and moving images) and social languages (for example, ritual language, manners and negotiations).

The criteria covered by the descriptor **attitudes–values** cover the ethical, personal and social dimensions of learning. This includes levels of intrinsic motivation (for example, keenness to learn), leadership, curiosity, collaboration, interpersonal strengths (for example, friendships and reciprocity), intrapersonal skills (for example, self-assurance and confidence), ability to handle and respond to change, care and consideration of self and others, respect, self-discipline, determination and judgement.

The criteria group called **practical skills** refers to the range of skills a person needs to become an effective learner at any given age. This includes physical skills (for example, skipping, running, dancing, holding a pen, handwriting, drawing, typing, playing an instrument and signing); conceptual skills (for example, measuring, composing, analysing and evaluating); information and communications technology (ICT) skills (for example, computer skills, camera skills and online/internet skills) and learning skills (for example, using a library, researching, interviewing and reporting).

The fifth criteria of **critical thinking** encourages children to recognize the strengths and weaknesses of certain ways of thinking, and based on this reflection to think in diverse and multiple ways. Critical thinking is evident in the way learners can make corrections to other learning, are aware of their own learning (reflection on learning), adopt a stance of open-mindedness, gather information from a range of sources, make statements based on evidence, build relationships between different pieces of information or skills, see things from several points of view, ask interesting questions and identify their personal strengths and weaknesses as a learner.

The potential of the framework

The above suite of criteria groups is illustrative of attempts in research and practice to broaden the perspective on stated features of assessment or, more specifically, to value a range of learning that may fall outside official assessment requirements. They represent an instance of assessment extending to recognizing and documenting reflective, creative and critical learning practices, raising these to prominence in the decision making and judgement that teachers and students engage in about learning and accountability. Of special interest is how the framework accommodates the use of ICTs and the related digital capabilities such as online and internet skills as well as more traditional technologies including handwriting. The potential of the framework is that it offers a wide view of learning that can *count* for assessment. Moreover, its intended operation as a web-based portal permits it to integrate ICT content, and the increasing use of technologies in monitoring and mediating learning. In common with other work on e-portfolios, it shares the interest in giving a range of parties including students, parents and administrators, access not only to student work samples, but also to various representations of assessment and reporting data against accepted institutional standards.

Next, we consider a different framework for assessing how students use and create knowledge online. It shares with the first framework an overall interest in student learning, assessment and meaning-making, though it takes a particular focus on digital literacy and multi-modal working.

Framework 2

As suggested earlier, using, creating and sharing knowledge online calls for specific skills, strategies and ways of working, many of which are different from print-based ways of reading, writing and communicating. The second framework and the discussion presented here draws on the body of work by Kimber and Wyatt-Smith (2008, 2009, 2010) and conceptualizes two strands: (i) using existing knowledge, texts or materials; and (ii) creating and sharing new knowledge, texts and materials. Within this framing, categories of desired learning are identified, namely e-proficiency, e-credibility, e-designing and trans-modal facility, as shown in Table 8.1 and outlined below. They are understood to be connected and interactive, and do not constitute a hierarchy, with trans-modal facility being the synthesizing feature in terms of working within and across modes of representation.

E-proficiency within this framework is understood to be inclusive of basic technological competencies and also extends to more critical and applied usage. For example, demonstrations of being 'net-savvy' might begin with the ability to search for, locate and retrieve relevant information on the internet, but being e-proficient will ensure that the user knowingly selects from a variety of search engines and databases to suit different purposes and contexts, rather than automatically selecting a single search engine. The e-proficient user will have more advanced working knowledge of a range of software protocols and fine functions. From this perspective, an accomplished user has a wider choice of options in creating a quality digital product and in understanding how others' digital texts have been designed. All these skills enable production as distinct from consumption of digital products and are foundational to any creative design possibilities using digital media. In effect, e-proficiency involves digital capabilities that can be built upon and extended towards more purposeful, critical and ethical use, and production of knowledge in online environments. This applies to participation in social networking sites as much as it does to more formal activities online, associated with, responding to and producing texts for classroom assessment.

E-credibility is taken to refer to discrimination in selection of sources, and critical ways of thinking about sources of information, corroborating evidence and ways of valuing and evaluating different perspectives. Drawing on Haas and Wearden

Table 8.1 Assessment framework for using, creating and sharing knowledge online

Use existing knowledge texts or materials	Create and share new knowledge texts or materials
Trans-modal facility Ability to work with and across source texts, technology platforms and modes of representation to create a new digital text whereby critical thinking about content and concepts is balanced with the aesthetics of design	
e-proficiency	
• Ability to locate and retrieve information in written, visual, auditory, digital modes, using a variety of search engines, databases, and strategies • Ability to use a range of software efficiently and fluently • Ability to keep efficient records of source texts for tracking purposes	• Ability to select software and mode of display appropriate for selected audience, the medium and type of content • Ability to exploit the affordances of the software and achieve particular effects in accord with the intended audience/ purposes
e-credibility	
• Ability to establish accuracy, currency, reliability and trustworthiness of sources (sites and authors) • Ability to discern how values and ideologies are operating in source texts and how these work to represent people, cultures, places and eras • Ability to make a discriminating selection of sources, balance viewpoints and find corroborating evidence • Ability to formulate a position on a topic by informed use of a range of source materials • Ability to identify and examine how elements of a text (verbal, visual/ auditory channels) work to communicate and 'normalize' a position	• Discriminating choice of material resources for display or communication • Discriminating use of selected sources • To formulate, communicate and defend as appropriate a position, distinguishing it from other possible positions • Ethical/scholarly acknowledgment and use of all sources
e-designing	
• Ability to identify/discern the potential of source material and to select for (a) new applications and (b) appropriate mode/s of display • Ability to utilize sources ethically (e.g. with accurate representation and proper acknowledgements) • Ability to be receptive to the contributions of others	• Ability to assemble, compose or design an aesthetic, creative combination/ transformation or treatment of existing sources and materials into new, cohesive representations or text (e.g. colours, fonts, spatial layout)

Source: Kimber and Wyatt-Smith (2010), reproduced with permission.

(2003), this notion assumes importance through the invisibility of the internet and the need for constant credibility and verifying the 'truthfulness' or trustworthiness of sources and reported claims. This involves being able to accept or reject indicators of reputed expertise where informed corroboration may be difficult to ascertain. Several researchers have made the point previously that many young people seek instant corroboration from networked friends (Flanagin and Metzger, 2008), rather than informed 'experts'. As the authors of the framework argue, with so much erroneous and misleading information available on the internet, young people need to be able to develop ways to apply discriminating evaluations for themselves, with educators having the opportunity to play a vital role in this area.

E-credibility is also significant when young people's growing propensity for digital text creations are considered (Lenhart et al., 2007). With speedy communication to wide audiences, concerns about plagiarism and intellectual copyright are raised, as are the practices of copying, pasting, remixing or morphing others' work into students' own creations. Ethical use and appropriate acknowledgement will inform trans-modal facility and form part of the level of e-credibility of the user.

E-designing is the visible process and instantiation of creativity. It is a useful way to allow creative thinking about design options, explore different solutions to problems, innovations, transformations or original creations. It can include synthesizing ideas and accommodating different viewpoints, as well as the technological e-proficiency to exploit the functions of software or technology tools. E-designing can include being playful with the tools in ways that are not possible without mastery knowledge of how they can be used for effect. Several researchers have found that academic progress and improved student performances can result from students as designers of multi-modal texts (Kimber et al., 2007; Walsh, 2007). Further, The New London Group's (2000) notions of Designing and the Redesigned supported the proactive reshaping of available designs in imaginative ways. As suggested earlier, evaluative practices at the core of e-proficiency and e-credibility also permeate e-designing, though here their critical and ethical dimensions are balanced by creativity and a sense of the aesthetic.

Trans-modal facility is taken to refer to the synthesizing, connecting element that marks the successful integration of the other three elements. This element recognizes the multiple channels and modes of communication at play in meaning making, both as producer and receiver. It also recognizes how the characteristic speed of communication today makes possible new ways to connect, engage and respond, with both local and global reach. The potential therefore lies in learner agency as learners operate within and across modes, across various platforms and activities. This is where more expert others, or what we refer to as 'digital cultural guides', can play a vital part. They are the online users and producers with both technical knowledge and expertise, and insider knowledge about the ways of knowing, being and making meaning accepted within particular online communities.

The potential of the framework

The elements of this second framework resonate with the emphasis placed on incorporating evaluative criterial knowledge and digital literacies into foundational knowledges (Kimber and Wyatt-Smith, 2009) and with the research-based principles for assessment for learning (Assessment Reform Group, 2002), drawing those principles more closely into digital learning contexts. It presents opportunities for taking up an evaluative and a creative stance, both in the use of knowledge and in the production of knowledge and related new textual material. Those moments for transition between location, selection, copying and transforming material require evaluative consideration on a constant basis, and especially in the creation of new texts, in line with the discussion on ethical decision making given earlier. All this mirrors the connectivity of networks, the speed of accessing and transforming digital texts, and the complex interplay between both activities as characterized by screen-based activity whereby users can be, simultaneously, users, consumers and producers of digital texts.

An area for further development and closer consideration lies in the notion of connectedness and sharing knowledge, particularly the collaborative ways in which young people interact online. In addition, when the nature of community knowledges is considered in the context of online informal (that is, outside of school or university) learning, wider opportunities for collaboration and sharing of feedback, with community experts as well as peers, are provided.

In this framework, cognitive, creative and the aesthetic aspects can come into view for holistic consideration of learning processes and qualities in performance. The identified features are intended to be portable, with potential relevance to a range of disciplines, depending on the assessment tasks or projects students are undertaking. Further, their intention is to support learners' and teachers' thinking and talking about quality in digital practices, and inform self-monitoring and improvement.

The extension of the frameworks considered in this chapter would be to the online use of exemplars and standards. This has potential to occur at local and system levels, with the posting of e-portfolios or samples of student work to illustrate achievement and to provide concrete examples of how standards are satisfied. It could also include assessment exemplars in the form of quality assessment tasks with accompanying student work, offering valuable inputs for year-level planning. Digital assessment banks also have potential to support teachers' judgement practices, especially when they are used in the context of digital moderation, whereby teachers post and share student work within their school and regional communities of practice.

As Wiggins (2013) records in his thoughts on education:

I tweeted yesterday an interesting news item in Erik Robelen's blog in Education Week that a few states … are seriously looking into some sort of assessment of creative thinking as part of the whole 21st century skills/ entrepreneurship movement. I think it is a great idea, with a lot of potential for leveraging change.

Wiggins (2013) concluded, quite simply: 'On assessing for creativity: yes you can, and yes you should'. More than this, however, he reflected on student feedback on surveys and reported that he:

ran across an interesting pattern of dislikes: rubrics that squash creativity. This is a worrisome misunderstanding: students are coming to believe that rubrics hamper their creativity rather than encouraging it. That can only come from a failure on the part of teachers to use the right criteria and multiple and varied exemplars. If rubrics are sending the message that a formulaic response on an uninteresting task is what performance assessment is all about, then we are subverting our mission as teachers.

Also quite simply and in response: We agree!

Review questions

Now, to return to the original provocative question we asked at the start of the chapter: What do you think educators know about the life of the people they teach outside school? By extension, what value do you place on community knowledge that students bring with them to school?

In considering these questions, take a moment to think about your own experience of the fit (or lack of fit) between the enacted curriculum and official assessment requirements of your own education, on the one hand, and on the other the knowledge and literacy capabilities that you developed in your familial and community contexts.

In your experience as a student and a user of technology, do you agree with the view that assessing the quality of learning with technology requires different assessment principles and practices from those associated with print-dominant classrooms?

What are the implications for formative and summative assessment, if students can use social networking and other digital tools to access expert advice and feedback on their learning? What is the changed role of the teacher in this scenario?

In considering your own experiences of using knowledge online in producing assignments and your experiences of designing a new multi-modal text, what assessment criteria and standards were used to assess the work? Were these salient to the actual learning that occurred and the work you produced? How effective were they in informing you about features of quality, and did you use them to monitor your progress both during the production of the work and on its completion?

References

Allen, B. and Coleman, K. (2011) 'The creative graduate: Cultivating and assessing creativity with eportfolios', *Proceedings Ascilite*, 4–7 December. Hobart, Australia.

Assessment Reform Group (2002) *Assessment for Learning: 10 principles. Research-Based Principles to Guide Classroom Practice*. Available at: www.assessment-reform-group. org/CIE3.PDF.

Bamford, A. and Thompson, D. (2005) 'Transforming student assessment to liberate pedagogy', *Snapshots*, 3 (2): 17–21.

Beach, R., Clemens, L. and Jamsen, K. (2009) 'Digital tools: Assessing digital communication and providing feedback to student writers', in A. Burke and R.F. Hammett (eds), *Assessing New Literacies: Perspectives from the Classroom.* pp. 157–76.

Bearne, E. (2009) 'Multimodality literacy and texts: Developing a discourse', *Journal of Early Childhood Literacy*, 9 (2): 156–87.

Becker, K.L. (2006) 'Unlearning: A people development issue for sustainable change and innovation', in *7th International CINet (Continuous Innovation Network) Conference*, 8–12 September, Lucca, Italy.

Bereiter, C. (2002) *Education and Mind in the Knowledge Age.* Hillsdale, NJ: Erlbaum.

Buckingham, D. (2007) *Beyond Technology: Children's Learning in the Age of Digital Culture.* Cambridge, UK: Polity Press.

Coiro, J., Knobel, M., Lankshear, C. and Leu, D.J. (2008) *Handbook of Research on New Literacies.* New York: Lawrence Erlbaum Associates.

Cumming, J. and Wyatt-Smith, C. (eds) (2001) *Literacy and the Curriculum: Success in Senior Secondary Schooling.* Melbourne: ACER Press.

Engestrom, Y. (1987) *Learning by Expanding.* Orienta-Konsultit Oy: Helsinki.

Engestrom, Y. (1999a) 'Innovative learning in work teams: Analyzing cycles of knowledge creation in practice', in Y. Engestrom, R. Miettinen and R-L. Punamaki (eds), *Perspectives on Activity Theory.* Cambridge, UK: Cambridge University Press. pp. 377–404.

Engestrom, Y. (1999b) *Learning by Expanding: Ten Years After.* Introduction to the German edition, titled *Lernen durch Expansion.* Marburg: BdWi-Verlag (Reihe Internationale Studien zur Tätigkeitstheorie, Bd. 5; translated by Falk Seeger).

Flanagin, A. and Metzger, M. (2008) 'Digital media and youth: Unparalleled opportunity and unprecedented responsibility', in M. Metzger and A. Flanagin (eds), *Digital Media, Youth and Credibility,* The John D. and Catherine T. MacArthur Foundation Series on Digital Media and Learning. Cambridge, MA: The MIT Press. pp. 5–28.

Haas, C. and Wearden, S. (2003) 'E-credibility: Building common ground in web environments', *L1 – Educational Studies in Language and Literature*, 3: 169–84.

Hipwell, P. and Klenowski, V. (2011) 'A case for addressing the literacy demands of student assessment', *Australian Journal of Language and Literacy*, 34 (2): 127–46.

Kimber, K. and Wyatt-Smith, C. (2008) 'Assessing digital literacies: Can assessment ever be the same?' in L. Unsworth (ed.), *New Literacies and the English Curriculum.* London: Continuum. pp. 328–54.

Kimber, K. and Wyatt-Smith, C. (2009) 'Valued knowledges and core capacities for digital learners: Claiming spaces for quality assessment', in A. Burke and R. Hammett (eds), *Assessing New Literacies: Perspectives from the Classroom.* New York: Peter Lang Publishing. pp. 133–56.

Kimber, K. and Wyatt-Smith, C. (2010) 'Secondary students' online use and creation of knowledge: Refocusing priorities for quality assessment and learning', *Australasian Journal of Educational Technology*, 26 (5): 607–25.

Kimber, K., Pillay, H. and Richards, C. (2007) 'Technoliteracy and learning: An analysis of the quality of knowledge in electronic representations of understanding', *Computers and Education*, 48 (1): 59–79.

Lee, M.J.W. and McLoughlin, C. (2007) 'Teaching and learning in the Web 2.0 era: Empowering students through learner-generated content', *International Journal of Instructional Technology and Distance Learning,* 4 (10): 21–34.

Lenhart, A., Madden, M., Rankin Macgill, A. and Smith, A. (2007) *Teens and Social Media.* Washington, DC: Pew Internet and American Life Project.

Leu, D.J. Jr. (2000) 'Literacy and technology: Deictic consequences for literacy education in an information age', in M.L. Kamil, P. Mosenthal, P.D. Pearson and R. Barr (eds), *Handbook of Reading Research,* Vol. 3. Mahwah, NJ: Erlbaum. pp. 743–70.

Leu, D.J. Jr., Kinzer, C.K., Coiro, J. and Cammack, D. (2004) 'Toward a theory of new literacies emerging from the Internet and other information and communication technologies', in R.B. Ruddell and N. Unrau (eds), *Theoretical Models and Processes of Reading,* 5th edn. Newark, DE: International Reading Association. pp. 1568–611.

McClay, J.K. and Mackey, J. (2009) 'Distributed assessment in ourspace: This is not a rubric', in A. Burke and R.F. Hammett (eds), *Assessing New Literacies: Perspectives from the Classroom.* New York: Peter Lang. pp. 113–32.

McLoughlin, C. and Lee, M.J.W. (2008) 'Mapping the digital terrain: new media and social software as catalysts for pedagogical change', *Proceedings Ascilite.* Melbourne: Australia.

McWilliam, E. (2005) 'Unlearning pedagogy', *Journal of Learning Design,* 1 (1): 1–11.

New London Group, The (2000) 'A pedagogy of multiliteracies: Designing social futures', in B. Cope and M. Kalantzis (eds), *Multiliteracies: Literacy Learning and the Design of Social Futures.* London: Routledge. pp. 9–37.

Nonaka, I. and Takeuchi, H. (1995) *The Knowledge-Creating Company: How Japanese Companies Create the Dynamics of Innovation.* New York: Oxford University Press.

Paavola, S. and Hakkarainen, K. (2005) 'The knowledge creation metaphor – An emergent epistemological approach to learning', *Science & Education,* 14: 535–57.

Pink, D. (2005) *A Whole New Mind: Moving from the Information Age to the Conceptual Age.* New York: Riverhead Books.

Rowsell, J. (2009) 'My life on Facebook: Assessing the art of online social networking', in A. Burke and R. Hammett (eds), *Assessing New Literacies: Perspectives from the Classroom.* New York: Peter Lang Publishing. pp. 95–112.

Sadler, D.R. (1985) 'The origins and functions of evaluative criteria', *Educational Theory,* 35 (3): 285–97.

Sadler, D.R. (1989) 'Formative assessment and the design of instructional systems', *Instructional Science,* 18: 119–44.

Sefton-Green, J. (2003) 'Informal learning: Substance or style?' *Teaching Education,* 13 (1): 37–51.

Sefton-Green, J. (2008) 'Is informal learning the new "new literacies"?' in conversation with K. Mallan, A. Bruns and J Coates, Queensland University of Technology, Brisbane, 27 May.

Sefton-Green, J. (2009) 'Epilogue', in A. Burke and R. Hammett (eds), *Assessing New Literacies: Perspectives from the Classroom.* New York: Peter Lang Publishing. pp. 193–7.

Selfe, C.L. (ed.) (2007) *Multimodal Composition: Resources for Teachers.* Cresskill, NJ: Hampton Press.

Walsh, C. (2007) 'Literacy in the new media age: Creativity as multimodal design'. Paper presented at Critical Capital: Teaching and Learning, AATE and ALEA National Conference, Canberra.

Wiggins, G. (2013) 'On assessing for creativity: yes you can, and yes you should', *Granted, but ... thoughts on education by Grant Wiggins*. Blog, available at: http://grantwiggins. wordpress.com/2012/02/03/on-assessing-for-creativity-yes-you-can-and-yes-you.

Wyatt-Smith, C.M. and Cumming, J.J. (2003) 'Curriculum literacies: Expanding domains of assessment', *Assessment in Education: Principles, Policy and Practice*, 10 (1): 47–59.

Web extras

Bennett, D.E. and Davis, M.A. (2001) 'The development of a computer-based alternate assessment system', *Assessment for Effective Intervention*, 26 (3): 15–34.

Vasudevan, L. and Campano, G. (2009) 'The social production of adolescent risk and the promise of adolescent literacies', *Review of Research in Education*, 33 (1): 310–53.

9

Futures-oriented assessment

Overview

In this chapter we consolidate our position that it is time for the 'masterful teacher', using the facility of digital and emerging technologies, to engage with futures-oriented approaches to assessment. The key propositions presented earlier support our contention that assessment needs to be reconsidered in the light of current developments. We argue that with major international curriculum and standards-driven reform, policy developers, academics, teachers, students and the public need to be aware of the accountability demands and their effects on assessment policy and practice. We see this as a time of transition for assessment, with the merging of traditional modes of written examinations, school-based and teacher assessment with online, digitally mediated forms of assessment. Such developments evoke a rethinking of learning and assessment from a measurement of the acquisition of knowledge, to participation and active engagement in processes of assessment as communities of learners, through to knowledge creation by means of the technological transformation of assessment. This development in thinking about assessment, we argue, requires the teacher to utilize a network of knowledges and develop a repertoire of assessment skills and understandings.

Introduction

In this chapter we return to a theoretical framework that helps to explain and make explicit the connectedness of assessment, curriculum and teaching, and we reiterate our framing of what constitutes futures-oriented assessment. The turning point for assessment, as evident in Chapter 8, has come with digital and emerging technologies that provide alternative modes for assessment of student learning, moving beyond traditional paper-and-pencil examinations and tests, and teacher or school-based assessment to use of online and digital media.

During this time of transition for assessment it is helpful to consider the different conceptions of learning, and their relationships and influences on approaches to assessment. However, before we do so, we relate relevant developments in thinking about assessment to situate our position. In this century, major shifts in assessment practices and approaches have arisen from the move towards the development of human capital, defined as:

> The knowledge, skills and competencies and other attributes embodied in individuals that are relevant to personal, social and economic well-being. (OECD, 1999: 11)

As evident in Chapters 4, 7 and 8 of this book, students are no longer assessed exclusively using only paper-based, multiple-choice tests or written examinations. Rather, included in the types of assessment of student achievement are complex tasks that require students to demonstrate their understandings and skills of analysis, problem solving, resilience, creativity and the like. The implications for teachers are the relevance of being assessment literate and possessing a pedagogic repertoire of assessment skills and understandings that includes assessment design. In rigorous and cognitively demanding assessments, tasks are designed so that there is no single right answer: there can be multiple ways to answer, to analyse or to solve the problems, or to consider issues posed. Such a shift in assessment design brings to the fore teachers' judgement and decision-making skills and their competence in assessing students' learning. In Chapters 2 and 5 we explored how teachers can develop their judgement and decision-making practices using standards in contexts of curriculum and standards-driven reforms.

The policy drivers for recent curriculum and assessment reforms were analysed in Chapter 2, where we explained how PISA has become influential in national education policy making. We discussed some demonstrable changes to national curriculum and assessment systems, as in Germany's response to what has been described in that country as 'PISA shock'. We argued that what has become apparent is that PISA is being used and to some extent 'integrated within national or federal policies and practices of assessment and evaluation, curriculum standards and performance targets' (Breakspear, 2012: 27). Internationally, external accountability for system improvement and performance enhancement has gained significance in the context of a global knowledge economy.

The advancement of knowledge in this century has seen an intensification of the work of 'knowledge-workers', with systems seemingly uncertain about how to keep pace with the developments of the processes of knowledge advancement. Knowledge creation 'requires changes in attitude, not only on the part of the individual knowledge worker, but on the part of the whole organization' (Drucker, 1999: 156). This includes educational organizations such as schools, universities and government agencies. We have seen how governments have responded to the demands of knowledge advancement by the introduction of curriculum change and achievement standards that ostensibly have been described as 'futures-oriented'. For curriculum that is oriented towards a more sustainable and generative future for the next generation, we have argued how teachers can no longer focus on 'the basics' and the acquisition and reproduction of knowledge. Standards associated with quality and authentic pedagogy that include higher-order thinking, profound knowledge, substantive conversation and connections to the real world beyond the classroom (Anyon, 1981) form part of the pedagogic repertoire of the 'masterful teacher'.

Sociocultural views of learning are central to how we have framed assessment as a social practice involving interactive communicative processes. How teachers interact with and learn about their students in the dialogic interchange takes prominence from this view, as explicated in Chapter 3. The values reflected in such an assessment system are intended to disrupt traditional views that focus on acquisition of knowledge and measurement to an understanding whereby participation with others and creation of knowledge are valued. We have also argued how such a view helps to develop a more culture-responsive pedagogy and assessment practice with the capacity to address issues of equity.

Towards futures-oriented assessment

In conceptualizing the transition towards futures-oriented assessment, an emergent epistemological approach to learning, described as 'trialogical', has been illuminating for us. From this trialogical approach, learning is seen as 'a process of knowledge creation which concentrates on mediated processes where common objects are developed collaboratively' (Paavola and Hakkarainen, 2005: 535). Learning from this epistemic view values knowledge creation and articulation processes over the assimilation and recall of existing knowledge and participation in known and established practices. From this view of learning futures-oriented approach is taken to assessment, with the use of technology to leverage opportunities for greater collaboration in the mediated processes of knowledge advancement, particularly given that such processes are crucial in a knowledge-based society. Futures-oriented assessment of learning focuses on knowledge building, discovery and innovation, developing new materials and conceptual artefacts, either individually or collaboratively within cultural contexts (Paavola and Hakkarainen, 2005).

Drawing on the emergent epistemological approach to learning of Paavola and Hakkarainen (2005) and Watkins' (2003) views of learning, we now explicate the implications for futures-oriented assessment. The metaphor of learning as acquisition of knowledge or the view of learning as 'being taught' (Watkins, 2003: 40) involves didactic, teacher-dominated and monologic approaches to teaching. From this perspective, and as evident from past approaches, assessment tends to privilege written tests with correct answers that reflect teaching and instruction, with a focus on how much the student has learnt. Present conceptions of learning as a process of participation in learning communities for co-construction as well as 'individual sense-making' (Watkins, 2003: 40) rely on more dialogic forms of instruction. Assessment from this view of learning as participation has been oriented towards performance and demonstrations of learning, with evidence of sense-making and meaning. From a futures-oriented perspective learning is viewed as knowledge creation and development of new materials and conceptual artefacts. The knowledge creation metaphor focuses on the processes of building knowledge and the creation of 'mediating artefacts within cultural settings' (Paavola and Hakkarainen, 2005: 541). Assessment from this view focuses on knowledge generation through the use of technology, mediating artefacts and social interactions within authentic and collaborative settings. Assessment tasks involve collaborative solutions and knowledge generation involving skills of creativity and a trialogic approach. An overview of key concepts that unpin our view of a trajectory towards futures-oriented assessment is summarized in Table 9.1.

Table 9.1   Towards futures-oriented assessment

Views of learning	Time frame	Dominant mode	Assessment form
Process of acquisition and adoption of what has been taught – subject matter, knowledge and representations	Past	Monologic Teacher-dominated Didactic	Written exams Correct answers Measurement – how much has been learnt Answers reflect instruction
Process of participation in learning communities with co-construction of knowledge and individual sense-making	Present	Dialogic Participation in learning communities	Performance and demonstration Dialogue Evidence of sense-making and meaning
Process of creativity and developing new materials and conceptual artefacts, building knowledge as individuals and in groups using mediating artefacts	Future	Trialogic ICT-mediated Digital learning environment	Collaborative, generative Creating and developing new material and conceptual solutions Critical and reflective forms of learning Authentic tasks using ICTs

Implications for the 'masterful teacher'

What, then, are the implications of futures-oriented assessment practice for the 'masterful teacher'? In Chapter 8 we discussed the new priorities for education of digital literacy capabilities, creativity, innovation, problem solving, resourcefulness and resilience. While we acknowledge the importance of the new and emerging technologies, we emphasize that these are digital tools, and we highlight the importance of developing teachers' assessment capabilities and assessment literacies. Throughout the book we have stressed the important role of teachers in assessment design and that teachers need well-developed disciplinary knowledges and an appreciation of how such knowledge intersects with community knowledge, digital literacies, criterial knowledge and understandings of quality.

As we look to the future we recognize that with emergent technologies and the creation of 'mediating artefacts within cultural settings', which teachers will have at their disposal, implications for the 'masterful teacher' are that a repertoire of assessment skills and understandings will still be required. With a futures-oriented approach to assessment teachers and students will be able to focus on quality, creativity, originality of learning and the use of knowledge. Judgement and decision making using evidence and standards will remain relevant in discerning, monitoring and providing feedback for the improvement of such knowledge and learning.

Teacher education needs to keep pace with such developments. While traditionally the focus has been on developing pre-service teachers' disciplinary knowledge, we are suggesting that a repertoire of knowledge and understandings now needs to involve multiple literacy knowledge, which includes assessment, curriculum, digital and screen literacies. As suggested in Chapter 8, the 'masterful teacher' will understand the importance of this in a rapidly changing world, in order to take account of community knowledge and sociocultural contexts through social networking and school-based activities involving parents and local community. The 'masterful teacher' has an understanding of the lives of the people she or he teaches, including outside of school.

Criterial and standards knowledge that indicate the qualities valued in the performances, demonstrations or processes of learning will continue to be important. As evident in Chapter 7, policy and resource support for teachers' practice in times of curriculum and assessment change will continue to be significant in the support and growth of the 'masterful teacher'. We have argued throughout the book that with adequate system-level resources and support, together with teacher professionalism and commitment to the improvement of learning for all students, exemplary enacted pedagogic and assessment practices can provide a level of coherence between system-level accountability demands and site-level practice, to develop sustainable assessment cultures. This is yet another role and responsibility for the 'masterful teacher'.

Educational researchers will continue to conduct research and development in the field of futures-oriented assessment, to provide understandings and new knowledge about how new ways of being and thinking are shaped in cultural contexts by existing and emergent technologies. If futures-oriented assessment is to foster creativity, innovativeness and agility with change then educational researchers will continue to work with schools and education departments to maximize the opportunities presented by the digital revolution. Today, businesses and commercial enterprises are engaged in assessment design and delivery through the internet, bringing further challenges for the classroom teacher and schools. While the involvement of industry partners is welcomed in the field of education, the maintenance of standards is a concern that requires continuous research and development by educators and the 'masterful teacher'. Professional teachers accept responsibility for the quality of their work. Critical inquiry into one's practice, self-assessment and self-regulation are skills required for the development of futures-oriented assessment and the enactment of such practice.

Conclusion

The global context of major curriculum and assessment reform has been addressed in this book's focus on standards, teacher judgement and moderation, with the case for intelligent accountability of high-quality, innovative and futures-oriented assessment to address external accountability demands, on the one hand, and quality, equity and learning on the other. We have brought together the accountability and improvement agenda through analysis of moderation practice and, in so doing, have highlighted the significance of teachers' competence in judgement and decision making. We also described the dual functions of quality assurance to demonstrate comparability of teacher judgement and consistency in the use of standards and capacity building, whereby teachers engage in meaningful learning about what counts as quality. Assessment develops relevance and meaning through teacher involvement in moderation practice, through which new insights and knowledge about teaching and the qualities of valued learning are generated.

A set of principles underpinning assessment practice that acknowledges the use of achievement standards in judgement practices, as exemplified in examples of teachers' practice in Chapters 4, 5 and 7, demonstrated the importance of teacher assessment literacies and teacher assessment. In Chapter 8 we introduced a futures-oriented approach to assessment founded on a trialogic approach (Paavola and Hakkarainen, 2005). We illustrated how the rapidity of change through new and emerging technologies has brought with it changed communication practices, including new ways for knowledge creation and meaning making to occur. Given this, we reiterate a position taken by many writers in the field of assessment: teachers are central to realizing quality assessment. However, in contemporary times the role of the teacher needs to extend beyond traditionally accepted boundaries of what teachers and students do in classrooms. It is through changed classroom practices of the types we have presented in this book that students can develop knowledge of the curriculum and know-how in discerning quality in their own work. Further, it is through classroom practice in the hands of the masterful teacher that students can develop their analytic and creative skills, with new technologies to use and create knowledge in ways not available in earlier times. Futures-oriented assessment that supports teacher judgement and the classroom use of standards is essential in providing students with knowledge-generating opportunities in preparation for their futures.

References 📖

Anyon, J. (1981) 'Social class and school knowledge', *Curriculum Inquiry*, 11 (1): 3–42.

Breakspear, S. (2012) 'The policy impact of PISA: An exploration of the normative effects of international benchmarking in school system performance', OECD *Education Working Paper*, No. 71. OECD Publishing. Available at: http://dx.doi.org/10.1787/5k9fdfqffr28-en.

Drucker, P.F. (1999) *Management Challenges for the 21st Century*. Oxford: Butterworth-Heinemann.

OECD (Organization for Economic Cooperation and Development) (1999) *Measuring Students' Knowledge and Skills: A New Framework for Assessment*. Paris: OECD.

Paavola, S. and Hakkarainen, K. (2005) 'The knowledge creation metaphor – An emergent epistemological approach to learning', *Science & Education*, 14: 535–57.

Watkins, C. (2003) *Learning a Sense-maker's Guide*. London: Association of Teachers and Lecturers.

Web extra

Wiener, L. (2002) 'Assessing systemic reform's "Learning by All": Who evaluates learning by policy analysts?' *Educational Policy*, 16 (2): 239–63.

Index